THE BAMFORDS
A FAMILY HISTORY

BY SARAH HARTLEY

Dedicated to the descendants of Samuel Bamford

Copyright © Sarah L. Hartley – 2018

address: 59 Lancelot Dr. Palm Coast, FL 32137
email: mssarahhartley@aim.com

ISBN 978-0-578-41753-0

Editor: Danielle Lieneman
Interior layout and cover design: Nicole Sturk

Table of Contents

Preface vii

Excerpt "Armorial Families" 1

Derivation of Bamford 3

Notable Bamfords 5
    Less notable Bamfords 6

The Bamfords 7
  Samuel Bamford 7
  Charles Bamford 14
  Edwin Bamford 18
    Thornton Hough 21
  The JCB Bamfords 24
  The Fourth Earl Ferrers 25
    Arrest and trial 27
    Execution 29
    Conclusion 31
  Bamford Brothers 35
    New Investments 45
    Back to the Business Known 55

A Felony 59
   The Split 60
   The Waring Connection 62
   The Passing of an Era 66
   Arthur John Jones Bamford 73
   Anne Bamford 89
   Major Charles and Dorothy Bamford 94
   Edwin Scott Bamford 99
   Anne Nash Bamford 105
   Charles Francis Kreitmair Bamford (Frank) 106
   Doris Betty Bamford (née Holloway) 112
   Arthur Ingram Bamford 120

The Kreitmairs 123
   Wiguläus von Kreittmayr 123
   Karl Joseph Benedikt Kreitmayr 130
   Francis Joseph Benedict Kreitmair 133

The Holloways 137
   John Alexander Holloway 137
   William Claude Holloway 140
   Sydney Charles Holloway 144
   John (Jack) William Holloway 146

The Citroens 151
   Barend Roelof Citroen 151
   Joseph Barend Citroen 155
   Minerva Motors 160
   Another Motor Car Connection 179

Bamford Family Timeline 185

Postscript 191

Additional family trees not previously displayed 193

Appendix I: Will of Samuel Bamford the Elder 205

Appendix II: Will of Charles Bamford 213

Appendix III: Will of Arthur John Jones Bamford 221

Appendix IV: Will of Edwin Bamford. 223

Appendix V: The Honourable Anne Hawke —
Letters of Administration 231

Appendix VI: Honourable Harold Brooke Hawke –
Letters of Administration 233

Appendix VII: Will of Francis Joseph Benedict
Kreitmair 235

Appendix VIII: Will of David Citroen 243

Appendix IX: Lehigh Zinc Iron Company v. Bamford 257

Appendix X: Famous owners of Minerva's. 263

Appendix XI: References in Wiguläus von Kreittmayr
article 265

Appendix XII: References in article by Jeri L. Jones 269

Additional Family Information 271

About the Author. 279

Preface

When I first started writing about my family genealogy some years ago, I had no idea of the story that was about to unfold. There was talk from the elders in my family about the wealth of previous generations of Bamfords and that they were in the meat exporting — or was it importing business — but that was about it. As I dug deep into my family history, I kept finding more information and, with the help of many sources, was able to piece together an incredible story. The first few chapters lay the foundation to the story and contain many names and dates which are of historical interest, but not that exciting to read.

The family that holds this book together is Charles Francis Kreitmair Bamford (Frank) and his wife, Doris Betty Holloway (Dorrie) — my father and mother — as the book details the lives of not only the Bamfords, but the Holloways, the Kreitmairs, and the Citroens, Frank and Dorrie's ancestors.

Using Google, Wikipedia, various genealogy websites, mostly Ancestry. co.uk, some professional researchers, and various family members from the past and present, history began to be revealed. As each new nuance presented itself, further digging was required. The research was exciting at times, but often it was frustrating, as connections could not always be made or stories verified. Another source of useful material were the

Last Wills and Testaments of some family members. These are shown in the appendices.

The information in "The Bamfords: A Family History" is, to the best of my knowledge and belief, all true; any speculation is so stated. The most frustrating part of the research was on the female lines of a family working backwards due to the surname change, so there are gaps in the narrative presented here. Plenty of additional information is out there, ready to be uncovered by those so interested.

The census records in the United Kingdom are an incredible source of information. The first one available for public viewing is from the year 1841 and then every 10 years thereafter. However, the last available for public viewing is the 1911 census, with the 1921 census to be released in January 2022 and the 1931 census was destroyed during World War II. Unfortunately, there are no such census records in Germany, where the Kreitmairs originated. All information has to be found in church records, so the researcher not only has to know from which town the individual was born, married, or died, but also which parish. In the case of the Kreitmairs, there is also a change in the spelling of the surname from the original spelling of Kreittmayr.

Through my research and several trips to England and Wales to uncover as much information as possible, I met many wonderful and helpful people, such as Arthur Williams, whom I accidently met in the Kings Head, a pub in Llanrhaiadr. I mentioned to him that I was trying to find the grave of Arthur John Jones Bamford; not only did he show me the grave, but it turned out that we were distant cousins! And the Vicar of St. Dyfnog, Llanrhaiadr, who, after I barged into the church during the tail end of her communion service, invited me to join them all for tea and biscuits. Then there was Jill Hope, churchwarden, who was so helpful to my sister Jayne and me when we were visiting St. Barnabas Church, Bromborough in the Wirral, and she kindly gave us each a water colour of the church. And while visiting old family homes, I met Mrs. Heather Craven, who lives at Misterton Hall, and so kindly showed me around her home when I arrived unannounced. The same was true with Mr. and Mrs. George Begg of Pentre Celyn, who not only gave my brother David, his wife Jo and myself tea but graciously gave us a guided tour of their home. In the Wirral, there was also Susan Nicholson, Honorary Archivist of the Bromborough Society, who supplied me with crucial information regarding Brookhurst and Bromborough. Then there were relatives such as Michael Cave, who provided much needed Citroen family information, and Corrine Hastilow, who unearthed details of Eleanor Bamford's wedding to Samuel Waring, Charles Bamford's baptism record and has been a great source of early Bamford material. And of course, my immediate family members gave me much support, information and needed encouragement over the years, including my nephew Carl Bamford, who provided me with a colour picture of the Bamford Coat of Arms used on the cover. My heartfelt thanks go to you all.

Sarah Hartley
(Peter Bamford)

Excerpt "Armorial Families"

By Arthur Charles Fox-Davies
Jack Publisher 1 January 1895

BAMFORD

ARTHUR JOHN JONES BAMFORD, Gentleman, Lord of the Manor of Misterton. *Born* April 25, 1857, being the third son of Charles Bamford and his wife, Hannah Clifford, daughter of John Yerl. *Clubs* — Leicester Conservative (Leicester), Conservative (Liverpool), County (Rhyl). *Livery* — Light coat, with red collar, piped with red silk. Red waistcoat. **Armorial bearings** — He bears for **Arms**: Argent, a fesse engrailed between two annulets in chief, and as many mascles in base gules: and for the **Crest**, on a wreath of the colours in front of a dexter arm embowed holding a flagstaff proper, therefrom flowing a banner argent, charged with a mascle gules, three annulets interlaced of the last; with the **Motto**, "Perseverantia vincit." *Married*, October 15, 1879, Anne, eldest daughter of Thomas Nash of Worcestershire; and has *Issue* — (1) Charles Arthur Bamford, Gentleman, born July 27, 1880; (2) Edwin Scott Bamford, Gentleman, born April 23, 1886; and Anne Nash. *Estates* — Misterton Hall and Brookhurst, Bromborough, Cheshire. *Postal address* — Misterton Hall, Lutterworth, Leicestershire.

Derivation of Bamford

The surname 'Bamford' is derived from various habitational places (the two main ones being in Lancashire and Derbyshire). The villages were named in old English as beam as in 'tree', 'beam' + ford as in a drivable road across a stream, i.e. a ford with a plank bridge for those who wished to keep their feet dry. Beamford became Bamford[1].

---

1. This information is from www.houseofnames.com/bamford-family-names

Notable Bamfords

(None Related)

William Bamford of Bury: High Sherriff of Lancashire, 1787 (Bury is about 3.5 miles from Bamford, Lancashire)

Samuel Bamford (1788-1872): English reformer and poet

Captain Edward Bamford VC, DSO (1887-1928): British officer in World War I who received the Victoria Cross

Joseph Cyril Bamford (1916-2001): English businessman, founder of the JCB heavy machinery company

John "Jack" Bamford (b. 1937): English, youngest person to have received the George Cross

James Bamford (b. 1946): American bestselling author and journalist

Maria Bamford (b. 1970): American stand-up comedian.

LESS NOTABLE BAMFORDS

William Bamford: English convict from Lancaster who was transported aboard the 'America' on April 4, 1829, settling in New South Wales, Australia

In Ian Fleming's books, James Bond's first car was a Bamford Martin, the forerunner to the Aston Martin; Robert Bamford was a principal investor with Lionel Martin a car enthusiast.

The Bamfords

SAMUEL BAMFORD

George III was on the throne and William Pitt the younger was prime minister. The year was 1791, and Samuel Bamford was born in Chesterfield, Derbyshire. If young Samuel had been able to read, he could have read the first issue of The Observer, the world's first Sunday newspaper. The recently formed United States was in its infancy. George Washington was completing his first term as president and the first 10 amendments to the United States Constitution had been passed, creating the United States Bill of Rights. Back home, the Priestly riots in Birmingham were occurring; the rioters main targets were religious dissenters, the most controversial being Joseph Priestly who sympathised with the French revolutionaries[2].

Ten years previously, in 1781, Mary Jones was born and later became Samuel's wife in January 1813, marrying in Wolverhampton. They settled down in Wednesbury, Staffordshire, living on the High Street, where Samuel was a pork butcher. He later became a cattle dealer, and his involvement in the meat business ultimately proved fortuitous for him and two of his sons.

---

2. Information from en.m.wikipedia.org

DESCENDANTS OF SAMUEL BAMFORD

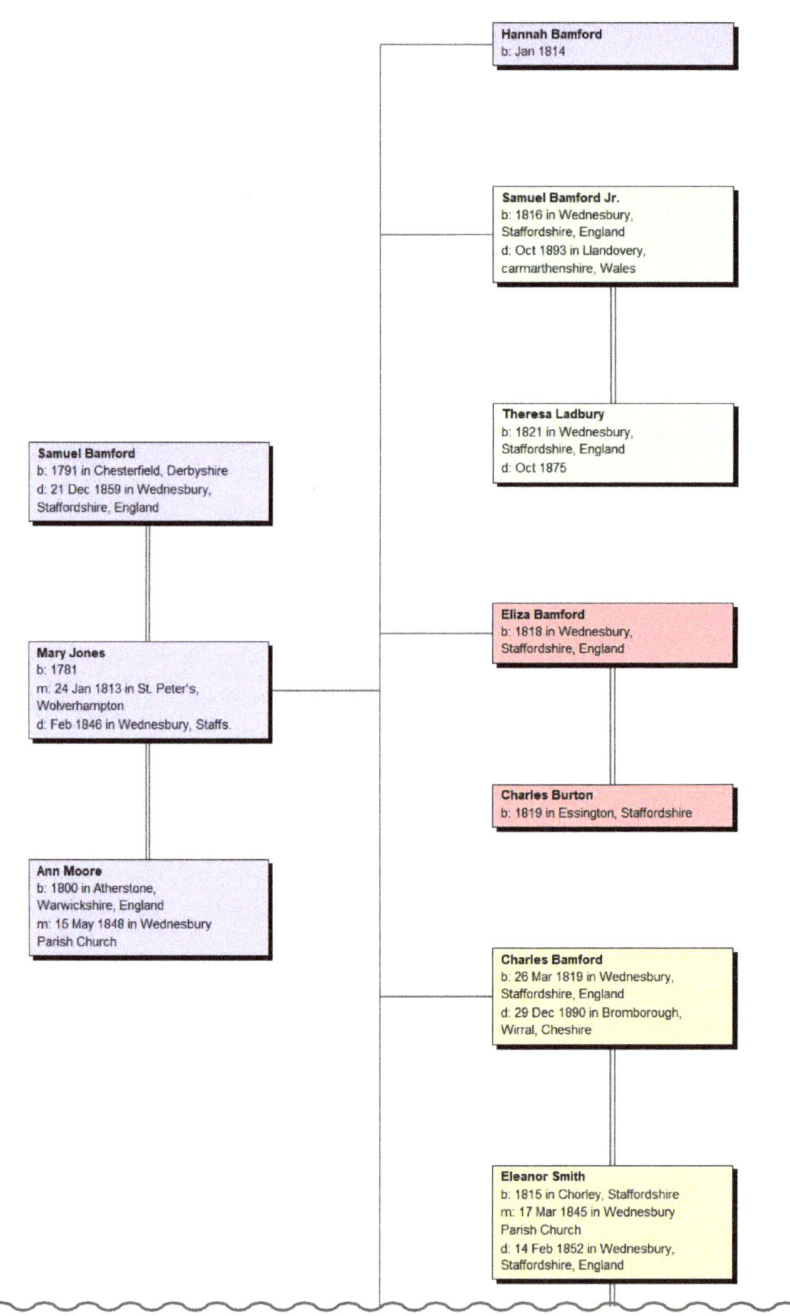

The Bamfords

Hannah Clifford Yerl
b: 1828 in Butterfield, Wednsbury, Staffordshire (maybe Butterhill)
m: 01 Feb 1853 in Seighford Parish, Stafford, Staffordshire
d: 11 Dec 1886 in Broohhurst, Bromborough

Mary Bamford
b: Jan 1820 in Wednesbury Staffordshire

Edwin Steer
b: 22 Feb 1825 in Croydon, Surrey
d: 16 Dec 1890 in Croydon, Surrey

Edwin Bamford
b: 1823 in Wednesbury, Staffordshire, England
d: 03 Apr 1894 in Cheshire, England

Elizabeth Evason
b: 1826 in Upton, Cheshire
m: 1853
d: Apr 1888 in Cheshire

Louisa Bamford
b: 1826 in Wednesbury, Staffordshire, England

Samuel and Mary had seven children: Hannah, Samuel Jr., Eliza, Charles, Mary, Edwin, and Louisa, who was born in 1826 when Mary, her mother, was 45 years old. Eliza married a butcher and Mary married a provision dealer and both families lived and worked in Wolverhampton. Mary's husband, Edwin Steer, was an alcoholic and after Mary's death he was invariably in trouble with the law for either assaulting people or not paying his debts, usually small amounts even though he had the money. Hannah, the eldest child remained unmarried but unfortunately, little is known about Louisa other than her birth year.

Samuel Bamford, Jr., the eldest son, was born in 1816 in Wednesbury and almost certainly worked with his father as a pork butcher for a short while after he left school, but it was not the career for him.

Having decided that a change in careers was necessary, and much to the disappointment of his father, Samuel Jr. became a draper, setting up business down the road from his father's business on the High Street in Wednesbury. His business was next to the Ladbury's, who were druggists. As it turned out, he didn't have to look far to find his future wife; he married the girl next door, Theresa Selina Ladbury around 1841. They had five children.

Samuel Jr. and Theresa's first three children were born in Wednesbury, but sometime after 1847 and before 1853, Samuel, Jr. decided on a career in farming, and he purchased 31 acres in Stock and Bradley, Worcestershire, with some financial help from his brother Charles. The farm is where the other children were born. At some point after 1861, Samuel Jr. decided to move to another larger farm in the lush farming area of Kerry's Gate, near Abbey Dore in Herefordshire, probably with the help of a small inheritance from his father. It is interesting to note that Frederick, the eldest son, and his wife Emma emigrated to Australia in 1877, the same year that they married, and Frederick died in Perth, Western Australia in 1927. John Hobbins Bamford and

DESCENDANTS OF SAMUEL BAMFORD, JR.

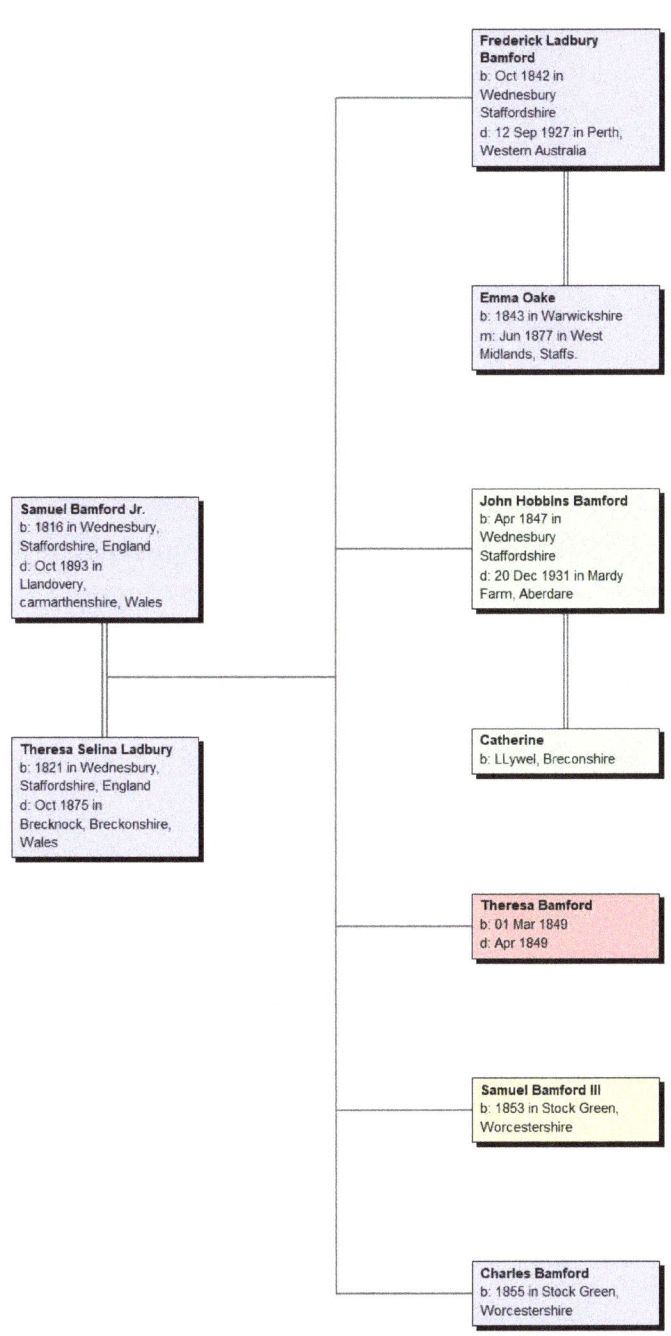

Catherine, farmers in Aberdare, Wales, had six children, but both Samuel and Charles remained unmarried.

Unfortunately, Mary, the wife of Samuel Sr. died at the age of 65 in 1846 and was buried at St. Bartholomew's in Wednesbury. Two years later, Samuel remarried, a widow by the name of Ann Moore, who had two sons, one a teenage son, William who was still living at home. According to the 1851 census, the three of them lived at Earps Lane in Wednesbury. On their marriage document, Samuel's father is listed as Samuel, a forgeman, and her father, William Matthews, a mechanic. It is likely that Ann was unable to read or write, as she signed with a mark on the marriage document[3].

Samuel Sr. was a hardworking man eager to make something of his life. The money he made he reinvested into property mainly on the High Street in Wednesbury. Both Charles and Edwin were working as pork butchers and it is believed that around 1842 Samuel left the business to his two sons and started a new business as a cattle dealer. The two brothers worked well together and formed a formal partnership, Bamford Brothers, in 1845. According to the 1851 census records, Samuel Sr. was listed as a retired cattle dealer at the age of 60.

Samuel Sr. and Ann were able to have 11 years together until Samuel passed away just before Christmas in 1859. At the time of his death he had managed to acquire The Old Royal Exchange, Public House on the High Street and six other properties on the High Street as well as 2 properties in Earp Lane and a plot of land there. These properties together with his own house on Sansome Lane were bequeathed to his wife and children. Charles received the pub and an adjoining house, and all the others received one house each with the properties on Earps lane being sold off. The complex details are divulged in his Will, Appendix I. The end result is that Samuel Jr. actually receives very

---

3. Information provided by Corinne Hastilow

little from the bequests of his father underscoring Samuels's disdain for his eldest son Samuel Jr.

However, the real story is about the middle children of Samuel Bamford Sr.: Charles, who was born in Wednesbury, Staffordshire in 1819, and Edwin, born in 1823, also in Wednesbury. The brothers were ambitious but uncertain, as all teenagers are, as to where their lives would take them. They could not have foreseen the large fortunes they were to make.

CHARLES BAMFORD

Charles was working as a pork butcher when he met Eleanor Smith from Chorley, Staffordshire. Not much is known about her except that she was three years older than Charles and that they married in 1845, when Charles was 27 years old. They settled down on the High Street in Wednesbury and had two children, Charles Smith in 1848 and Eleanor in 1850. In the 1851 census, which was taken on 30 March 1851, Charles listed his occupation as a cattle dealer and victualler[4]; the children were

Charles Bamford

---

4. The term victualler normally means someone licensed to sell alcoholic liquor or selling foods or other provisions.

now aged 3 and 1. The census also showed that they had visitors: Mary Smith, probably Eleanor's sister-in-law, with her two children, James, aged 2, and Charlotte, aged 1. What bedlam and a happy house that must have been with four children under the age of 3! They also list two others living with them: Eliza, a housemaid, and George, a brewer! So, what was going on? What trade was Charles involved in, and why is George on the payroll? It is known that his father Samuel owned a pub, The Old Royal Exchange, and it is probable that Charles helped him, if not completely handled, the pub's affairs. So, George was probably brewing beer for the pub. Like his father, Charles was determined to be successful in business, willing to put his hand to anything, and had taken over his father's business as a cattle dealer upon his father's retirement.

Later that year, in October, there was tragedy in the family: little Eleanor died. Maybe Mary was there to help her sister-in-law Eleanor with the sick child. At that time, it was not unusual for young children to die due to sickness, but it did not make it any easier on the parents. Undoubtedly, both Charles and Eleanor were heartbroken.

Four months later in 1852, disaster struck yet again. At the age of 39, the elder Eleanor died, leaving Charles with his 4-year-old son. It must have been exceptionally hard for both father and son. Eleanor's cause of death is not known: it may have been some deadly sickness, complications during childbirth, or perhaps even a broken heart. Whatever the cause, Charles wasted no time finding a new mother for his child. He probably already knew Hannah Clifford Yerl, as she was a local girl, and they became engaged and were married in January 1853 in Seighford parish church by licence. In the marriage documents, Charles' occupation is listed as a farmer in Kings Norton, which according to the marriage documents, was where he lived[5]. The farm was probably more of an investment than a career change. Even though Hannah was nine years his junior, it was a good marriage, by all accounts. They had five children of their own.

---

5. Information provided by Corinne Hastilow

DESCENDANTS OF CHARLES BAMFORD

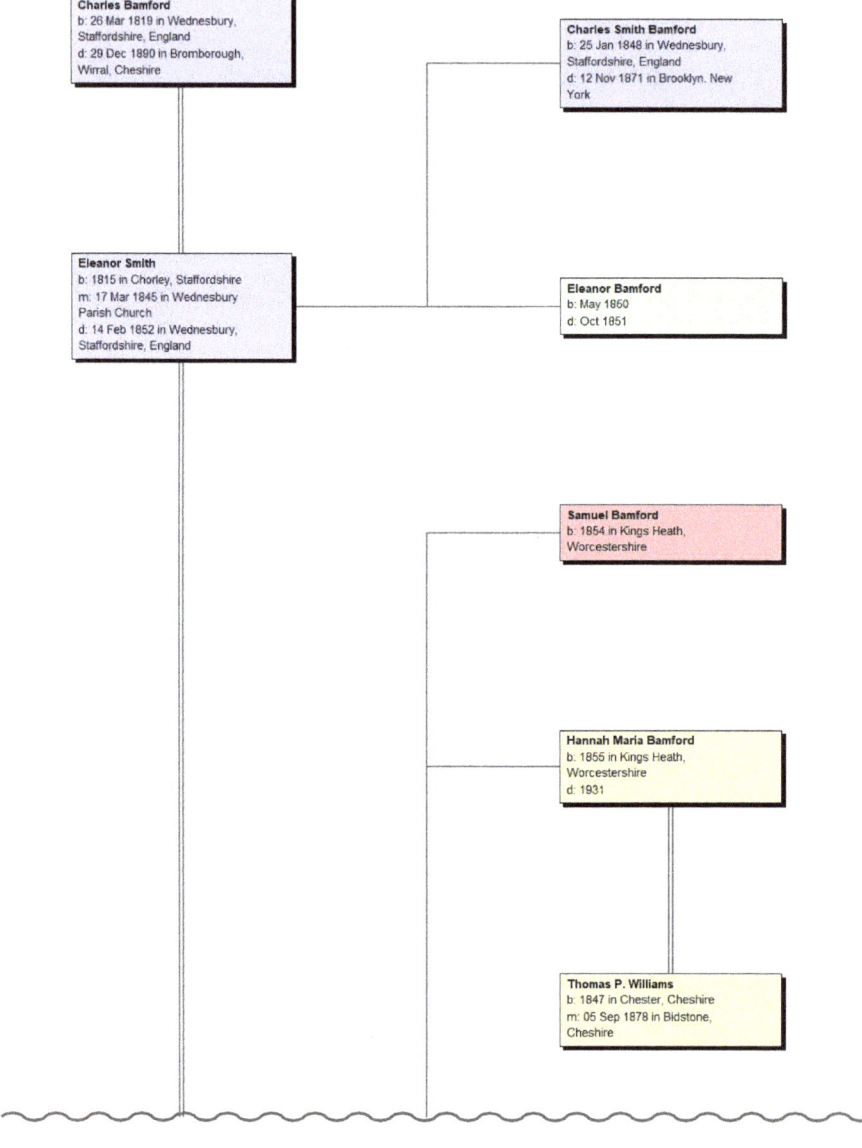

The Bamfords

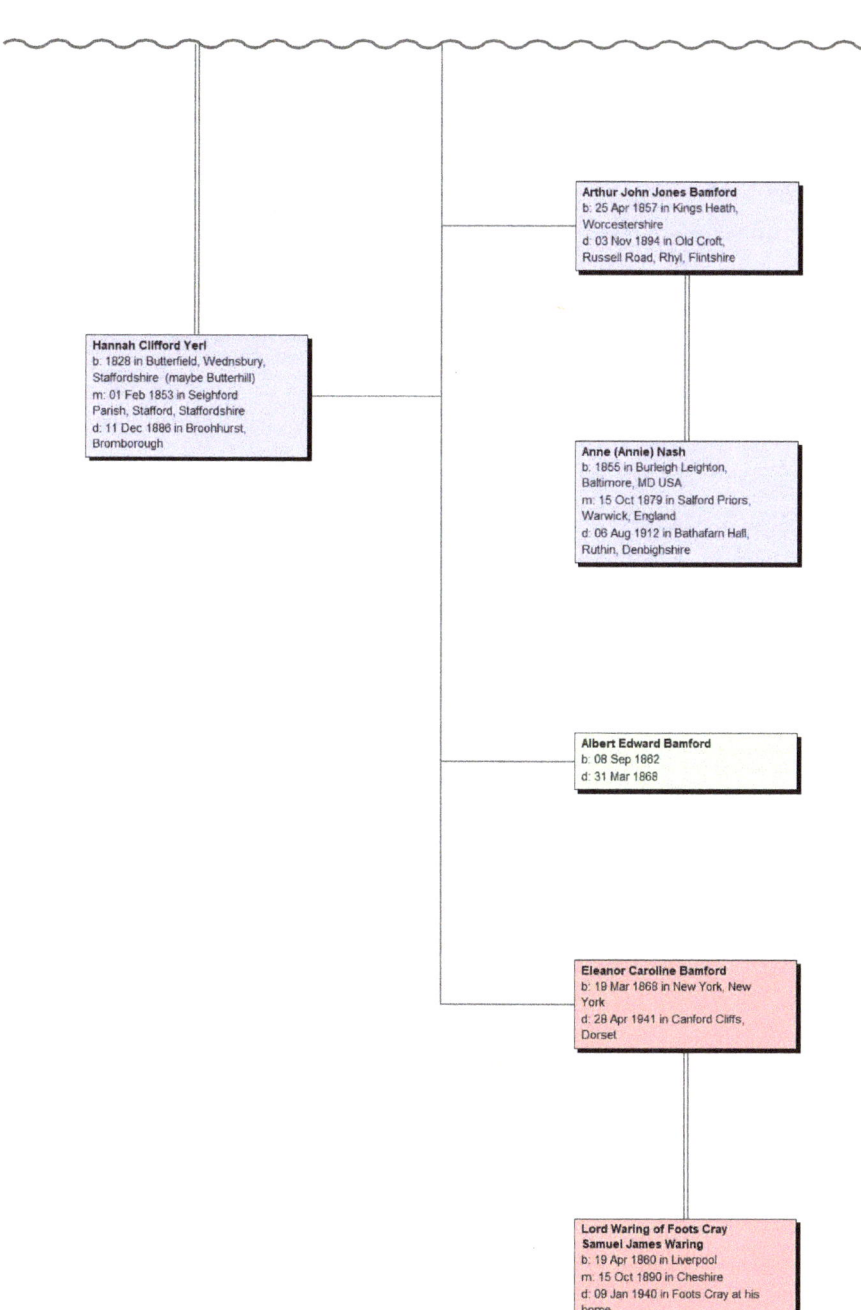

EDWIN BAMFORD

Edwin was born in 1824 in Wednesbury, Staffordshire, like his brothers. And like his father and brother Charles, he worked in the meat business as a pork butcher. He met Elizabeth Evason from Upton, Cheshire, who was two years younger than him, and they married in 1853, the same year as Charles' second marriage. One wonders if they used the new railway system to travel to meet each other or if they travelled the 70 miles by carriage or horseback. Their marriage was prolific, with seven children.

Research did not uncover a date of death of the eldest son, Edwin. It is believed that he went into the church and became the vicar of Kingston, presumably on Thames, or it could have been Jamaica! In the will of Edwin the father (found in Appendix IV), this son was hardly mentioned. Right at the end, it states that any property not previously bequeathed should be divided equally between his two daughters and Edwin, the two daughters having already been left substantial real estate and personal property. There is no mention of Mary Elizabeth in her fathers will, and so it is assumed that she died at a young age, so common in those days.

Little information could be found about William Evason, Edwin's third son, after the 1881 census. At that point he was living at Raby Hall in the Wirral with his father and mother and working with his father in Liverpool. It is believed that he never married. In his fathers will, it was mentioned that William was bankrupt and that he was left an annuity of £260 to be paid at the rate of £5 per week, to be used for his personal use only. Any other use would void the legacy and he would receive nothing. It is probable that William had a gambling problem. By the 1891 census he was no longer living at Raby Hall, and it is unlikely he was working with his father in Liverpool. He died at the age of 38, one year after his father, in 1895. Edwin's bequest to his son was not so punitive, as £5 in 1895 converts to approximately £604 in today's money, using an annual inflation rate of 3.85 percent.

DESCENDANTS OF EDWIN BAMFORD

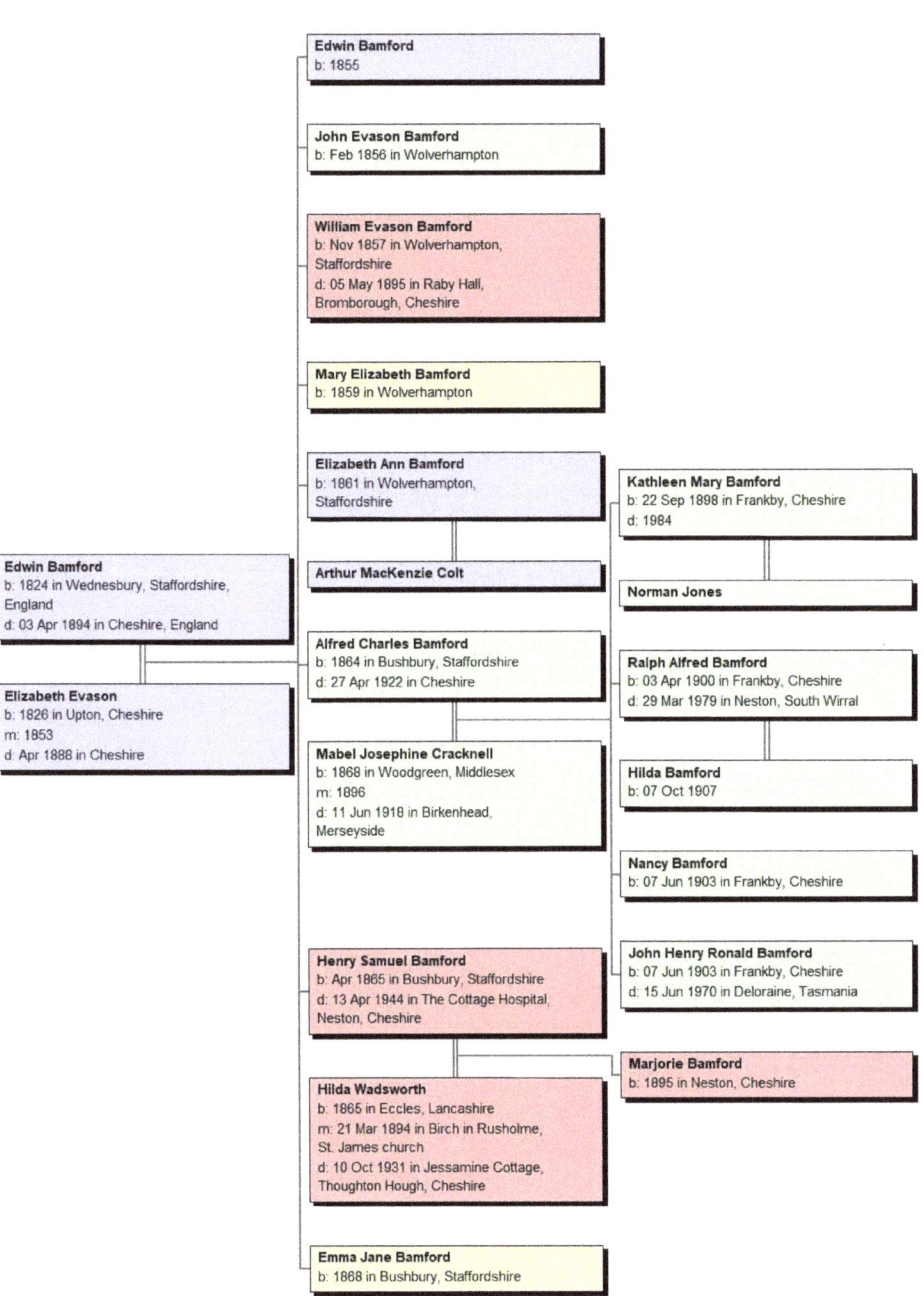

Alfred Charles Bamford married Mabel Josephine Cracknell in 1896. They had four children.

Henry Samuel Bamford married Hilda Wadsworth from Eccles, Lancashire in 1894 and had one child, Marjorie. Henry and Hilda purchased, or maybe built, Thornton Hall in Thornton Hough. The home includes many beautiful oak carvings, including a carving of the Bamford Family coat of arms and an ornate ceiling made of leather and embossed with mother-of-pearl. It is now a four-star hotel and spa.

DESCENDANTS OF ALFRED CHARLES BAMFORD

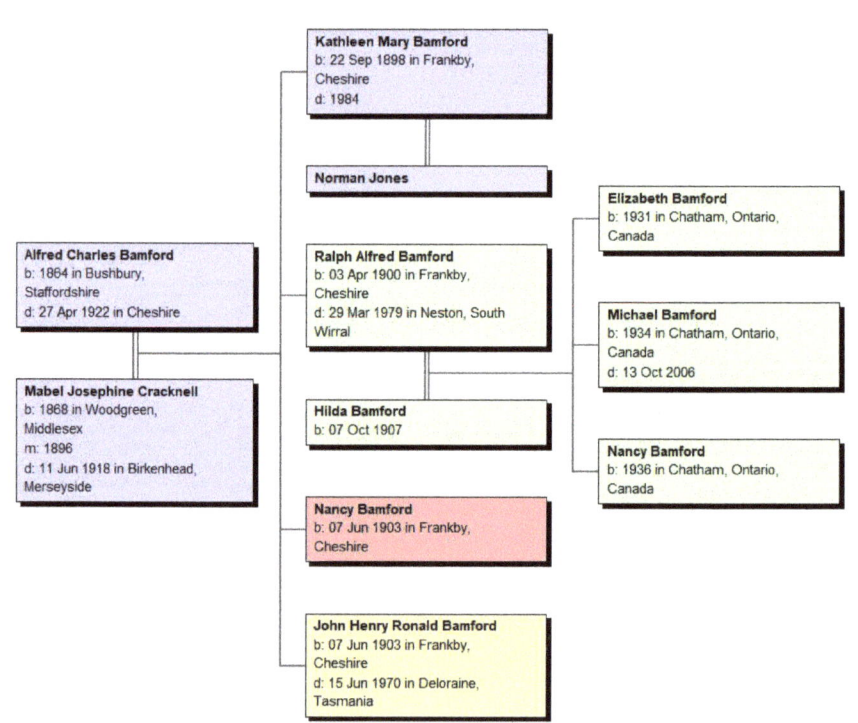

Thornton Hough

The village includes some notable buildings, including Thornton Hall, once the home of wealthy shipping merchants, the Bamford Brothers of Liverpool. It is believed to have been built in the mid-1800s and was transformed into a hotel in 1954. Many of its original features remain intact, including oak carvings and the ornate mother-of-pearl embossed ceiling in the Italian Room[6].

Of Edwin (the elder) Bamford's great-grandchildren Kathleen Mary Bamford married Norman Jones in 1922 and lived in Bryn Mair, N. Wales.

Ralf Alfred Bamford was called up to serve in the army at the age of 18. Fortunately for him, World War II had just finished, and he was honourably discharged two years later. He (or the family) decided that

Thornton Hall with Bamford Coat of Arms adjacent to sign

---

6. Cheshire Life 2012

Original entrance hall

Oak carving of the Bamford Coat of Arms (Note the banner argent has broken off)

he should go overseas, so he went to Cleveland Ohio in 1920. He stayed for six months, working for the Cleveland Provision Company, a meat packing company. On his return home he went back to work at the family business in Liverpool. He met and married Hilda (b. 1907), maiden name not known. They had only one son, Michael, who was born in Chatham, Ontario. He was the only boy to carry on the Bamford line from Edwin. Ralf emigrated to Chatham, Ontario, Canada in 1927 after his business, Bamford Brothers, ceased trading around 1925. It was there where he started to farm tobacco, mainly a dark tobacco used in pipe smoking. It is believed that his son Michael died in Canada, but nothing is known about his family.

John Henry Ronald Bamford remained unmarried and died in Deloraine, Tasmania, having travelled all through his life. He never went into the family business. Maybe he was a remittance man.

Marjorie Bamford, Henry and Hilda Bamford's daughter, attended St. George's School in Ascot. No other information could be found.

THE JCB BAMFORDS

A question often asked is, "Are we (the Bamfords) related to the JCB Bamfords from Uttoxeter of the excavator business fame?" We know all the relatives of Charles Bamford, and there are no connections there, but what about Samuel and Edwin Bamford's families? JCB stands for Joseph Cyril Bamford, who started the business in 1945 after World War II. He was born on 21 June 1916, and it has been extremely difficult to find out information about his ancestors. However, a family tree of the male side of his family was found on the Vintage Farm Machinery site of Henry Bamford & Sons[7].

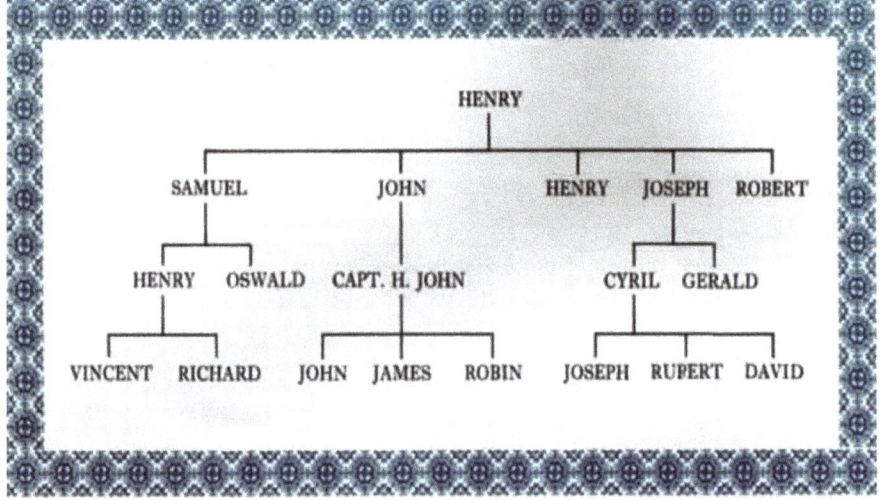

Joseph Cyril Bamford was the son of Cyril Bamford, with brothers Rupert and David. They were born into a recusant Catholic family, and none of the first names match any of the first names of the children or grandchildren of Samuel or Edwin in a corresponding time frame. Therefore, we are not immediately related to the JCB Bamfords. Given the Catholic connection, one would have to go a long way back to find a common relative; however, with their close proximity to the Samuel Bamford family in Staffordshire, it should not be ruled out.

---

7. Information and family tree from www.henrybamfordandsonsuttoxeterengland.co.uk

THE FOURTH EARL FERRERS

The following story is of interest, as Margaret Clifford is related to the Charles Bamford family. All information comes from Capital Punishment U.K.[8]

Laurence Shirley, the 4th Earl Ferrers, was born on the 18th of August 1720 and has the dubious distinction of becoming the last peer of the realm to be hanged as a common criminal.

---

8. Story from www.capitalpunishmentuk.org courtesy of Richard Clark

He inherited the title in 1745, at the age of 25, and with it the family estates in Leicestershire, Derbyshire and Northamptonshire. The main residence was at Staunton Harold Hall about two miles from Ashby-de-la-Zouch in Leicestershire.

From 1743, he had been having a relationship with Margaret Clifford, the daughter of his land agent Richard Clifford, with whom he had 4 illegitimate daughters between 1744 and 1749. Like most people in his position he needed at least one male heir to inherit the title and the estates, so in 1752, he married Mary, the 16 year old sister of Sir William Meredith of Henbury in Cheshire.

It was not a happy marriage, Mary lived in fear of the Earl's constant drunken rages and violent outbursts and also his womanising (it seems that the relationship with Margaret Clifford continued during the marriage and she went to live with him after the dissolution of it). In the end, things got so bad that Mary obtained a separation from him by an Act of Parliament in 1758. This was a most unusual step for that time and she would have had to show very strong grounds to obtain the separation.

As part of the separation arrangements, it was agreed that Mary should receive an income from the rents from some of the properties on the estate. As a result, control of the estate was vested in trustees, one of whom was an old family steward, John Johnson, who reluctantly became the receiver of these rents. Unsurprisingly, Mr. Johnson was disliked by Ferrers, particularly after he had found out that Johnson had paid his wife £50 without his approval and presumably also because he hated the fact Johnson had power over the estate. It has also been suggested that the Earl suspected that John Johnson and Mary were having an affair. Mary later re-married — to Lord Frederick Campbell, dying in a fire at her house in 1807.

On Sunday, the 13th of January 1760, Ferrers paid a visit to Johnson and invited him to visit the Hall on Friday, the 18th. Before John

Johnson arrived, Ferrers sent away his mistress, Margaret Clifford, the children and the male servants. When Johnson arrived at the Hall, he was shown into the Earl's study and a discussion of business matters took place. A heated argument soon erupted and around 3 o'clock in the afternoon Ferrers shot Johnson. He was not fatally injured by the bullet and was given some treatment at the Hall for his wound and put to bed there. Dr. Kirkland from Ashby-de-la-Zouch and Johnson's daughter, Sarah, were also sent for. The Earl continued to abuse and threaten Johnson through the evening before finally falling into a drunken stupor, thus allowing Dr. Kirkland to remove him back to his own house where he died the following morning. Ferrers had apparently told Sarah Johnson that he would take care of her family should her father die, on condition that they did not bring a prosecution against him.

Arrest and trial

It was Dr. Kirkland, assisted by a number of local men, notably a collier named Curtis, who disarmed and arrested the Earl the following day. The inquest on Mr. Johnson brought in a verdict of death by wilful murder and so Ferrers was remanded to Leicester prison. As a peer, he could not be tried at the Leicester Assizes so he was transferred to the Tower of London and committed to the custody of Black Rod on the 14th of February to await trial.

The trial opened at Westminster Hall on the 16th of April 1760 before the Lord High Steward, Lord Henley and was to last 2 days. The Attorney General, Sir Charles Pratt, and the Solicitor General, Sir Charles Yorke, led for the prosecution. They brought as witnesses, Dr Kirkland, Sarah Johnson and the 3 women servants who were present at the Hall at the time of the murder.

Ferrers conducted his own defence, as all defendants had to in those days. He had been dissuaded by his family from trying to claim that the shooting of John Johnson was justified. He therefore attempted a defence of insanity, a condition for which he was able to offer considerable evidence — just about everyone who knew him thought he was mad. He later maintained however, that he had only done this at the insistence of his family, and that he had himself always been ashamed of such a defence. It is easy to understand why the family were so concerned at the prospect of the damage to their reputation and the shame of having a prominent member of it hanged as a felon.

One witness, Peter Williams, gave an account of what happened when the Earl came to collect a mare that he had left in the care of the Williams family. Ferrers was unhappy with the way that the horse had been cared for and hit Mrs. Williams and seriously injured Peter Williams with a sword. The Solicitor General pointed out that this was no proof of insanity or eccentric behaviour. He went so far as to say that if a man couldn't take such action against a negligent servant, then everyone present would be in the dock! This gives you an idea of the way the nobility of the time saw life — they were above the law, Ferrers clearly thought he was. He did not really seem capable of understanding that it was wrong for a man in his position to shoot Mr. Johnson.

At the end of the trial, his fellow peers decided that Ferrers was legally sane. Although he had presented a strong defence in an articulate manner, it was difficult to see that there was any other verdict open to them. They had each, individually, to find him guilty of murder, which they did and therefore there could only be one sentence — hanging by the neck until dead followed by dissection, to be carried out on Monday, the 21st of April in pursuance with the conditions of the Murder Act 1752. This Act specified that execution was to take place within two days of sentence unless that would fall on a Sunday.

In view of the importance of the prisoner and to allow time for suitable arrangements to be made, the hanging was stayed until Monday, the 5th of May. The thought of a public hanging at Tyburn appalled

Ferrers — it was the death of a common criminal and he petitioned the king to be allowed to be beheaded instead — the death of a nobleman. Beheading was not a legally available punishment for murder, only for treason committed by a peer. Thus, the sentence had to stand, and he remained in the Round Tower awaiting the trip to Tyburn.

It is said that on the night he was sentenced to death he played picquet (early 16th century card game) with the warders. He led a very good life style in the Tower — effectively if you could afford it you could get whatever you wanted in prison at that time. The only privilege he was not permitted was visits from Margaret Clifford. He made his will, leaving £16,000 to his 4 daughters by Margaret, and £200 to Sarah Johnson. The king, George II, duly signed the Writ of Execution on the 2nd of May.

Execution

The hanging of a nobleman was a major public spectacle as well as a wholly unusual event. A special new gallows was constructed at Tyburn for the occasion. It comprised of a scaffold covered in black baize reached by a short flight of stairs. Two uprights rose from the scaffold, topped with a cross beam. Directly under the beam there was a small box like structure, some 3 feet square and 18 inches high, which was designed to sink down into the scaffold and thus leave the criminal suspended. There were even black cushions for the Earl and the chaplain to kneel on to pray before the hanging. Every seat in Mother Proctor's Pews was taken and there was a huge crowd around the gallows, held back by the customary Javelin men.

For the hanging, Ferrers wore his wedding suit, a light-coloured satin one embroidered with silver, saying "he thought this at least as good an occasion for putting them on as that for which they were first made". As we have seen before, it was considered important to look ones best at one's execution.

At nine o'clock on the Monday morning, Ferrers' body was demanded of the keeper of the Tower, by the sheriffs of London and Middlesex. It had been agreed that Ferrers could make the trip to Tyburn in his own landau[9] drawn by six horses. He was accompanied in this carriage by Mr Humphries, the Chaplain of the Tower and Mr Vaillant the sheriff. Ferrers said he "was much obliged to him and took it kindly that he accompanied him."

The procession to Tyburn was led by a troop of cavalry, with Ferrer's landau behind them, guarded on both sides, followed by the carriage of Mr Errington, the other sheriff, a mourning-coach-and-six, containing some of his lordship's friends, a hearse for the conveyance of his body to Surgeons' Hall after execution, and another contingent of soldiers. Huge numbers of people had turned out to watch the spectacle and it took 2-3/4 hours to complete the journey to Tyburn. Ferrers remarked that he thought "so large a mob had collected because the people had never seen a lord hanged before." (The last execution of a lord was that of Simon Lord Lovatt who was beheaded on Tower Hill for treason on 9 April 1747)

---

9. A landau is a four-wheeled convertible carriage so that it can be open or closed

Rev. Humphries, the chaplain, told Ferrers "that some prayer should be offered on the scaffold, and asked his leave to repeat at least the Lord's Prayer;" to which Ferrers replied, "I always thought it a good prayer, you may use it if you please."

When they finally got to Tyburn, Ferrers told Rev. Humphries "I perceive we are almost arrived; it is time to do what little more I have to do." He gave Sheriff Vaillant his watch and presented 5 guineas to the chaplain. He had also brought the same sum to give to the hangman, Thomas Turlis, however, he handed it to the wrong man, and there was nearly a fight between Turlis and his assistant.

Ferrers and Mr. Humphries then kneeled together on the two black cushions and said the Lord's Prayer. Ferrers concluded by saying "Lord have mercy upon me, and forgive me for my errors." He then mounted the "drop" where his arms were tied with a black silk sash, and the rope placed around his neck. He final words were to ask Turlis: "Am I right?" A white nightcap which Ferrers had brought with him, was pulled down over his head. He had declined to give the signal to the hangman himself, so this was done by the sheriff. So sometime around noon, the platform sank down leaving the Earl suspended. The mechanism had not functioned properly and Ferrers' feet were still virtually in contact with the platform. He writhed slightly for a short period before becoming still. Horace Walpole reported that it took 4 minutes for him to die. The body was left to hang for the customary hour before being taken down and placed in the coffin for transport to Surgeon's Hall and dissection. A woodcut was made of the body in its coffin. After being dissected and the body put on display until the evening of Thursday, the 8th of May, when it was returned to his family for burial in St. Pancras church. Twenty-two years later, the body was taken back to Staunton Harold to be re-interred in the vault.

Conclusion

It was generally accepted that there was mental instability in Laurence Ferrers, but it was greatly exacerbated by his extremely heavy drinking.

He could behave quite normally when sober but was totally out of control when drunk. It would seem that Ferrers' drinking was also the principal cause of the breakdown of his marriage.

There was clear evidence of premeditation and planning in the murder and of normal "sane" behaviour before and after it. He had invited Mr. Johnson to the Hall and sent out his mistress and children and his man servants — perhaps because they may have tried to stop him.

There is also his supreme arrogance, probably resulting from his position and the power it gave him as a feudal employer and landowner. It seems hard to understand today, but Peers really still did think they were above the law in the mid-18th century. Physically and verbally abusing servants was deemed perfectly normal and acceptable.

It was expected of nobleman that he would know "how to die" and how to put on a good show for the public and in this Earl Ferrers did not disappoint. Nor did the Sheriffs of London, as they had to obtain funding for and have designed and built the new gallows and arrange for the cavalry etc. to provide what was perceived by many at the time as a great day out. Compare the treatment of Ferrers with that of the common felons who were hanged at Tyburn.

Margaret Clifford lived another 25 years and died in 1785, aged 63. She was buried at Breedon on the Hill where she was born.

What an interesting story, but what has it to do with the Bamford family? Well, Margaret Clifford's first cousin, John Clifford (b. 1729), married Hannah Gorse (b. 1746), and one of their two children was Mary Clifford (b. 1791), who married John Yerl in 1824 at St. Mary's Church in Lichfield. They had five children, one of whom was Hannah Clifford Yerl, who married Charles Bamford after his first wife, Eleanor Smith, had died. That means that Margaret Clifford and Hannah Clifford Bamford were second cousins once removed. Yes, it's a stretch, but they are related all the same. The following simplified family trees of the Clifford family may help one understand the relationship.

One of Hannah Bamford's sisters was Mary Ann Yerl, who married James Gretton in 1848. At first their marriage was fine. They had

DESCENDANTS OF WILLIAM CLIFFORD

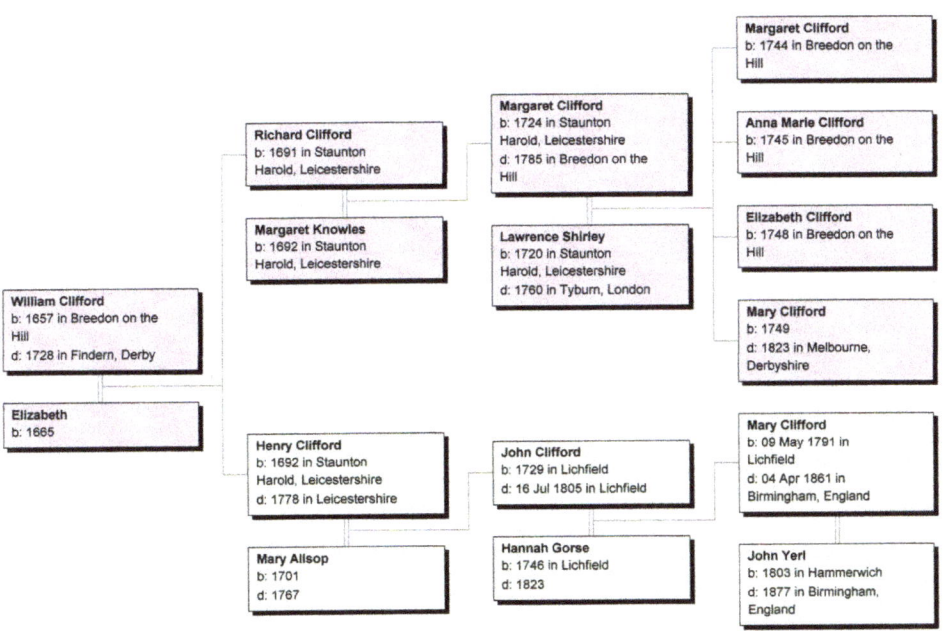

DESCENDANTS OF JOHN CLIFFORD

four children, a son and three daughters. However, things began to sour, and they split up, as divorce in Victorian times was scandalous. In 1868, James had an illegitimate daughter, named Lily, by his new "wife" Helena. It would appear that he set up home down the road with Helena: on the 1871 census for Aston, he was living on Aston Road with Helena and Lily, together with his four children from Mary Ann. Mary Ann went to live with her sister and brother-in-law, Hannah and Charles Bamford. Unfortunately, James Gretton's fortunes went downhill, and in the 1881 census he lives only with his daughter Lily at 61 Miller Street, Aston with no sign of Helena. By 1889, James Gretton is a lodger in a lodging house at 93 Belmont Row (by Curzon Street) and he eventually died in the Workhouse Infirmary in 1899[10].

Lily supposedly never married. On the 1901 census, she is a housemaid at the Birmingham Eye Hospital, and eventually died in 1950, aged 82

Mary Ann Gretton (nee Yerl) also had an illegitimate daughter, named Mary. Charles and Hannah Bamford were supportive of both Mary Ann Gretton, Hannah's sister, and the child. In the 1881 census, Mary Ann is with the Bamford's at Brookhurst, Bromborough, Cheshire, and Mary is with William Yerl and his second wife Sarah (her uncle and aunt) in Salford Cheshire. Whether they are just visiting or are living there is not known, probably the latter.

Mary Gretton (the illegitimate daughter) was a bridesmaid at her cousin Eleanor Bamford's wedding to Samuel James Waring (later Lord Waring of Foots Cray, who started the Waring furniture store in London and later merged to become Waring & Gillow a department store on Oxford Street), and Mary was also a mourner at Charles Bamford's funeral.

Mary Gretton died in her 80s in Bournemouth in the 1950s; she, like Lily, never married.

---

10. Paul Gebhard, Ancestry.com

BAMFORD BROTHERS

As brothers, Charles and Edwin were close. Of course, like all brothers and business partners, they had their differences of opinion, but that was good. It forced them to look at the issues before them objectively. But whatever problems they encountered, they almost always came to an amicable agreement — almost. Their father was a pork butcher and then a cattle dealer, and, both of them worked in the meat industry starting in their mid-teens. In the 1851 census (Charles, age 32 and Edwin, age 27) were listed at 8 Prescot Rd. (probably an inn) in the Parish of West Derby, Liverpool. This residence and business was owned by Alfred Webb, a victualler, who lived there with his two sons, two daughters, a son-in-law and 16 visitors. All the visitors, including Charles and Edwin, were cattle dealers, butchers, cattle salesmen, and cattle drivers. In fact, many on the street had the same type of occupants, many with numerous servants, especially the lower numbered houses. What they were all doing there is anyone's guess.

The term victualler is a bit confusing. In Britain it generally means either a person who is licensed to sell alcohol or the formal name for the landlord of a public house. It can also mean a person providing or selling food or other provisions. Now, later in life, both Charles and Edwin list their professions as provision merchants, although in the 1861 census Charles lists his profession as an auctioneer. For anyone paying attention, you'll note that Charles Bamford was counted twice in the 1851 census. Once when he completed the form and included his family and two servants, including George the brewer, and again when he was a visitor at 8 Prescot Rd. with his brother Edwin!

It is known is that the brothers started a business together, called Bamford Brothers, which eventually specialised in bacon, ham, and cured meats. One source stated that Bamford Brothers was started in 1845, which is quite possible, as at that time they were working together as pork butchers. The first mention of provision merchant was in Edwin's 1851 census form, which states he was a cattle and provision dealer. Ten years later, in Edwin's 1861 census form, he is listed as both a provision merchant and a hide, skin, and fat broker, while Charles' census form listed him as an auctioneer. According to Charles' son Arthur, between 1858 and 1861, Charles was the largest wool salesman in the Midland counties, with offices in Birmingham and Bingley Hall being used as a warehouse. At that time, he was living at 5 Jennens Row in Birmingham with his family and first mother-in-law, Anne Smith.

But it was Edwin, the younger brother, who found that the Provision Merchant business was very profitable and persuaded Charles to give up his other pursuits, which included, cattle dealer, victualler, farmer, auctioneer, wool salesman, and skin and hide broker — an activity that was mentioned in his father's probate records — and concentrate on the provision business, as did Edwin. Interestingly, Bingley Hall was Great Britain's first purpose-built exhibition hall, as it officially opened in 1850, although Charles held an auction there of livestock in September 1849. In an advertisement in the Staffordshire Advertiser announcing the auction, it states that Bamford Brothers had offices on Albert Street, Birmingham; Cleveland Street, Wolverhampton; and Vicar Lane/Smithford Street, Coventry[11].

However, in early 1862 Charles fell ill, and while recuperating, his doctor suggested he take a holiday to help with his recovery. So, at the age of 43 in October 1862, Charles took a trip from Liverpool to New York aboard the Cunard ship "Australasian," Cunard's first iron screw steamship.

While convalescing, Charles felt improved enough that he decided to investigate business opportunities for Edwin's and his new business venture. He concentrated on the business they knew best: the meat business; since they would be shipping to England, it was to be the cured meat business.

---

11. Information provided by Corinne Hastilow

Cunard steamship S/S Australasian[12]

The trip was very encouraging, and the brothers saw tremendous opportunities. Two further trips were made by Charles in March and October of 1863, first to New York and then to Canada. Naturally, Canada was intriguing because it was a colony of Britain and easier to do business there, even though it was still a young and mainly undeveloped area. The United States of America was not so united at that time, as they were in the middle of their civil war (1861-1865), which made the prospect of a new business venture all the more difficult.

The prospect couldn't have been too damaging, as the brothers ultimately decided they would concentrate their business in the United States, importing ham, bacon and other cured meats. Edwin would handle business affairs in England, while Charles would set up the business in the United States. He made many trans-Atlantic trips, traveling between the two countries every six months, always in the spring

---

12. Picture from www.NorwayHeritage.com

or autumn, until October 1865, when it is thought that he started to live in New York at the age of 46.

First, he (representing Bamford Brothers) became a member of the newly created New York Produce Exchange. His membership number was 73, which is pretty impressive considering Exchange membership later numbered several thousand. There he befriended Frank A. E. Cott who had offices at 430 Produce Exchange, New York. Because of these connections, Charles made him his New York agent. He also employed the services of Sperry and Barnes of New York and New Haven Connecticut as shipping agents. He wasted no time.

During the American Civil War, pork was in great demand to feed the Union Army, and the Chicago meat packing industry grew exponentially during that time. The stockyards were huge, one square mile[13]. Since Charles and Edwin were in the pork business, it was obvious that he had to have contacts in Chicago. A trip there proved very beneficial, as he came to know the Nash family. Thomas Nash, an Englishman by birth and around Charles' age, had been in the meat packing business since 1857, along with his younger brother, John. Charles may have known of the Nash Family before he went to Chicago, as Charles' elder brother, Samuel, had his small farm in Stock and Bradley, Worcestershire, near Dodderhill, Worcestershire where the Nash family lived[14]. As meat packing businesses go, it was a medium-sized firm; Charles and the Nash's got along well together. They struck up some sort of partnership and the Bamford Brothers were in the meat packing business. With Edwin back in England selling the pork products as quickly as Charles could ship them, business was booming[15].

---

13. Chicago, now known as the Windy City was known as Porkopolis back then!
14. It is interesting to note that Thomas (b. 1824) was the fifth child and John (b. 1837) was the 14th child, out of a total of 17!
15. It is possible that Charles alone became partners with the Nash's, not Bamford Brothers.

When Charles moved to New York, naturally he brought his family with him. It is not known where in New York they lived, but it is possible they lived above the premises on 18 Broadway, which he had purchased. But in 1868, tragedy struck. His third son with Hannah, Albert Edward Bamford died. He was only 5 years old. It was heart-breaking for Hannah, who had already lost her fist son, Samuel Bamford, soon after birth. Albert's cause of death is not known but was probably due to smallpox. By this time Charles was financially secure and was able to purchase a fairly large plot (no.16198 Sec. 151/159) in the Green-Wood Cemetery in Brooklyn, New York. It is here where Albert was buried. Green-Wood Cemetery is a very large cemetery where many of New York's affluent are interred. Due to its beautiful architecture and history, the cemetery has been designated a National Historic Monument. For Hannah it was a bitter sweet year, as she also gave birth to her fifth child and second daughter, Eleanor Caroline.

Green-Wood Cemetery gate looking out

Green-Wood Cemetery chapel, looking from the hill[16]

By 1871, the brothers were making good money and Edwin Bamford lived in a lovely home in Tettenhall, Wolverhampton, called Washington House. However, there is no record of Charles Bamford in the 1871 census, as he was living in the United States.

Washington House, Tettenhall, Wolverhampton[17]

---

16. Pictures of Green-Wood Cemetery from Wikipedia.org
    Entrance gate credited to Beyond My Ken
    Chapel credited to Bestbudbrian
17. Image from www.blackcountryhistory.org

Later in 1871, tragedy struck Charles Bamford's family yet again. On November 12th Charles Smith Bamford passed away at the age of 22. He was Charles' first son by his marriage to Eleanor Smith and undoubtedly was working with his father in New York. The probable cause of death was smallpox, about which he had written to his father a year earlier.

Home Brooklyn, Nov. 10th. 1870

My dear Papa,

Your form enclosing list of sales oc oc came to hand in due course. Perhaps you were very much surprised to learn of me being taken down so sudden with the small pox. I assure you it has been a fearful drawback to me, but that God who has mercy on me and only afflicted me lightly and I am now fast recovering, I expect to be able to go down from my hospital on Sunday. I tell you I was the luckiest young man in America to meet with the kind family I am with. When the City Authorities said I must go to the Flushing hospital they replied he shan't go. The officer then said, you will all have to be vaccinated then, they replied without a murmur, all right, and all have been vaccinated, servant and all. They have cooked and fussed beyond explanation and done everything that possibly could be done. I hope some time to pay them. You had no need worry about me getting along all right and I hope by this day week to be able to write you a letter that will be more easy to read than this which is written under many difficulties. I must close with lustlove to all at home, hoping this will find you all in good health and spirits as I am happy to say I am fast improving.

I remain
Your Affectionate Son
Charles

Charles' grave is near his half-brother, Albert, in the Green-Wood cemetery. Charles the elder had now seen three of his four sons die at a young age and was probably quite protective of his remaining son, Arthur John Jones Bamford, now 14 years old.

By early 1872, Bamford Brothers, were shipping considerable amounts of ham, bacon, and cured pork to Britain, and their wealth was rapidly increasing. They purchased a shop store and premises at 156 West Street, New York on the southern tip of Manhattan and also acquired a packing plant on the west side of 42nd street. While Charles was expanding the business in the United States, Edwin was busy moving the business to Liverpool, needing to be close to the port of entry. The brothers purchased two properties, 10 Mathew St. and 16 Button St., both close to the docks.

The premises 10 Mathew Street was a fairly large four-story brick property with warehousing and offices on the upper levels and a cellar below. In the late 1950s, the upper floors were still being used as a warehouse, but the cellar became a nightclub with popular music of the day being played there. The club was known as The Cavern, which later earned worldwide fame when The Beatles regularly performed there in their very early days. During the 1960's, a wide variety of popular acts appeared at the club, including The Rolling Stones, The Yardbirds, The Hollies, The Kinks, Elton John, Black Sabbath, Queen, The Who and John Lee Hooker. Future star Cilla Black worked as the hat-check girl there[18].

Mathew Street was historically the centre of the wholesale fruit and vegetable market, but it's doubtful that the Bamford Brothers business dealt with fruit and vegetables in addition to their meat business. Tragically, British Rail used a Compulsory Purchase Order to demolish warehouses 8-12 Matthew Street in 1973 in order to build a ventilation shaft for Liverpool's underground railway. Typically, the shaft was never built, and although developers tried to renovate the original club, it was too badly damaged. Eventually a new building was built that used many of the original bricks and included a replica of The Cavern.

---

18. Wording from en.m.wikipedia.org

The original 10 Mathew Street with the Cavern Club[19]

Meanwhile, back in the United States, family lore suggests that Charles was busy selling bacon to the American and Canadian Indians! After all, he brought back to England a beautiful beaded Indian "cap" and a clay "peace pipe." Unfortunately not much more is known, but the cap is still in the family and the peace pipe was stolen in a robbery of Dorrie Bamford's home. Whether he was selling to the Indians or not is up to you to decide.

Both brothers needed homes close to Liverpool, so Edwin sold his home in Tettenhall and moved into Raby Hall in Raby Mere, which is located in the Wirral, sometime around 1870. As was a common practice at the time, he rented the hall, which had beautiful views over the countryside. Charles, who was mostly living in the United States, either purchased or rented Greenbank at 63 Park Road South, Claughton, Birkenhead, just across the Mersey from Matthew Street.

He also purchased Llanrhaiadr Hall, near Ruthin in North Wales. It was a large estate with good farmland in the beautiful Clwyd Valley. In his will, he also mentions that he owned farmland in Llangwyfan and Llndydyreoog, which were adjoining farms that, in total, covered about 3½ miles in length.

---

19. Cavernclub.org

Llanrhaiadr Hall circa 1930

Llanrhaiadr Hall, Nr. Ruthin, North Wales as it is today. It is now a care home.

New Investments

In 1872 Charles persuaded Edwin of the need to diversify. Subsequently, they purchased a Zinc mine in Lancaster County, Pennsylvania. The story is best told by David Bachman Landis, who wrote this in 1892.

Mineral Deposits and Works of the Hempfields[20]
(Words in italics added)

Every one of the forty townships in Lancaster County (Pennsylvania) has some earth deposits, or mineral veins, of a more or less productive value. And these ores and minerals have a history. It is not generally known, and may even seem surprising, that our local lands (lauded the country over as farms of the finest agricultural fertility) have evidences of silver, nickel, zinc, lead and coal; while those ores and deposits more commonly recognized, like iron and limestone formations, are in evidence at numerous localities. It is the purpose of this present sketch to give a graphic history of the mines in various portions of East and West Hempfield townships, where the writer happily spent his boyhood days. I shall divide this article into several parts, the first treating on Zinc and Lead. About one and a-half miles east of the pretty village of Landisville is the small settlement of Bamfordville (its post office now being named Bamford). Directly northeast from the Harrisburg turnpike, and bordering on Snipe or Snapper creek (a branch of the Little Conestoga), is a famous deposit of lead and zinc ores, the discovery of which, including their development, will prove interesting to the present generation. Away back, during the time of the Mexican War, a fence-maker, Samuel Pickel (who died at Landisville, December 8, 1883), was engaged in digging post-holes for a fence on the farm of Henry H. Shenk. These two

---

20. Title: Mineral deposits and works of the Hempfields / by D. B. Landis.
    Publisher: Lancaster, Pa. Lancaster County Historical Society, 1903/1904

men at that time thus accidentally found some lead ore in rock taken from these small openings. Samples were examined by Dr. Fahnestock, a chemist of Lancaster, whose analysis showed zinc, lead and traces of silver. Soon after Mr. Pickel's original find of mineral, buildings were erected on the Shenk farm, and the manufacture of oxide of zinc, for painting purposes, was carried on for a brief period. This was by the Lancaster County Mining Company, composed of Christopher Hager, John Shenk, David Hartman, Christian Bachman and David Longenecker. They were granted perpetual mining privileges (as recorded in Book F, page 499, Lancaster Recorder's office), on the property of Henry H. Shenk, comprising one hundred and five and a-half acres, for the consideration of $25,000, under date of December 13, 1847. Afterwards the buildings were torn down, and most of the wood material was used up in a large barn yet standing at Musselman's Mill, East Hempfield Township. The writer believes the credit for this original discovery of a deposit of lead and zinc ores was first given in print in the defunct Landisville Vigil, published by him, during 1883.

A Famous Transaction

The mines lay idle for a number of years, when, about 1872, a traveling mining expert happened to hear of this neglected spot of alleged hidden wealth; and this sharper, named Captain Tamblin, at once sought an interview with the Lancaster County Mining Company, of which Mr. Shenk was one of the interested stockholders. The Captain shrewdly saw how anxious the Shenks were to have the mine-farm off their hands, and he secured a promise of a rich recompense should he procure a buyer. He immediately left for the metropolis of New York; and afterward came across Charles Bamford, a member of the millionaire firm of Bamford Bros., pork packers, with offices in Chicago, New York and Liverpool, England. Captain Tamblin at once fell into the good graces of the rich Englishman, and, after telling him of a wonderful mine of zinc in Lancaster County, he succeeded in getting Mr. Bamford interested in the matter to such an extent that the pork packer offered the wily Captain a sum of money if he secured the mine for him. The Captain had left Mr. Bamford a rich specimen of zinc mineral. Mr. Bamford had seen this taken from an old shaft in the mine, and he took it to an assayer soon after. The examiner of minerals at once pronounced it a good specimen, yielding about seventy-five per cent.; at the same time stating his belief that it was not from Lancaster County, but from the distant State of Colorado. The assayer said: "There is such a thing as salting a mine."

Mr. Bamford seemed to take the hint, and, one night, came on to Landisville, without anyone's knowledge of his presence and purpose. Quietly he went down the shaft of the old mine about midnight, and, with the aid of a lantern and pick, broke off at several places from supposed solid rock, pieces of the mineral. These he exultantly took back to the New York mineral assayer and awaited his opinion of their worth. One specimen yielded some forty per cent, and the others about half that. Although not as good as the piece Captain Tamblin procured, the specimens which Bamford secured himself were good enough to convince him of the value of the mine; and he purchased it forthwith. Then the Captain again showed his adroitness at winning lucre for himself by getting Bamford's consent to erect great works at these deposits and to fit them out with first-class machinery. Without first wisely digging after a supply of zinc, large furnaces were erected, one of which a hurricane blew over before completed. It was, however, immediately finished, in brick and wood, and a large sum of money spent for various crushing and separating machinery, much of which was of necessity imported from Wales. The most expensive and intricate machinery was placed in a four or five story "Jig-house." It is said that the Captain made a snug percentage on all this complicated work for which he contracted. While thousands of dollars had thus been foolishly spent (as Messrs. Haldy and Howry, late of the Lancaster County National Bank, could verify when living), on work above ground, the tricky Tamblin found that it was becoming rather uncomfortable for him, and he suddenly departed for new fields of labor, with no little fortune.

Developing the Mines

Under the new management of Mr. Spillsbury, a practical mining engineer, the works and mines were operated for some time. Search was then made for veins of zinc, sometimes moderately successful, and just enough to keep the furnace fires lit; but, as a rule, most deposits of the mineral being found in "pockets," which soon became exhausted. Finally, the Bamford brothers, after having spent nearly $300,000 in the fruitless effort of developing these mines to a paying extent, closed up the works in the fall of 1877. Possibly few mining plants in Eastern Pennsylvania had so complete arrangements for making their own necessities as the zinc works at Bamfordville. Here there were, besides tool houses, carpenter and blacksmith shops, special places for making, and ovens for baking, their own firebrick, used in lining the furnaces; and here, also, were made by skilled labor the peculiar clay crucibles and retorts wherein the crushed zinc was reduced to metal. These men, most of them, received $100 and over a month; and, like many of their kind, spent all of their earnings each month. Most of them were of foreign descent—Welsh, Spanish, French and Italian; and ale was their daily drink at the family table, with American beer and whisky as side lines on a pay-day. During the Centennial era, about 1876, when the smelting furnaces were in full blast, I spent not a few summer evenings at the zinc mines, watching the brawny men, as they sang odd melodies, "roast" the crushed ore in low, hot ovens, with small fire-doors; then "charging" the crucibles at the smelting section with the brownish product, and capping the retorts with long, funnel-shaped hoods—around the circular openings of which, when all were at a white heat, the most peculiar, deadly-looking flames and fumes played in weird-like, flickering lights. The heat was so intense that almost every day new retorts had to be put in place of cracked ones, before an entire section of a furnace was rebuilt, after being chilled. The pouring of zinc into the familiar molds was very fascinating to me, the molten metal flowing like silvered water from the long ladles of the furnace men. These blocks of zinc were probably an inch in thickness and 8x16 inches in size, with the top regularly stamped with the firm's name, an emblem symbolizing strength or quality in centre, and location at bottom of plate. For a time all material had to be hauled from or to Landisville station, necessitating heavy teams and much labor; but before the close of the works a special siding was connected with the Pennsylvania railroad opposite the Bamford works.

The Last Company

The mine farm, after 1877, for about six years, was in the charge of David Uren, an intelligent Welshman. As may be supposed, the fine buildings and costly machinery naturally depreciated in value from non-usage. In this condition the Lehigh Zinc and Iron Company, of Bethlehem, Pa., leased the mines for a period of ten years, from April, 1883. The terms of the lease were that the owners of the mines were to receive a royalty of $1 per ton on all ore taken from these mines, and $1.50 on all ores that came from other mines elsewhere that were to be cleaned at the concentrating works of this place. In June of that year this same company leased the Widow Kauffman property, in East Hempfield Township; but little was accomplished there, more than taking some small lots of zinc ore from the place. Under the skilful superintendence of Captain P. O. Dwyer, the

Bamford works were operated until October of the same year, when, owing to innumerable difficulties with the machinery (which had become almost valueless, through some years of idleness), and on account of there not being enough mineral on hand to make it pay, the mines and works were again closed late in the fall of 1883. Mr. Dwyer left for his home, in Friedensville, Lehigh County. Mr. Heckscher, a member of the Lehigh Company, then came on and had most of the loose articles of the Bamford mines removed and shipped to his smelting works at Bethlehem. In a disagreement on the terms of a contract, the Messrs. Bamford, in November, 1885, secured a verdict in their favor in a suit with the Lehigh Zinc and Iron Company, in the United States Court at New York. *(This case was appealed and went all the way to the United States Supreme Court who found in favour of the brothers and awarded them $3,201.58, see Appendix IX. Unfortunately it took a long time to reach the US Supreme Court and the verdict wasn't given until 1893, after Charles' death.)* The original case provided for the payment of $1,000 per year in case of further non-usage of the mines, or for the full carrying out of the contract if the works were operated. The buildings around the old zinc mines are now in a state of desolation and decay. As early as 1884 and 1885 there were large cave-ins at the main shaft and open cuts of the mines; and water now fills the various pits to within ten feet or less from the surface. The main shaft having been 110 to 120 feet in depth from the level, one can easily comprehend the great body of water that had to be pumped from these mines. During this operation, a large steam-pump, capable of hoisting a barrel of water at a stroke, was one of the sights to be seen there.

Bamfordville (which name, by the way, was first given to it by the writer) sprang up in the vicinity of these works. It is rather a quiet village now. It is in the heart of a thrifty tobacco region. Faint hopes are entertained by some of its steadfast settlers that brighter days are ahead for the village. Probably a thorough search underground may yet bring forth a vein or veins of purer zinc-bearing rock. It is the belief of the writer that the frequent evidences of zinc, lead and traces of silver along the meadows of Snapper creek, cropping out, as they do, in various farms toward the south of East Petersburg, may sometime result in starting an industry more profitable than it was to the Bamford brothers.

In the Landisville Virgil in March 1884, the following was extracted from an article:

Directly after the Centennial era, a brass band was organized at the zinc works, Bamfordville, of which Chas. Bamford's son, a full-fledged Englishman, was a conspicuous member. Frank Watson of Landisville and William Clegg, a cornetist, belonged to this band, which enlivened the mining settlement for a few seasons[21].

It was undoubtedly Arthur J. J. who was in the band, as his brother Charles had passed away before the Centennial. However, it is doubtful he stayed very long, as he was busy helping his father and finding a wife.

The following picture depicts the Bamford Zinc and Lead Smelter as it appeared around 1888 after being abandoned some years earlier. The brick stack survived in a ruined condition until the late 1940s. Smelting furnaces were located along the walls of this building. Ore buggies can be seen among weeds at right.[22]

---

21. Contributed by Corinne Hastilow — www.archive.org
22. Picture and description from a piece entitled Lead and Zinc in Lancaster County by John W. W. Loose, extracted from the Lancaster County Historical Society and provided by Corinne Hastilow

The village of Bamfordville became the town of Bamford, Pennsylvania. In the picture below, the large building in the northeast quadrant is a new Kellogg's Cereal plant on the site of the Bamford zinc mine. The railroad beside the property was originally a siding put in place by Charles Bamford.

> According to Jeri L. Jones in her article "The Bamford Zinc Mine" (references in Appendix XII) the four different owners of the mine sank three shafts, which had an average width of 12 feet. The richest ore was found at the 75-foot level, with the ore never exceeding 12 percent zinc. It is estimated that about 25,000 tons of ore and waste rock have been removed from the mine since its discovery. Freedman (1972) estimated that approximately 3,000 tons of zinc was recovered. The cost of producing a pound of zinc in 1877 was $0.05; the sale price from $0.07 to $0.11 (Frazer, 1880).

Bamford, Pennsylvania[23]

Although Bamford was not one of the more famous Lancaster County collecting spots (compared to Cedar Hill quarry and Pequea mine, for example), Bamford has produced an interesting series of zinc and associated minerals. Primary minerals include galena, sphalerite, calcite, pyrite, saddle-shaped dolomite crystals, and Chalcopyrite.

It would be reasonable to assume that the great majority of the zinc recovered was done by Charles Bamford, as he had the mechanisms for large scale production, and the company that leased the mine from him did not produce very much, hence the subsequent law suit. As a conservative guess, let's assume he mined 2,500 tons of the 3,000 tons (net tons) extracted and that he made an average profit of $0.04 a pound. That would have produced an income of $200,000. Considering he invested $300,000 in equipment, there seems to be a shortfall of

---

23. Picture taken from Google Earth

$100,000[24], a substantial sum in the 1880s. This shortfall would have been minimized by the sale of other minerals mined there. The Bamford mine is now a part of Pennsylvania's rich mining history.

After the highs and lows of the Zinc mine, Edwin lost all interest in the mining business, but not Charles. In his will, there is mention of,

> ...all my farms containing about two hundred & thirty one acres & nineteen one hundredth of an acre together with the works, engines & machinery known as the Apple River & Galena Lead Mining property situate at Apple River in Davis County in the State of Illinois.

Apple River, IL[25]
(The large 'patch' in the centre of the photo is possibly the lead mine.)

---

24. $100,000 in 1880 is worth approximately $2.4 million today.
25. Image from Google Earth

He also mentions "all my interest in the Silver mines in Nevada in partnership with the Joel A Sperry of Newhaven Connecticut for which I paid ten thousand dollars", Joel Sperry being his shipping agent.

Back to the Business Known

Returning to the meat importing business, Charles, the true entrepreneur of the duo, was always looking for new ideas. The idea of having cheap "fresh" American meat in England always intrigued him. In May 1878 there appeared an article in publication "The Inter Ocean," which read as follows:

SHIPPING BEEF TO ENGLAND

> Mr. Charles Bamford, a commission Merchant of Liverpool, New York, and Philadelphia, and Mr. Edward Gibbons, of John Gibbons & Sons, of Liverpool, are at the yards in the interest of livestock shipping trade to Europe. They have been on tour of inspection through the country, looking for the most favourable points at which to purchase cattle. They are fully up to the times as to methods of transportation, and predict that before many years the business of shipping live beef cattle to England will be immense. It is necessary now that vessels be built especially for the trade.

Bamford Brothers began their import business using only cured pork meats such as ham, bacon, etc. Early cooling systems involved the use of ice, which was not at all satisfactory on transatlantic voyages, as the ice melted much too quickly. Shipping water was not profitable! But by the early 1800s, artificial refrigeration was invented, and by 1834 the first working vapour-compression refrigeration system was built. The first commercial ice-making machine was invented in 1854, and by the 1880s, ships with refrigeration on-board were making long voyages. So, the idea of shipping live cattle to England was dropped, and

Bamford Brothers were shipping not only cured meat, but frozen pork and beef.

In 1879, Charles was spending more time in Britain and decided to buy Brookhurst, a large family house with 43 acres of farmland in Bromborough, Cheshire. It was close to Raby Hall, where Edwin lived. Soon after moving into Brookhurst, Charles donated eight bells to St. Barnabas Church, Bromborough in memory of his late son, Charles Smith Bamford. Each bell has an inscription written by the Reverend Edward Dyer Green, who was instrumental in building the present church and was rector from 1860 to 1907.

The inscriptions are as follows:

> First Bell: When the full ring its tuneful voice shall raise
> Let me be first to lead the call to praise
>
> Second Bell: Gladsome we peal from out the Church's tower
> To God's great glory and his Love and Power
>
> Third Bell: To worship duly Heaven's Almighty Lord
> Our sweetest chimes unite with one accord
>
> Fourth Bell: When wedded love makes two as one abide
> Their joys we share and spread it far and wide
>
> Fifth Bell: From Mersey's banks sounds for our sacred glee
> And courts responsive echo from the Dee
>
> Sixth Bell: Aloft are we but loftier points the spire
> That heavenward man should raise his heart's desire
>
> Seventh Bell: May every strain melodious we outpour
> Stir all who hear, God's goodness to adore

Eighth Bell: Gloria in Excelsis Deo
                (Latin for Gory to God in the Highest)

The bells were installed in 1880, weigh 4½ tons (approximately 4,100 kilograms) and cost £800, approximately £96,700 today. The plaque in the church is inscribed as follows:

In fond memory of Charles S Bamford who departed this life on 12 November 1871, in the 24th year of his age: his father Charles Bamford of Brookhurst dedicated these eight bells, and had them placed in the Parish Church of Bromborough A.D. 1880[26].

Brookhurst from the south[27]

---

26. All information regarding the bells supplied by Jennifer Hope, churchwarden and Steven Hughes, the bell captain
27. Photos from Somerville Preparatory School prospectus circa 1940s, courtesy of Susan Nicholson

Brookhurst Entrance Hall

St Barnabas Church in the Parish of Bromborough, Cheshire

A Felony

With all people or companies of any means, there are always unscrupulous individuals trying to conceive ways to relieve them of their assets. This certainly was the case with the Bamford Brothers. The following was reported in the New York Sun newspaper on 4 January 1884[28].

> CHICAGO, Jan. 3 — About Christmas time the detective agency in this city (*Pinkertons*)[29] received a telegram from Sperry & Barnes of New York and New Haven, the American agents of the large commission house of Bamford Brothers that their exchange clerk, E. H. Kobbe, had absconded after forging and converting to his own use $100,000 in exchange. The agency at once went to work upon the case and soon ascertained that Kobbe was here *(in Chicago)* in company with John R. Van Arsdale, and that they were spending money freely. Van Arsdale returned to New York where he was arrested. On Friday last, Kobbe was arrested in a house of ill repute in this city. He was on the point of starting for Mexico with an inmate of the house. Four hundred dollars in money was found on his person, and $1,200 worth of furs and silks, which he had lavished on the woman, were also taken possession of.
>
> Kobbe forged bills of exchange on Bamford Brothers, which were readily disposed of to Jesup, Patten & Co., he being recognized as the exchange clerk of the firm, and had the checks made payable to his own personal order, instead of that firm. He opened an account with another bank, collected the amount of Jesup, Patten & Co.'s checks, invested the money

---

28. Source Newspapers.com
29. It is interesting to note that Pinkertons Detective Agency was started in 1850 by Allan Pinkerton and is now a large company still in business today. Allan's son John handled the Bamford case.

in Government bonds, and absconded. The Pinkertons say that he confessed that his gains were fully $100,000. He was taken to New York the same day where he was arrested, and on Sunday last he took the detectives to the upper part of New York, where they recovered from a dry cistern, encased in hermetically sealed drain pipe, and wrapped in oiled silk, Government bonds to the amount of $20,000. Going thence to Brooklyn, *(behind Van Arsdale's mother's house)* another piece of drain pipe yielded $25,000. It is not known here whether any more money has been recovered. Kobbe is well connected, and once occupied a responsible position with the Inman line, and his brother is now chief clerk in that office.

This case was big news, mainly because of the large amount of money involved. $100,000 in 1884 was worth about $2.5 million in 2017. There were reports of the affair in newspapers all over the United States. The outcome for Kobbe is not known, but it is assumed he went to prison. The New York times reported that the Bamford Brothers sued Van Arsdale in the New York Supreme Court for $5,000 that was still unaccounted for, plus $6,000 for their expenses, including John Pinkerton's fee and Charles' trip to the United States for the case, plus $2,500 of the Bamford's money that Van Arsdale had spent. Again, it is not known how the case ended, but it is supposed that Bamford Brothers probably won after reading how involved Van Arsdale was with Kobbe. It's doubtful that he could come up with the money to repay them and probably went to a debtor's prison.

The Split

It is often the case in family businesses that brothers or a father and son relationship is good for business, but when cousins become involved, major problems occur. In 1886, Edwin had two sons in the business, Alfred, aged 22 and Henry, aged 21. Another son, William, had gone bankrupt and was no longer in the business. Charles had his only remaining son, Arthur, in the business, aged 29. There was plenty of friction, and it wasn't pleasant. The business was still thriving, so a solution needed to be found.

In the 6 April 1887 edition of the London Gazette the following notice was published.

> Notice is hereby given, that the Partnership formerly carried on by us the undersigned, Charles Bamford and Edwin Bamford, at 20, 22, 24 and 26 Cheapside, Liverpool in the county of Lancaster, as Provision Merchants, under the style of Bamford Brothers, was, on the 26th day of March last, dissolved by mutual consent. The said Charles Bamford will in future carry on business at 20, 22, 24, and 26, Cheapside Liverpool, in co-partnership with Mr. John Nash and Mr Arthur J. J. Bamford, under the style of Bamford, Nash and Bamford. The said Edwin Bamford will in future carry on business at 10 Matthew Street, Liverpool, in co-partnership with his sons Alfred Charles, and Henry Samuel, under the style of Bamford Brothers. All debts due to and from the late partnership will be received and paid by the said Charles Bamford. — dated this 2nd day of April, 1887.
>
> *Charles Bamford*
> *Edwin Bamford*

Wow! Word spread like wildfire though Liverpool, New York, and Chicago. The fabulously wealthy Bamford Brothers had dissolved their partnership. Charles kept his membership of the New York Produce Exchange, but neither Edwin nor his sons ever joined. John Nash, Anne Bamford's uncle, was now a partner, and it is likely that he was running the United States side of the business while Arthur ran the business at home in England.

Charles Bamford kept a firm hand of all his business affairs until his health began to deteriorate about two years before his death. The day-to-day running of the business was now in the hands of Arthur and John Nash, with Charles keeping distant eye on things.

Earlier in the autumn of 1886, Charles' wife Hannah died at the age of 58. He had now seen four of his seven children die and had survived two wives. It must have been hard for him. This was all on top of the process of breaking up the Bamford Brothers partnership. Brookhurst, his large house, was relatively empty, except for the servants, now that all his children and grandchildren had moved out. He was 68 years old now, and his health was deteriorating.

The Waring Connection

In the autumn of 1890, Charles' health deteriorated to the point that he was unable to walk his daughter, Eleanor Caroline, down the aisle. She had fallen in love with a cabinet maker from Sefton Park, Liverpool, and they were married on 15 October at St. Barnabas, Bromborough. The following is an article that appeared in the Birkenhead Advertiser.

Marriage of Miss Bamford at Bromborough

> The usually quiet village of Bromborough was *en fete* on Wednesday, the occasion being the marriage of Mr. Samuel J. Waring jun., son of Mr. S. J. Waring of Plas Ullet, Sefton Park, Liverpool, to Miss Eleanor Caroline Bamford, second daughter of Mr. Charles Bamford, of Brookhurst, Bromborough, Llanrhaiadr, Denbighshire and Misterton, Leicestershire.

> The high esteem in which the bride and her family are held in the district invested the happy event with unusual interest and the number of people who assembled in the neighbourhood of the Parish Church, Bromborough, in which the marriage was solemnised, would have filled the sacred edifice three times over. The church itself was tastefully decorated for the occasion.

Shortly after two o'clock the bride arrived and entered the church on the arm of her brother, Mr. Arthur J. J. Bamford C.C. She wore a dress of rich breche silk and duchesse satin, trimmed with deep old Brussels lace, her tulle veil being fastened by a diamond leaf ornament forming a pendant and brooch, the gift of the bridegroom.

Her bouquet was composed of white orchids, gardenias, orange blossoms, myrtle etc. Her bridesmaids were Miss Gretton, Miss S. Waring, Miss L. Waring, Miss Winnie Nash, Miss E. Turner, Miss Hesketh and two prettily-attired children, Miss Ethel and Miss Katie Williams daughters of Mr. Thomas Williams, J.P., Llewesog, Denbighshire *(brides nieces)*. The bridesmaids were attired in cream fancy cashmere and vieux rose silk dresses with hats of cream velvet, They wore brooches designed as a bar of gold with oriental pearls, forming a true lover's knot in the centre and with single pearls at the end, the gift of the bridegroom and carried bouquets of the choice exotics. Mr. James E. Waring, brother of the bridegroom, acted as best man.

As the bridal party proceeded up the centre aisle of the church, the choir, which preceded them, sang the processional hymn commencing "Father of Life, confessing". The officiating clergyman was Rev. E. Dyer Green, rector of Bromborough, who was assisted by the Rev. A. Ellerton and the Rev. G. C. Dieker, vicar of Birkenhead. The service was fully choral and at the conclusion Mendelssohn's "Wedding March" was played by the organist.

Between three and five o'clock Mr. and Mrs. Arthur Bamford gave an "at home" at Brookhurst which was attended by the wedding guests and others, to the number of about 600. A grand programme of music was rendered by the Childwell Quartette (Messrs. S. Kirkham, E. Edwards, J. Higginbottom, N. F. Burt and H. Whittingham, accompanist.)

The band of the 1st. L.A.V. played an excellent selection in a large marquee erected in the grounds. In the course of the afternoon the happy pair left for Oxford, *en route* for the Continent. The bride's travelling dress was of fawn cashmere trimmed with white and gold. Before taking their departure, the tenants of Llanrhaiadr estate of Mr. Bamford presented the bride with pieces of silver plate accompanied by a beautifully illuminated address, ornamented in the missal style by Messrs. Elkington. In the corner was written in antique characters, Queen Isobel's blessing on the wedding of the French Princess to Henry V: "God, the best maker of all marriages, combine your hearts in one"[30].

It seems that the wedding was a magnificent event. Obviously the Warings were from a well-to-do family, and their cabinet making business successful. In 1893, Samuel was given the task of opening a branch of the family furniture making company in London; four years later he merged the company with Gillow & Company to become Waring & Gillow and became chairman.

While Waring & Gillow continued to produce fine furnishing, they also built a department store on Oxford Street. It was at this store where later Charles Francis Kreitmair Bamford (see page 106) first started his working career. Samuel Waring made a considerable amount of money crafting exceptional furniture for the grand homes of Europe, along with furnishing large ocean liners and fine hotels. He owned two enormous homes himself, Gopsall Hall in Leicestershire and Foots Cray Place in Kent. He was generous with his time and money and was honoured in 1919 when he was created a Baronet of Foots Cray Place in recognition of his "public and local service." He was further honoured in 1922 and raised to the peerage as Baron Waring of Foots Cray Place in recognition of him being a, "Pioneer of decorative art in furnishing

---

30. Birkenhead Advertiser, Saturday 18 October 1890, copied off microfilm by Corinne Hastilow

…. [and a] Generous supporter of charities." Samuel and Eleanor had two children: Arthur Samuel Bamford Waring, who died unmarried in 1911 at the age of 19, and the Honourable Eleanor Gladys Waring (1894-1987), who married Captain Arthur Cunliffe Bernard Critchley (later Critchley-Waring).

Lord Waring had a love of sailing and was a commodore of the Royal Albert Yacht Club and owner of the yacht "White Heather," which he raced.[31] He was also a High Sheriff of Denbighshire for a term from 1907 to 1908.

White Heather (foreground) racing Britannia (George V's yacht) in Cowes 1925[32]

---

31. All Waring information from en.m.wikipedia.org and Grace's Guide, British Industrial History
32. Photo by Beken of Cowes in 1925

Lord Waring passed away in January 1940 at the age of 79, but with no male heirs the baronetcy and barony became extinct. Lady Eleanor Waring died the following year in April 1941.

The Passing of an Era

Arthur and John Nash were running Bamford, Nash and Bamford on a day-to-day basis, but Charles obviously kept an eye on things. He was feeling much better after being so ill at Eleanor's wedding and decided to travel to Liverpool and check on the business. Unfortunately, he caught a chill from which he never recovered. He died on December 29, 1890, at the age of 71.

News spread fast. Telegrams were immediately dispatched to all of his business associates and the New York Produce Exchange.

New York Times — Wed Dec 31, 1890

CHARLES BAMFORD
News reached the Product Exchange yesterday of the death in Liverpool, England of Charles Bamford, for many years a member of the Exchange and a leading figure in the provision trade. Mr. Bamford was born in England about seventy-three years ago. His first business venture was made in Wolverhampton, where he laid the foundation of what has since grown to be a great fortune. He was a man in middle age when he came to this city and established himself in the provision trade, his firm being Bamford Brothers. It had a packing house at Eleventh Avenue and Forty-Second Street.

Mr. Bamford joined the Produce Exchange soon after coming here, and was one of the committee appointed to buy the old Exchange building (since sold to the Government) from the person who then owned it. Although he returned to England some years ago, he kept up his membership in the Exchange until his death. Some time ago he left his old firm of Bamford Brothers, which was continued by other partners, and entered the firm Bamford, Nash & Bamford. His correspondents in this country were F. A. E. Cott of New York and Sperry & Barnes of New-Haven, Conn.

Mr. Bamford was possessed of large and valuable estates in Denbighshire and Leicestershire. He was interested in an Insurance company in Birmingham, and was the founder of a bank in that city. In banking circles in this city, too, he was well known. Mr. Bamford leaves two daughters and a son, all of whom are in England[33].

News of Charles' death was reported all over the United States. Articles have been noted in the following newspapers:

The World, NY, NY
Salt Lake Herald
The Record-Union, Sacramento, CA
Arizona Republic
Pittsburgh Daily Post
Pittsburgh Dispatch
Brooklyn Daily Eagle
The Courier Daily Eagle — Salt Lake City
Independent Record — Helena, Montana
The Sun, NY, NY

For example: **The Los Angeles Times — Sat, Jan 3, 1891**

CHARLES BAMFORD
A private cablegram announces the death at Liverpool of Charles Bamford, the founder of the great firm of Bamford

---

33. Source Newspapers.com

Bros., the most extensive dealers in American hog products in Great Britain[34].

His funeral and interment in the family vault in Bromborough Church was a grand but sombre affair with a special train being arranged to transport mourners from Liverpool to Bromborough.

The Denbigh Free Press Article 10 January 1891

THE LATE MR. CHARLES BAMFORD
LLANRHAIADR
A REMARKABLE CAREER

The remains of the late Mr. Charles Bamford, provision merchant, who died at his residence, Brookhurst, on Monday, in his seventy-third year of his age, was on Friday interred in the family vault in the Bromborough parish churchyard. There were present large numbers of sympathising friends, who were conveyed to Bromborough by a special train which waited on the 10.20 boat from the Liverpool Landing stage on Friday morning. The gathering at the grave-side was both numerous and representative, all the leading members of the provision trade being in attendance, in addition to troops of other friends of the late gentleman, who was greatly esteemed by all who knew him.

As already briefly announced, he caught a chill during a visit to Liverpool on Saturday, and death resulted from congestion of the lungs and bronchitis. He was head of the well-known firm of Messrs Bamford, Nash and Bamford, provision merchants, Cheapside, Liverpool; but for some time past he had ceased to take any active part in the business, the enfeebled state of his health confining him a good deal to Brookhurst, his

---

34. Source Newspapers.com

fine residence near Bromborough Station, on the Birkenhead and Chester railway. Mr. Bamford was born at Wednesbury, Staffordshire, in 1818 and received his early education in that town. He and his brother Edwin commenced as provision merchants some 40 years ago, in Wolverhampton and from 1858 to 1861 Mr. Charles Bamford was the largest wool salesman in the Midland counties. His offices for that business were in Birmingham, and he also used Bingley Hall as a warehouse. Taking an interest in the Volunteer movement, which was only then in its infancy, he granted that celebrated building to the citizen soldiers of the Midland capital for their drill, and his only surviving son, Mr. Arthur Bamford, now possesses a letter of thanks from the Mayor of Birmingham, acknowledging his kindness in the matter. (The) Deceased came to Liverpool in 1871, and along with Mr. Edwin Bamford carried on trade under the style of Bamford Brothers. Ten years before he was ordered to take a trip to America for the good of his health, and after having recovered, he immediately laid himself out to develop a new branch of the business for the supply of cheap food for the poor people of England. For this purpose he established packing houses at Chicago in conjunctive with Mr. John Nash, who now belongs to the firm of Bamford, Nash and Bamford. It was a mine of enterprise which proved very profitable, and Mr. Bamford quickly amassed a large fortune. Owing to the growing up of their sons the two brothers dissolved the partnership in 1887, Mr. Edwin going to Mathew Street and Mr Charles remaining at the old place in Cheapside. At that time the subject of this sketch took his son Arthur into the business with him and Mr. John Nash (previously his partner in America) also joined the firm. The deceased purchased two extensive estates — Misterton in Leicestershire (of which he became lord of the manor), and in Llanrhaiadr, in Denbighshire; and we understand that by his will he has left the former, together with Brookhurst, to Mr. Arthur Bamford, and the latter is to be divided between his two daughters Mrs Williams and

Mrs S J Waring, Jun. It is said that the Leicestershire property is worth £100,000 and the Llanrhaiadr, £70,000 to £80,000. Very few knew of the many acts of charity of the deceased, but it is known that he gave freely of his purse to relieve people in distress. He presented to Bromborough church its present peal of eight bells, and he furnished the vestry in the unique and quaint style called "Queen Canterbury". Altogether his career was a most remarkable one, illustrating many of those sterling qualities which make Englishmen great to commerce and industry.

The obsequies were conducted simply and without ostentation. The mourners and immediate friends assembled at the house, and the large number of representatives of the provision trade and others who had come from Liverpool by special train proceeded in carriages to the village of Bromborough, in the quiet churchyard of which the internment took place. The coffin, consisting of shell, lead and solid oak, with brass mountings, was conveyed in an open funeral car, which left Brookhurst at about noon, followed by the mourners in the appended order:-

First carriage: Mr Arthur Bamford (son), Mrs Bamford and Master Charles A Bamford.

Second carriage: Mr T Williams (son-in-law), Mr and Mrs S J Waring, jun. (son-in-law and daughter) and Miss Gretton.

Third carriage: Mr Edwin Bamford (brother) Mr Alfred and Mr Henry Bamford (nephews) and the Rev J Gott.

Fourth carriage: Mr and Mrs John Nash and Mrs S J Waring, sen.

Fifth carriage: Mr. John Bowker, Miss McKinnell and Mr Meadows Hancock

Sixth Carriage: Mr J Parry Jones (Denbigh) and Mr. Walter Cunliffe.

The coffin was covered in beautiful wreaths sent by Mr and Mrs Arthur Bamford, Mr and Mrs John Nash, Mr and Mrs S J Waring, jun. Mr Edwin Bamford, Mr H S Bamford, Mr A C Bamford, Mr and Mrs Thomas Williams, Mr and Mrs Williams (Llewesog) Mr Plumpton, the Liverpool Provision Trade Association, Master Scott Bamford and Miss Annie Bamford, the Rev J Williams, Mr J Parry Jones, Denbigh, Mr. S J Waring, sen. Mr and Mrs Cunliffe, Ethyl, Katie and Gladys, and Willie Williams (children of Mr Thomas Williams and grandchildren of the deceased) and Mr John Bowker

(List of attendees omitted)

The Rev John Williams, vicar of Llanrhaiadr read the lesson, and the rest of the funeral service was said by the Rev E Dyer Green, rector of Bromborough. The organist played the "Dead March" in "Saul" while the coffin was being borne out of the church by John Williams (the bailiff of the Llanrhaiadr estate), J. Jones, R Hughes (tenants), J Dunn (head gardener at Brookhurst), J Siddall and G Farrall (under gardeners), and W Wen and W Goodwin (warehousemen at Cheapside). After the body had been lowered into the family vault beside the remains of the late wife of the deceased, a muffled peal was rung, and then the spectators slowly left the churchyard. The funeral arrangements were carried out by Mr J Roberts, of Argyle Street, Birkenhead.

It's hard to determine the age of Charles at his death. In many articles and on the family vault it states that Charles was 72 years old when he died. However, his baptism records show that he was baptised on March 28th, 1819, and in those days, a baptism took place very soon after the birth. He died on 29 December 1890, so he would have been 71 years old. This is further corroborated by the census records, which were always taken on a Sunday around the first week of April, after Charles' birthday. In 1851, he stated he was 32 years old, 42 years old in 1861, 62 years old in 1881. It was a common practise in those days to talk of a person's age in terms of "in his such and such year." So, Charles was in his 72nd year when he died but was 71 years old. Birth date records were not recorded before 1 July 1837, so his exact birthday is not known but is estimated to be on 26 March, 1819.

ARTHUR JOHN JONES BAMFORD

It is probable that Arthur J. J. first met Annie Nash when he was quite young while on a business trip to Chicago with his father, Charles. Anne was born in Burleith-Leighton, Baltimore in 1855 and was the daughter of Thomas Nash, an Englishman and a Bamford Brothers partner in the meat packing business in Chicago. By all accounts, Annie was pretty and fun-loving. She was two years older than Arthur, but that didn't seem to matter. When Arthur's parents moved to New York around 1865, he obviously accompanied them, as he was only age 8. However, his boarding school was Liverpool College back in England. When he had completed his studies there, he went to Cambridge University at the age of 18. Annie and her parents had moved back to England when her father became ill, but it is not known whether Annie and her mother moved back to the United States or stayed in England, although it was probably the latter. Whatever the situation they had a flourishing courtship and married in 1879 in Salford Priors, Warwickshire. Arthur was 22 years old and Annie 24 years old. By that time, the Charles Bamford family had moved back to England permanently. Thomas Nash, Anne's father, had died in 1866 at the age of 42, having moved back to Stock and Bradley, England, and so she was given away by her elder brother, Arthur Nash of Salford Priors, Worcestershire.

Very soon after Arthur and Annie's wedding, Annie became pregnant and gave birth to Charles Arthur Bamford in July 1880. Initially, they lived at Brookhurst, Bromborough with Arthur's father and mother. In the 1881 census, it showed that also living with them was their son Charles Arthur (7 months old); Arthur J. J.'s younger sister, Eleanor; his elder sister, Hannah Maria Williams, and her husband, Thomas Williams, and their two daughters Ethel (1-year-old) and Catherine (2 months old); Mary Ann Gretton; and four servants. What a full house! While living at Brookhurst, Annie and Arthur had another child, Mary Hannah, born in 1881. Sadly, she lived only 13 days and was (eventually) buried in the family vault in St. Barnabas Church, Bromborough.

DESCENDANTS OF ARTHUR JOHN JONES BAMFORD

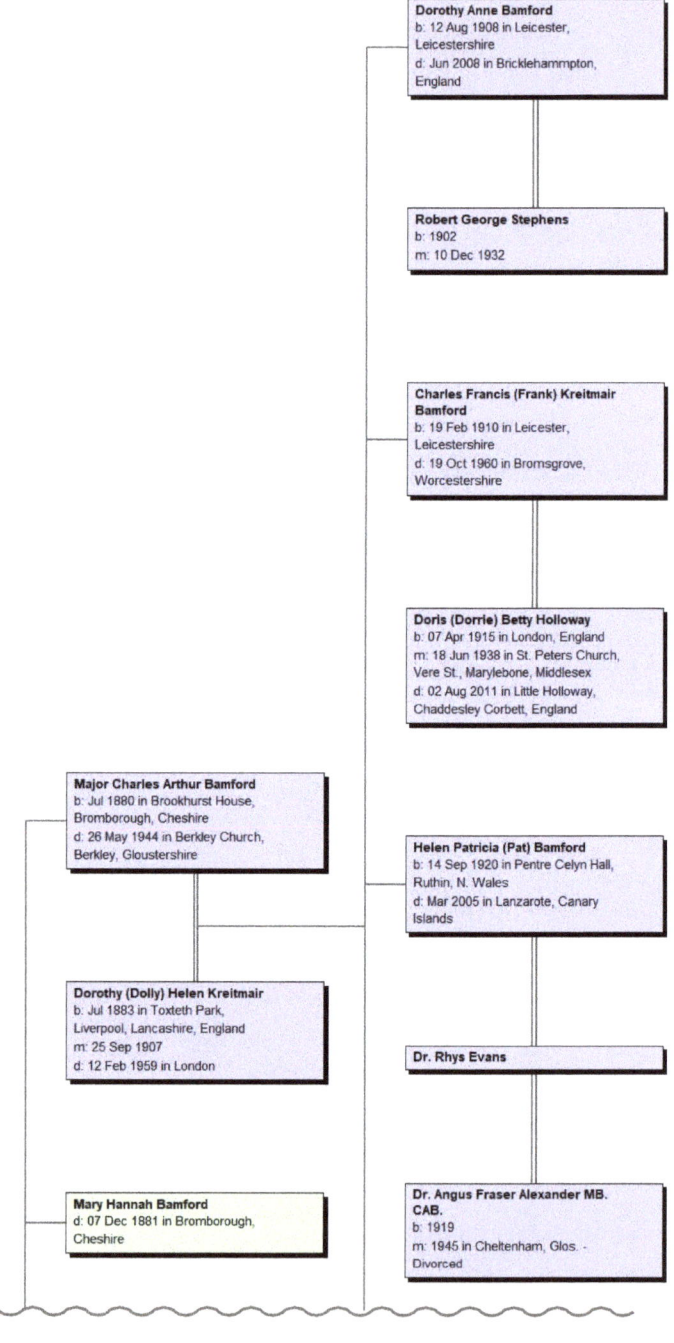

The Bamfords

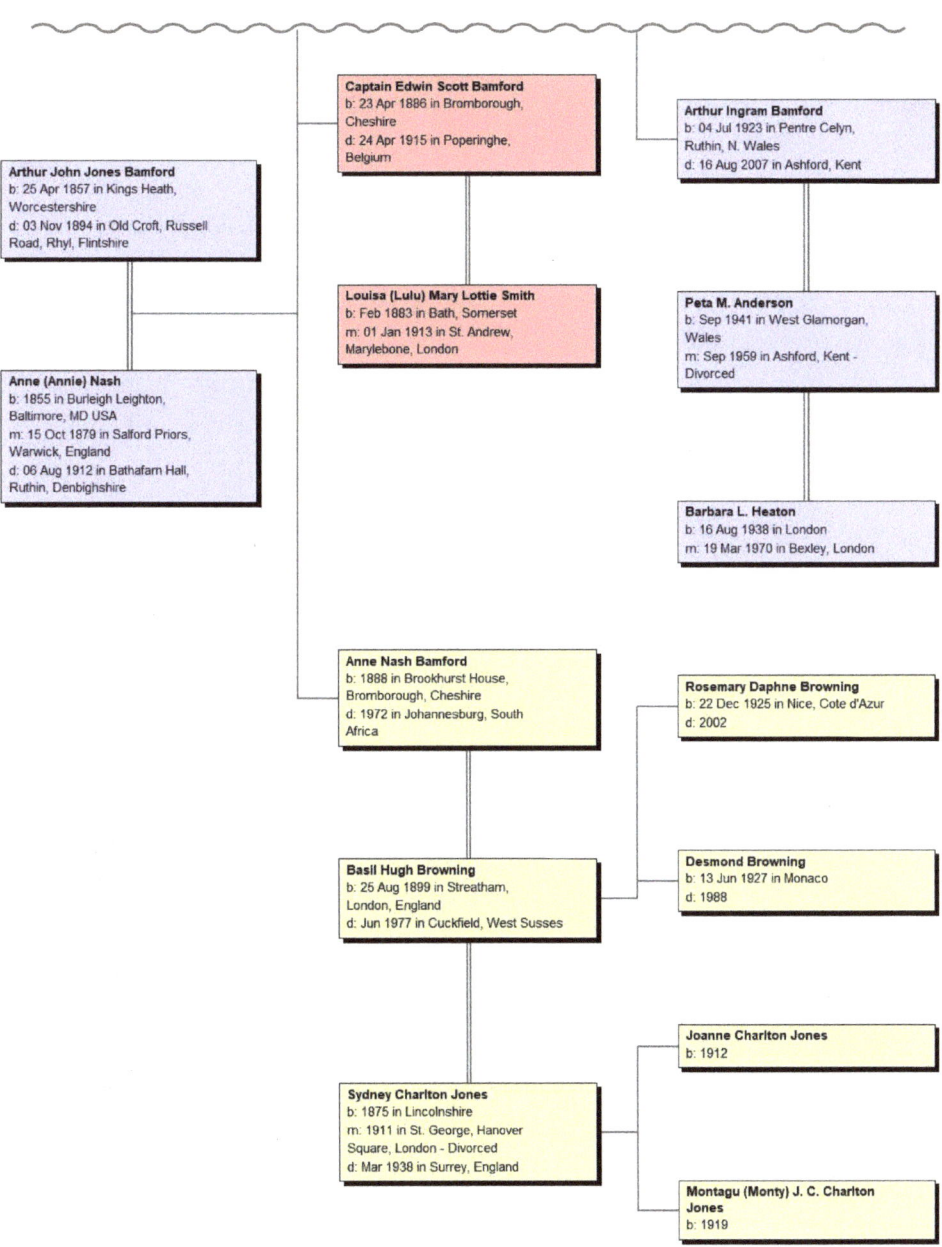

As part of his investments, Charles purchased the Misterton Estate in Leicestershire in 1885. The estate comprised 2,821 acres, including Misterton Hall, several farmhouses, and the Hind Hotel in Lutterworth. The estate also came with the right to appoint the Rector of Misterton.[35] The estate remained in Charles' name, but Arthur and Annie moved in and ran it. At Misterton, they had two more children, Edwin Scott (born 1886) and Anne Nash (born 1888). Misterton Hall was a good family house set in beautiful grounds. Arthur carried out several major projects there, including re-facing the west side of the house with red bricks in a Jacobean style and building two lodges, one at the entrance to Misterton Hall and the other on another corner of the estate.

Misterton Hall (2016) — notice the ship weather vane[36]

---

35. St. Leonard's, Misterton — Church guide
36. Considerable work on the house has since been done by the current owner, Mrs. Heather Craven, whose late husband was a builder.

View of some of the grounds at Misterton Hall from across the lake

Over the front door there is a wood carving of the Bamford family Coat of Arms

The Bamford family Coat of Arms was brought into existence by Arthur J. J. Bamford, who used it profusely. In the two lodges he built, the Coat of Arms and the Crest can be seen in several places. Arthur J. J. Bamford, Thomas P. Williams (Arthur's brother-in-law), and Francis J. B. Kreitmair (the father-in-law of Arthur's son, Charles Arthur) were contemporaries[37], and it is thought they all acquired a family Coat of Arms at the same time.

The front door of the lodge with the glass in lead Coat of Arms. Note the sheep and bull's heads in reference to his surrounding farms.

---

37. Information provided by Dorothy Stephens.

It was at Misterton Hall where Arthur's and Annie's three children, Charles, (Edwin) Scott, and Anne grew up and played. The grounds there are extensive, and it would have been a wonderful place for the children to explore. How much time Arthur was able to spend there with his family is questionable. With the dissolution of the Bamford Brothers partnership and the formation of a new one in the name of Bamford, Nash and Bamford, and his growing interest in politics in Liverpool, it is hard to see him having much time with his family. He was constructing two lodges on the grounds and running the Misterton estate, so he must have been stretched to the limit. One could see him spending a great deal of time on the trains.

After his father's death, Arthur J. J. was now head of the family. He had been left an enormous fortune, including the large estate of Misterton Hall, Brookhurst, the family home and farm in Bromborough, and all of his father's business undertakings. There were the numerous real estate holdings in land, buildings, and mineral mines in the United States, together with the investments in the Union Bank of Birmingham, the Bank of Liverpool, and the insurance company, also in Birmingham. He had been appointed to the Liverpool Board of the Norwich Union Fire Office. He was also an active Freemason.

Charles' investment in the Union Bank of Birmingham is interesting, as he was one of the original investors in the bank, which started in 1878. By 1883, the successful bank merged with the Birmingham and Midland Bank, which eventually, after many acquisitions, mergers, and name changes, became the Midland Bank in 1923. He also had an investment in the Bank of Liverpool, which in 1918 merged with Martins Bank to become The Bank of Liverpool and Martins Ltd. After a name change to Martins Bank, they were bought by Barclay's Bank in 1969.

The esteem Arthur held for his father, Charles, was naturally very high. He decided to erect a plaque in St. Dyfnog's Church in Llanrhaiadr, Wales, the parish in which Llanrhaiadr Hall was located, which now belonged to his sisters.

It is interesting to note that Llanrhaiadr is misspelled. Hard to change!

Arthur J. J. also donated an organ to his local church, St. Leonard's, Misterton in memory of his father.

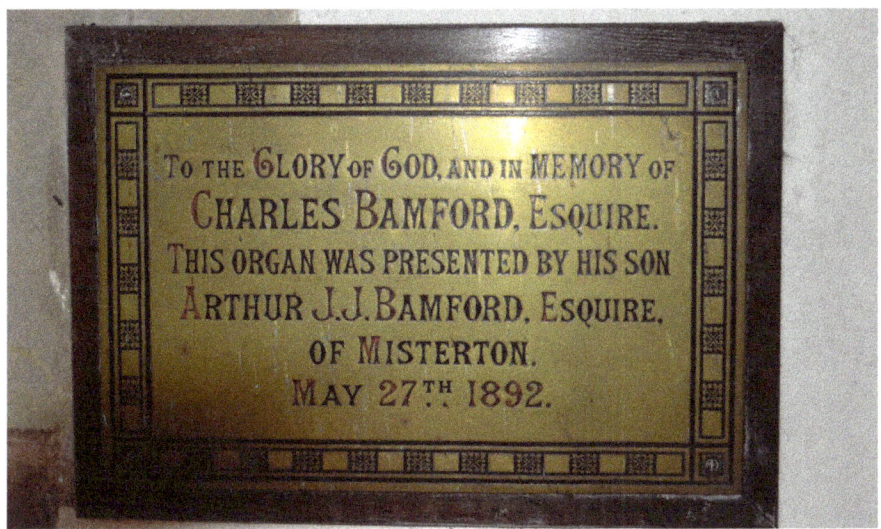

The oak panel sides of the organ, which has almost a thousand pipes, are adorned with the Coat of Arms of the Diocese of Peterborough and the Bamford Coat of Arms.

Arthur J. J. donated three stain glass windows in St. Barnabas Church, Bromborough, Cheshire in memory of his parents.

To the Glory of GOD and in pious memory of
Charles Bamford Esq.
Of Brookhurst Bromborough
Donor of the Ring of Bells in this Church Belfry
Who died December 29, 1890 age 72 years
And of Hannah Clifford his wife
Who died December 11, 1886 aged 58 years
These windows are placed by
Their affectionate son Arthur J. J. Bamford
"Honour the Lord with thy substance and with the firstfruits of all thine increase"

One of the three windows donated by Arthur J. J. Bamford

Besides the estates of Misterton Hall and Brookhurst, Arthur needed to attend to the family business, Bamford, Nash & Bamford, as well as his young family, including his wife Annie (35 years old), and three living children, Charles Arthur (10 years old), Edwin Scott (4 years old) and Anne Nash (2 years old).

Even with all this going on, Arthur decided to run for a Liverpool City Council seat. For some time, he had a strong interest in politics and was actively involved with the Conservative Party, both in Leicestershire and in Lancashire.

So, in 1889, Arthur ran as a Conservative in the St. Anne Street ward. It was a close election, but Arthur managed to prevail and held the seat for the Conservatives for a three-year term.

St. Anne Street Ward   **Votes**   **Percent**

Conservative: Arthur John Jones Bamford   640   43
Liberal: Jacob Reuben Grant 613   41
Henry Cartwright Gilmore   247   16

Majority   27
Registered electors   2,080
Turnout   1,500   72 percent

Conservative hold

The overall election results were as follows:[38]

Liverpool Local Election Result 1889							
Party	Seats	Gains	Losses	Net gain/loss	Seats (%)	Votes (%)	Votes	+/-
Conservative	7	0	5	-5	44	57	16,723	
Liberal	6	4	0	+4	50	18	5,163	
Irish Nationalist	2	2	0	+2	13	19	5,423	
Liberal Unionist	1	1	0	+1	6.3			
Labour	0	0	0	0	0	5.5	1,602	

It looks like the conservatives had a huge overall voter approval but may have been forced into a coalition with the Irish Nationalists. A good question would be, why the Conservatives lost five seats but the other parties gained seven seats. The St Anne Street, Liverpool Ward

---

38. Source: en.m.wikipedia.com

was one of the original wards established as a result of the Municipal Act 1835. It ceased to exist in 1952.

People who live in the Clwyd Valley in North Wales seem to love its beauty and quiet way of life. Since Llanrhaiadr Hall estate was willed to his sisters, Arthur was able to rent a home on the Llanrhaiadr Estate, a property known as Bryn Morfydd. In the 1891 census, Anne stayed there with two of her children, Edwin and Anne, her cousin, Mary Gretton, and nine servants. Charles Arthur was away at boarding school. There was no sign of Arthur in the 1891 census, so he was probably in the United States.

It must have been a busy trip. He undoubtedly met with Frank Cott, his New York agent; Joel Sperry, his shipping agent; and the New York Produce Exchange. He almost certainly visited the meat packing plant on 42nd Street and checked on his properties on Broadway and 157 West Street. And, no doubt, he met with his attorneys regarding the litigation with the Lehigh Zinc Company. Of course, he would have spent considerable time with his business partner, John Nash, in Chicago and probably went on to see the lead mine and surrounding farm land in Apple River, Illinois.

After staying at home for two years, Arthur made another trip to the United States in September 1893, possibly to finalise some deals with regards to the mining assets and maybe to celebrate his U.S. Supreme Court victory over the Lehigh Zinc Company. It was a little after this trip that Arthur's health began to flounder. He contracted tuberculosis (known as consumption in his day) and sadly died at the age of 37 in November 1894 in Old Croft, Russell Rd., Rhyl, North Wales.

Very little information could be found regarding Old Croft, but this home next door to the hospital and two streets from the sea is thought to be Old Croft. Living with his family with a highly contagious disease was out of the question, and at that time it was thought that fresh air

Believed to be "Old Croft," now a child care centre

and nourishing sustenance offered the best chance of recovery.[39] Old Croft seemed to provide him with these attributes. In August of 1894, knowing that he was unlikely to recover, he made his will (Appendix III). It was very basic, leaving everything to his wife, Annie, whom he adored. To Arthur, it was obvious that everything would then be passed onto his living children and grandchildren.

Anne Bamford was heartbroken. At the age of 39 she was now a widow, with Charles, aged 14, (Edwin) Scott, aged 8 and Anne, aged 6. They stayed in Misterton Hall, where Annie was now Lady of the Manor. This positon had many responsibilities, including Patron of St. Leonard's Church, which allowed her to appoint the rector.

A plaque was installed in the Chancel of St. Leonard's, Misterton by Anne in Memory of Arthur. It states:

---

39. History of Tuberculosis, www.faculty.virginia.edu

In loving memory of ARTHUR J. J. BAMFORD Esquire of Misterton who died at Rhyl November 3rd 1894 in his 38th year. And was interred at Llanrhaiadr, near Denbigh, This tablet was erected by his wife ANNE BAMFORD. "Lord, I have loved the habitation of thy house, and the place where thine honour dwelleth." Psalm 26.8

Samuel J. Waring, together with his wife, Eleanor Waring, Arthur's sister, donated the organ in St. Dyfnog's church, Llanrhaiadr in memory of Arthur J. J. Bamford. The plaque says:

To the Glory of God and in loving memory of Arthur J. J. Bamford late of Misterton Hall Leicestershire who died Nov. 4, 1894, aged 37 years, this organ is dedicated S. J. Waring and Eleanor his wife sister of the deceased of Foots Cray Place, Kent and Llanrhaiadr.

"The Peace of God which passeth all understanding."

In 1896 Samuel and Eleanor Waring also donated the choir stalls in St Barnabas, Parish Church of Bromborough in memory of her brother Arthur and parents, Charles and Hannah Bamford.

Arthur was educated at Liverpool College and then went on to Christ College Cambridge, matriculating in 1875 and was a Freemason in West Lancashire, Lodge 1570. According to the Bankers Magazine 1892, Arthur was appointed to the Liverpool Board of the Norwich Union Fire Office.

Oddly enough, Arthur was buried at St. Dyfnog's Church, Llanrhaiadr as opposed to St. Leonard's, Misterton, where he was Lord of the Manor, or St. Barnabas, Bromborough where his father, mother and baby daughter Mary Hannah were interred close to Brookhurst, the family home which he also inherited. Maybe it was because it was close to Rhyl, where he died. Or maybe, and most likely, it was because Mary Nash, mother of Anne Bamford (née Nash) is buried there, and she (Anne) purchased a double grave next to her mother's, where Arthur was buried, leaving a space between the two so that she could be buried between her mother and her husband.

ANNE BAMFORD

The provision business of Bamford, Nash & Bamford was now squarely in John Nash's hands, with Annie Bamford as a sleeping partner. Annie was John's niece. It is assumed that the business of Bamford, Nash and Bamford floundered, as there was no further mention of it in the press. Also, John probably stayed in Chicago to run the meat packing business there. It is possible, although unlikely, that Edwin's company, Bamford Brothers, picked up the pieces and bought John and Anne out.

Charles Arthur Bamford, Annie's eldest son, was sent off to boarding school at Uppingham in Rutland in September 1894, just before his father died. These circumstances were to reoccur some 66 years later when Peter Bamford went off to Ellesmere College, his public (boarding) school, and in his first term there, his father died.

In May, after Arthur died, Anne went on a 10-week trip to the United States, probably to determine what assets she had inherited. Much more research is needed in this area to know exactly what happened to Charles' investments. What is known, however, is that Walter T Nash (Anne's brother), Mary K. Scott of Chicago (Anne's sister), and Anne Bamford of Bromborough leased property in Chicago to E. J. Hosmer and John J. Fenn. This property was on the northwest corner of Indiana Avenue and 22nd Street 100' x 160' and they rented it from May 1st, 1890, for a period of 99 years. The lessees were to erect building costing not less than $100,000, with an option for renewal of another 99-year term at 6 percent of the appraised value, improvements to go to lessor at the end of term without compensation. The value was $10,000[40].

---

40. The Economist, a weekly Financial, Commercial and Real Estate Newspaper 4 April 1903 Valuation Supplement

Northwest corner of Indiana Avenue and 22nd Street, Chicago in 2017[41]

Back in England, Anne continued to reside at Misterton Hall while Charles Arthur Bamford and Edwin Scott Bamford, her sons were educated at Uppingham School, Lodge house.

Charles Arthur Bamford, having left school at age 16 or 17 with no business to join, decided to enlist in the army. He joined the Leicestershire Regiment as a 2nd Lieutenant after completing Officers Training Corps. His brother, Edwin Scott Bamford, age 16, was still at Uppingham, and his sister, Anne, was away at boarding school, as well. Anne (their mother) was living at Misterton Hall with seven servants. Also shown in the 1901 census was Sarah Anne Smith (age 46) — who was noted as her sister-in-law, but no evidence could be found to substantiate this — and her daughter, Laura Agnes Smith (16), staying as guests. However, Sarah Smith was to become Anne's son mother-in-law[42].

Charles Arthur Bamford was a career military man. He fought in the (second) Boer War 1889-1902, various other South African wars, and, of course, the First World War 1914-1918. He reached the rank of Major

---

41. Photo from Google Earth
42. See page 99

before retiring. In his grandfathers will, Charles was to inherit Brookhurst in Bromborough, with all its land, messuages, and hereditaments after the death of his father Arthur J. J. He was 14 years old when his father died, and it is probable that Anne rented it out until Charles became of age.

Serving with Charles in the Leicestershire Regiment was Captain Harold Brooke Hawke (The Honourable). Whether Charles, as a Second Lieutenant, was in the same company under the command of Captain Hawke is not known, but there was an introduction of Captain Hawke to Anne Bamford sometime after 1902. Perhaps it was at a Regimental Ball. Even though Harold Hawke was 12 years younger than Annie, the two of them embraced each other's company. It is certain that Annie liked the fact that Harold was titled and would be good company for her, and, more importantly, Harold was very attracted to Annie's wealth. Whether there was true love there or not, Harold proposed to Annie, and she accepted. The two of them were married at a civil service in 1906 and 3 months later at a church wedding at St. Mary's, Bryanston Square, Westminster. Annie loved the

Bathafarn Hall, Llanbedr-Dyffryn-Clwyd, Ruthin

Clwyd Valley in N. Wales, and rather than rent Bryn-Morfydd from her sister-in-law, Hannah Maria Williams, she purchased her own property there, Bathafarn Hall near Ruthin.

Very little is known about their marriage, but it is assumed that Harold helped Anne run the estates of Misterton and Bathafarn and manage the many investments she had. They were obviously trying to sell their mining assets in the United States, as John W. W. Loose reported in his Article "Lead and Zinc Industry in Lancaster County" that the Bamford zinc mine in Bamford, Pennsylvania was sold for $12,500 in 1906[43]. The proceeds were evenly split between Anne and the remaining issue of Edwin Bamford. It is worth noting that the land was purchased by Charles and Edwin for over $15,000 back in the early 1870s.

No doubt the Hawkes were living the life of Riley. But then their lifestyle began to catch up with them. After being unwell for a time, in August 1912, Anne passed away at Bathafarn Hall. She suffered a cerebral haemorrhage and had carcinoma of the liver and jaundice. There was some talk in the family that her death was suspicious, but the death certificate discredits that idea or that her will was destroyed, which was possible. It is extraordinary to think that with all the assets she owned that she would die intestate. The probate court awarded Harold Hawke, her husband, the sole beneficiary of her estate (Appendix V). Anne's three living children received nothing. When someone asked Charles Arthur why he did not challenge the situation in court, he said, "[he] didn't want to wash the family's dirty linen in public". It was more probable that he didn't have the finances available to pay the legal fees. When Charles approached the Hawke family to discuss the ownership of the Bamford family silver, he was told that it was available for purchase which is what he did! So, the immense fortune that Charles Bamford had accumulated during his lifetime completely vaporized from the Bamford family within 32 years of his death.

---

43. Information from the Lancaster County Historical Society.

The court order giving Harold Hawke sole ownership of Anne's estate was completed and signed on 23 June 1913. Within one year of Annie's death, The Honourable Harold Hawke died at Bathafarn Hall in July 1913, age 45. His death was also from a cerebral haemorrhage and chronic inflamed kidneys, less than one month after becoming the legal owner of the estate. The constant partying and hard drinking habits had finally caught up with them.

Harold Hawke had an elder brother, Baron Martin Bladen Hawke — Baron being his title, not a Christian name. Their father was Baron, The Reverend Edward Henry Julius Hawke, who died unexpectedly in 1887 at the Midland Railway Hotel, St. Pancras, Middlesex, leaving an estate of £191,897-6-7 (approximately £23 million in today's money).

After Harold died intestate, Martin Hawke, the elder brother, inherited everything (Appendix VI). There is good reason for the Bamford family to think that something smelled very fishy. However, nobody challenged the situation, so the status quo remained. Within the Bamford family, the saying was "Hawke by name and Hawk by nature". Baron Martin Bladen Hawke, generally known as Lord Hawke, lived nicely until he died in 1938 at the age of 78. He was an avid cricketer and played for Yorkshire and England, including five Test Matches and captaining Yorkshire for a record eight County Championships, and was President of the MCC. Martin Hawke had no children, so his title — and the Bamford inheritance — went to his younger brother, Edward.

MAJOR CHARLES AND DOROTHY BAMFORD

Major Charles Arthur Bamford and Dorothy Kreitmair

Dorothy (Dolly) Helen Kreitmair was born in 1873 in Toxteth Park, Liverpool, the eldest of three daughters of Francis Joseph Benedict Kreitmair, a cotton merchant, and Ann Eliza Gregg. She married Lieutenant Charles Arthur Bamford in September 1907. Although most of Anne Bamford's estate went to the Hawke's, Charles and Dolly had sufficient funds to live quite comfortably. Charles inherited Brookhurst, the old family estate, on the death of his father and his mother rented it out on his behalf. Just before he was married he decided to sell it, which he did in 1907 for £11,000 to the then current renter: Ernest William Tate, a son of Sir Henry Tate, the sugar refiner[44]. Initially, Charles and Dolly lived at The Chestnuts, Knighton Drive, Leicester, near Charles' regimental headquarters. Having finished fighting in South Africa and after the birth of their first two children,

---

44. Ownership information provided by Susan Nicholson

they decided to live in the Clwyd valley, an area where Charles had many happy memories spent with his father and grandfather. They were unable to find a suitable house to buy, but they did find a lovely home to rent, Pentre Celyn Hall. It came with "Park, gardens, lawns, stables, coachhouse, coachman's cottage, outbuildings and yards", together with "fields, meadows and grassland comprising an area of twenty one acres" for the annual rent of £83 plus an additional £2-10s for the sporting rights[45]. They signed a lease for seven years and then committed to a year-to-year lease at the same rent. Being a fairly large house, Charles and Dolly employed the services of a cook, nurse, parlour maid, housemaid, between maid, and a laundress, all living –in, and almost certainly a gardener.

Within 11 months of being married, Charles and Dolly had their first child, Dorothy Anne, in 1908. Their second child Charles Francis Kreitmair arrived just 18 months later, in 1910.

Strangely enough, it was 10 years before Arthur and Dolly had another child, Helen Patricia. Then, at the age of 40, Dolly gave birth to Arthur Ingram. Maybe World War I (1914-1918) had something to do with the long lapse between the children or maybe she had a difficult time getting pregnant for the third time. Being a military man, it is probable that Arthur was away a great deal before and during the war. It is interesting to note that Charles exited World War I, in 1918, as a captain while his younger brother Scott became a captain in 1909. Lieutenant Charles was probably very happy for Scott but must have been somewhat miffed! However, Charles eventually made the rank of major. Charles and Dolly moved to Charlton Kings, Nr. Cheltenham to be closer to Dorothy and Frank, who now lived in the Midlands, and Mig Kreitmair, Dolly's elderly aunt. They purchased a fairly large home there known as 'The Withyholt', where they lived blissfully with the help of six live-in staff. When World War II broke out, Charles was 60 years old and did not serve, having completed honourable service in the

---

45. Extracted from the lease.

Pentre Celyn Hall, Pentre Celyn, Nr. Ruthin, North Wales

Part of garden and back of Pentre Celyn Hall

Boer War and World War I. It was while he and Dolly were attending a funeral in May 1944 at Berkeley Church in Gloucestershire, which was not his local church, that he suffered a massive heart attack and died.

'The Withyholt' was certainly too big for Dolly to live in on her own. Arthur was now working in London, and Pat had recently married Dr. Angus Alexander. So, she (Dolly) moved to a smaller residence near Cheltenham and eventually moved into a nice flat at 14 Langford Place in St. Johns Wood, where Arthur also lived until he married Peta Anderson just after his mother had passed away. Both Charles and Dolly are buried in Charlton Kings cemetery.

DESCENDANTS OF CHARLES ARTHUR BAMFORD

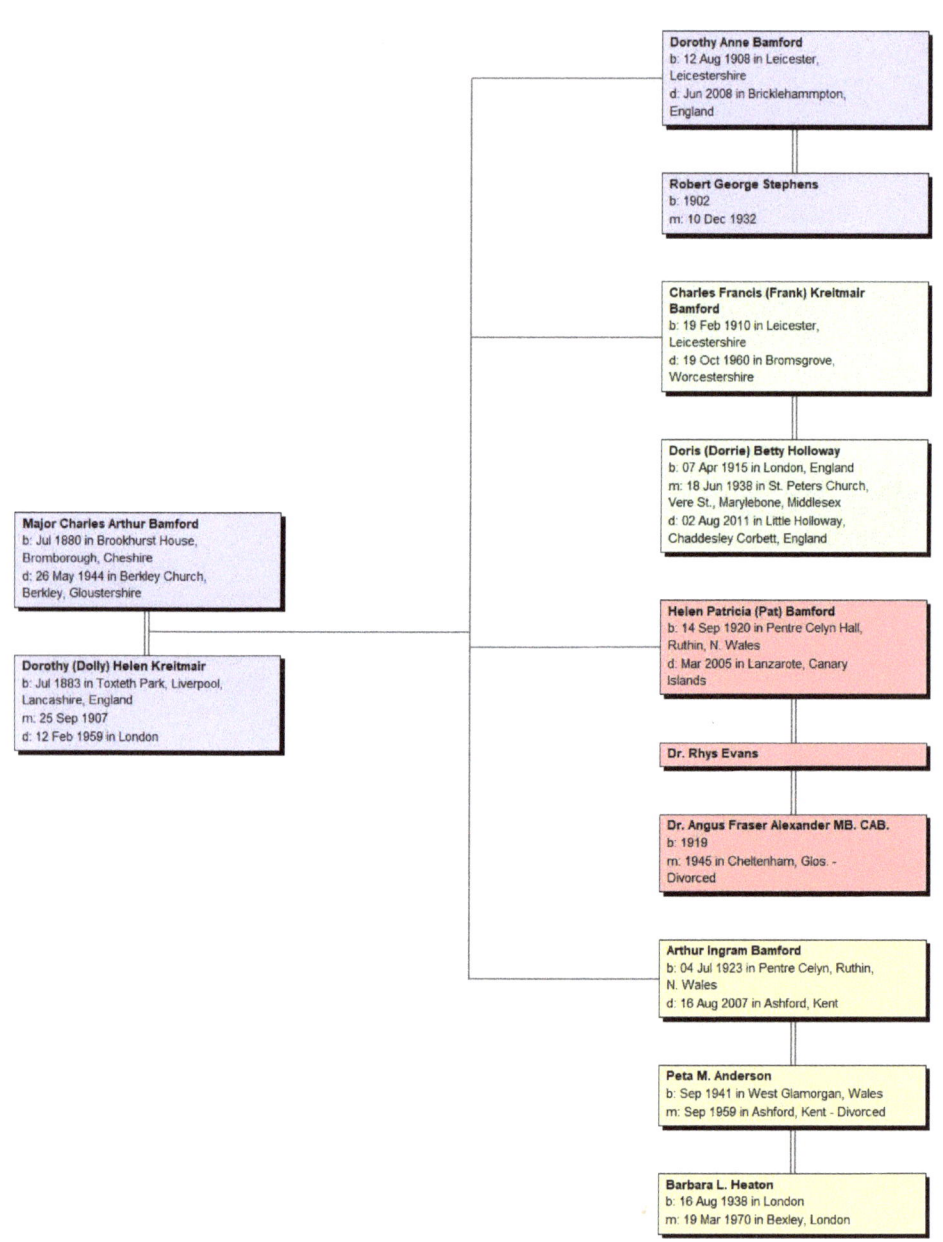

EDWIN SCOTT BAMFORD

Like his brother Charles, Scott decided on a career in the army and joined the Leicestershire regiment. For reasons unknown (maybe he wanted to see action) he transferred to the 1st Battalion of the York and Lancaster Regiment. He was soon posted to India where he stayed until World War I broke out. Louisa Mary Lottie Smith (Lulu) was the elder daughter and fourth child of Sarah Anne Louisa Smith and Walter Edmund Smith, both from Bath. In the 1901 census, Sarah was shown to be staying with Anne Bamford at Misterton Hall with her youngest daughter Laura. Anne listed Sarah Smith as a sister-in-law, but the connection could not be found, although there are several Smith's in the family. (She was to become the mother of Annie's future daughter-in-law, although Annie died five months before Scott married Lulu.) Even though Scott was spending most of his time in India, he found time to court and propose to Lulu. They were married in St. Andrew's, St. Marylebone, London on New Year's Day 1913.

After Scott and Lulu's wedding, it is believed that Lulu went with Scott to India. They lived in Dhukrani, Herbertpur, Dehra-Dun, in the north central part of India, and when Scott returned to England at the end of 1914, Lulu stayed in India.

Unfortunately for Lulu, their marriage was to be a short one. Like many young men at that time, Scott perished in the Great War at the battle of Ypres, having been wounded on his birthday at the age of 29. Lulu must have been devastated to hear the news of Scott's death, especially after only two years of marriage.

The following was a memorial to Scott.

Photos from the Imperial War Museum archives

War Memorials Project Source: Michael Doyle[46]
(written verbatim, words in italics added)

Their Name Liveth For Evermore: The Great War Roll of Honour for Leicestershire and Rutland

He *(Capt. Edwin Scott Bamford)* was the youngest son of the late Arthur John Bamford and his wife Annie Bamford, born 1854 in Baleman *(actually Baltimore)*, USA, (who remarried the Honourable Harold Brooke Hawke), she was the daughter of John Nash of Chicago, USA *(daughter of Thomas Nash of Chicago, brother of John)*. Edwin Scott was born in 1887 *(born 1886)* in Bromborough, Cheshire, he had one sibling, a sister Anne Nash Bamford, *(incorrect as Charles Arthur was his older brother)* born 1889 *(born 1888)* in Bromborough, also residing with the family was Edwin's cousin Mary Gretton,

---

46. www.leicestershirewarmemorials.co.uk/war/casualty/view/20720

born 1868 in Middlesex, in April 1891 the family home was at Bryn Marfyeed *(Bryn Morfydd)*, Church Lane, Llanrhaiadr in Kinmerch, Ruthin, Denbighshire, Wales. In March 1901 Edwin Scott was absent from the family home at Misterton Hall, Misterton, Lutterworth, Leicestershire, residing there was his widowed mother, living on her own means and Edwin's aunt *(future mother-in-law)*, Sarah Ann Smith, born in 1855 in Hanbury, Staffordshire, Edwin was residing as a boarder at Uppingham School, Stockerston Road, Rutland. Edwin married *(Louisa)* Lulu Smith in London on January 1st 1913, she was the only daughter of the late Edwin Whitney Smith of Bath. Edwin was educated at Uppingham, Rutland and later in Switzerland and joined the 3rd (Militia) Battalion of the Leicestershire Regiment from which he transferred into the York and Lancaster Regiment on the 6th July 1907, becoming a Lieutenant on the 1st February 1909. In that year he passed the Signalling course at Poona, India and obtained a certificate for Field Telephoning. In 1911 he took the Musketry and Machine Gun course at Satara, India and in 1912 the Physical Training and Swordsmanship at Poona, India where he was Gymnastic Superintendent for eight months, serving altogether seven years (1908-1914) in India. On the 12th March 1913 he was appointed the Battalion Adjutant and joined the British Expeditionary Force in France in January 1915. He had been promoted to Captain on the 5th September 1914, and was mortally wounded in action on his birthday, the 23rd of April 1915 during a charge at the second Battle of Ypres, and died at the Poperinghe Clearing Station the following day. The following abbreviated account of the circumstances attending his death was received from a brother officer: "On the morning of April 22nd the Battalion was resting — the men playing football — when the French troops came hurrying back completely overcome by asphyxiating gases. Immediately, on their own initiative without any command, our men fell in and moved off by companies from trenches near St. Jean

(Wieltje), with fixed bayonets across open country in broad daylight, with only two *(machine)* guns to support them, to fill in the gap left by the French, which the Canadians were unable to protect their flank. They made the attack through a hail storm of high velocity shell fire and Machine Guns at short range, which nearly wiped out the whole Battalion, leaving 300 out of the original 1200. In spite of the heavy casualties, they pushed on, as a Canadian officer remarked. "As if they were on parade", and eventually reached a field which was still under heavy fire. At the top of the field was a hedge on which the enemy's fire was concentrated, very few of the Battalion got past it. It was here that the Colonel *(probably A. G. Burt)* was killed outright, and Captain Bamford having done magnificent work during the whole attack, was mortally wounded." Some days after, General Plumer came to see the few survivors and congratulated them on their gallant attack. Had it not been made the Germans would have broken through. To use the Generals words, "They saved the situation". Captain Bamford was a keen sportsman and a first class shot.

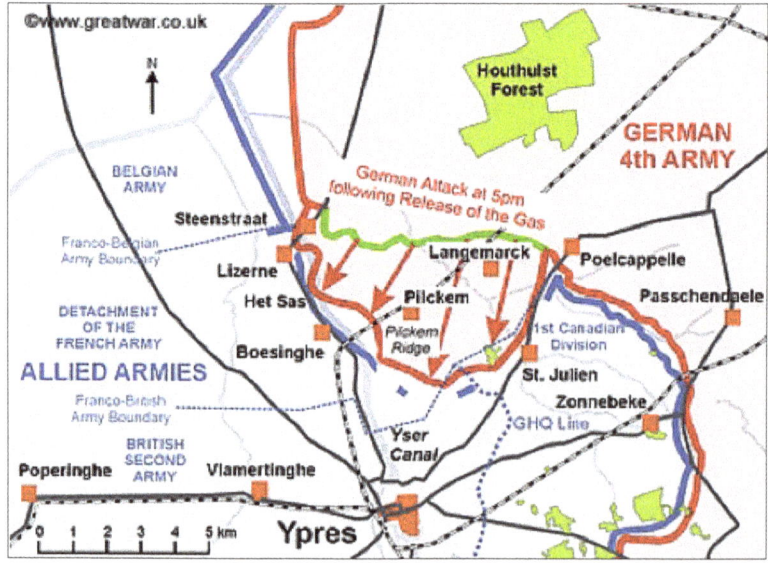

On Saturday May 8th 1915 The Leicester Chronicle and Leicestershire Mercury published the following article

"THE WAR." — DEATH OF CAPT. E. S. BAMFORD.

Captain Edwin Scott Bamford, adjutant of the 1st Battalion York and Lancaster Regiment, who has died of wounds, was the son of Mr. A. J. J. Bamford, of Misterton Hall, Leicestershire, and was in his 29th year. He was educated at Uppingham and in Switzerland, and was first commissioned in July 1907, and joined the 2nd Battalion (old 84th) at York. He left for India the following trooping season to join the 1st Battalion (65th), and came home at the end of last year to join a new division forming at Winchester for the front. Captain Bamford became Lieutenant in February 1909, adjutant March 1913, and Captain September 1914. He has served under four commanding officers, Colonel's Scholes, Howe, Daniells and Burt. His late commanding officer, in giving up the command, said the adjutant had never spared himself in working for the efficiency and well-being of the regiment.

Captain & Adjt., E. SCOTT BAMFORD. York & Lancaster Regt., 23rd April 1915, Age 29. He can now never mourn, a heart grown cold, a head grown grey in vain.

No further information concerning Lulu could be found in United Kingdom records, so it is likely that she remained in India.

Scott was buried at the Poperinghe Old Military Cemetery in Belgium. His grave Reference is II. L. 39[47]

Scott's gravestone[48]

Memorial to Scott Bamford in St, Leonard's Church, Misterton, Leics.

---

47. Photo by Phillip Soskin
48. Photo by John Charnock

ANNE NASH BAMFORD

Anne, born 1888, was the youngest child of Arthur J. J. and Annie. Like her siblings, she was brought up in Misterton Hall, but her schooling is not known. She was 6 years old at the time of her father's death and probably knew little of him. In her later years, she married Sydney Charlton-Jones in 1911 at St. George's, Hanover Square and they had two children, Joanne (b.1912) and Montagu (Monty) (b. 1919). The marriage ended in divorce and Anne re-married Basil Hugh Browning and had two more children, Rosemary (b.1925) and Desmond (b.1927). It is probable that the Browning's lived on the Côte d'Azur, as Rosemary was born in Nice and Desmond in Monaco. It is also probable that later in life they moved to Johannesburg, S. Africa, as that is where Anne died in 1972.

CHARLES FRANCIS KREITMAIR BAMFORD (FRANK)

Frank was the second child of Arthur and Dolly Bamford. He was born in Leicester, Leicestershire, where Lieutenant Charles Bamford was stationed. He first attended Ruthin School, a public school close to where he lived at Pentre Celyn Hall. It is believed that he was expelled from the school for accidentally setting the laboratory on fire, a feat nearly accomplished by his son Peter some years later. Thereafter, Frank attended Bromsgrove School, where he excelled in sports, winning both the 100-yard race and the 220-yard race. In rugby, he was awarded his 1st XV colours, and in his last term there was awarded the 'Victor Laudorum' on sports day for being the best all-round athlete.

Upon leaving school, he had no interest in a military career like his father but was more interested in industry and commerce. His great-uncle was Lord Samuel Waring, the founder and chairman of Waring and Gillows, a large London department store. It was at Waring and Gillows were Frank started his business career. If he was to become part of the senior management team, he needed to know the business of each of the stores departments. It was while he was learning about the carpet department that he visited Kidderminster, the home of British carpets, to learn about the manufacturing process. He joined Carpet Trades, one of the largest manufacturers at that time, and was guided by Frank Reed, their works manager. While he was there, he became fascinated by the industry and decided that it was an industry in which he wanted to be fully involved, specifically the manufacturing side.

Having left Waring and Gillows, he joined a small manufacturing company Frank Stone & Co., at the suggestion of Frank Reed, his mentor, with the understanding that a directorship and/or part ownership would become available at a later date. However, it soon became obvious to Frank Bamford (so many Franks!) that Frank Stone & Co. was not for him, and he began looking around for another investment opportunity. Probably with the help of Frank Reed again, he was introduced to Harry Dutfield, owner of Morris & Co, a small carpet manufacturing and shoddy dealer in Anchorfields, Kidderminster. (Shoddy is a by-product of waste or inferior yarn used to make felt.) Mr. Dutfield had union problems in Kidderminster and there was a lack of good fishing in area (Harry was an avid fisherman), so he decided to move to Axminster, Devon and revive the Axminster Carpet Company there[49]. In 1938, with the help of Winky Watmore, an investor, Frank purchased Morris & Co from Harry Dutfield.

1938 was a busy year for Frank Bamford, as in that year he also married Doris (Dorrie) Holloway, the sister of a good friend of his, Jack Holloway. Jack and Dorrie were living in London at 90 Hillfield Court, Hampstead while Frank was working at Waring and Gillows. They were married on 18 June 1938 at St. Peter's on Vere St., Marylebone. As Frank was working in Kidderminster, they initially moved into a flat at Comberton Mansions.

In 1939, Frank, again with the help of Winky Watmore, purchased the old Hoobrook Mill by the viaduct and moved the factory there from the Anchorfields site. The mill was a good solid three-story building on ample grounds that would be useful for future expansion. There were also air raid shelters on site, which at some point were converted into offices. However, on 1 September 1939 Germany invaded Poland, starting World War II, and the factory was soon commandeered by the government to manufacture webbing for the forces. It is believed that most of the webbing made was used for parachute harnesses. Frank, having hurt his hand in a loom, served in the Home Guard, which also enabled him to oversee the wartime manufacturing process.

---

49. The Independent, Obituary of Harry Dutfield

DESCENDANTS OF CHARLES FRANCIS (FRANK) KREITMAIR BAMFORD

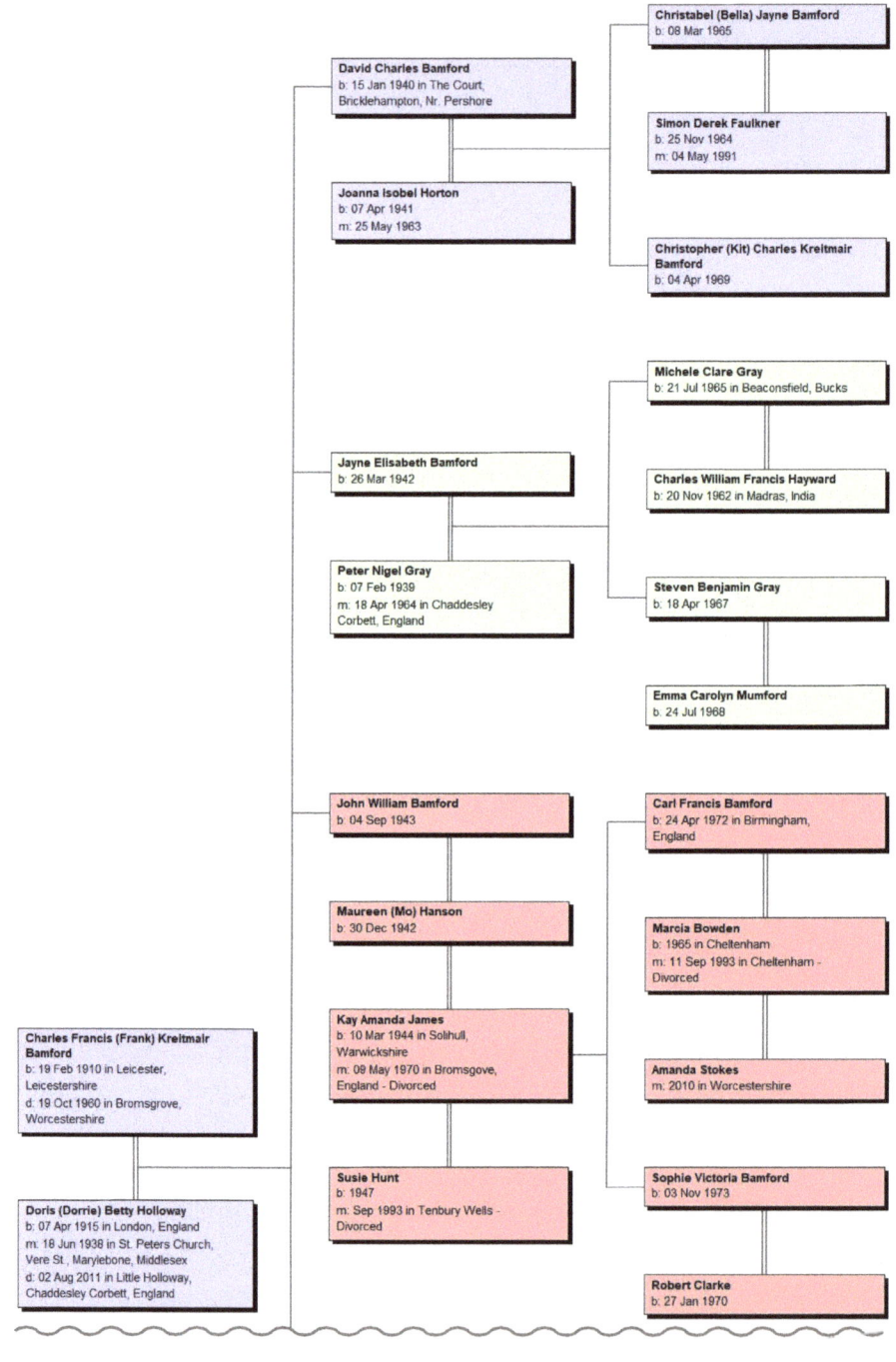

The Bamfords

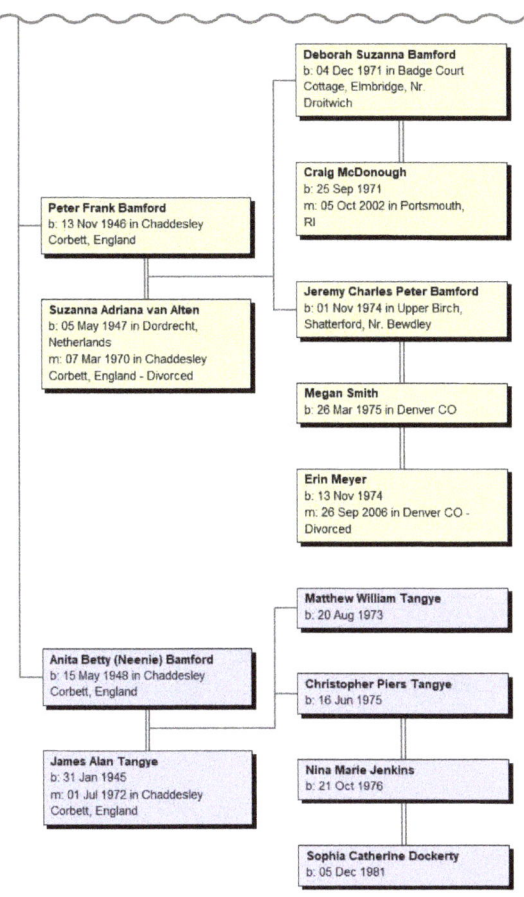

Hoobrook Mill circa 1905[50]

In January 1940, Frank and Dorrie had their first child, David Charles, and later that year they purchased Yesselcote, a good size Victorian family home set in approximately 2½ acres of gardens and orchard. Yesselcote, located in Chaddesley Corbett, Worcestershire was the perfect home to bring up their future family of five children.

At the end of the war in 1945, the factory was in a position to start manufacturing carpets again and continue the shoddy side of the business. For the next five years, carpet orders slowly increased, and Morris & Co. gradually expanded. By 1950, Frank was confident enough in the business to be able to repay Winky Watmore his investment. It is almost certain that Dorrie help him financially in this regard. Even though the business was doing well, most of the profits were either being reinvested into the business or used to pay for the private schooling of five children.

---

50. Picture of a poster in the Carpet Museum, Kidderminster

Letterhead[51]

In 1958, David Bamford left Uppingham School and joined his father in the business while also attending the Community College in Kidderminster to learn the carpet trade. Unfortunately, in the latter part of 1959, Frank was not feeling well and had exploratory surgery. It was determined that he had cancer. By August 1960, he was becoming weak and very thin. So, with the help of his financial advisers, Bertie Rose and Len Barrows, and legal adviser Godfrey Russell, a plan was put in place to avoid inheritance tax. In August, 1960, a new company was incorporated by the name of Morris & Co. (Kidderminster) Ltd, of which Dorrie became the overall largest shareholder, and trusts were set up for the five children. On 19 October 1960, at the age of 50, Frank succumbed to his illness.

---

51. Photo of the letterhead taken at the Carpet Museum, Kidderminster

DORIS BETTY BAMFORD (NÉE HOLLOWAY)

Doris, affectionately known later in her life as Dorrie, was the second child of William Claude Holloway and Elisabeth (Betty) Holloway (née Citroen). Doris was born in 1915 at 35 Grove End Rd., St. John's Wood, London. One month before her fifth birthday, her father passed away after a long illness at age 43. Betty with her two children, Jack and Doris, then moved to 8 Hamilton Place, just around the corner from their previous home, close to Lords Cricket Ground and London Zoo in Regents Park. It was a more manageable home than the one on Grove End and, more importantly, perhaps, it was just down the road from where David Citroen, Betty's father had purchased a large home — Number 44.

Late in 1928, Jack was away at boarding school, and it was decided that Doris should go to a school in Eastbourne, close to where her grandparents now lived at Trevin Towers. Betty was living in London alone when she learned that her mother, Doris' grandmother, Sarah Citroen, became ill. So, Betty moved to Eastbourne to help take of her mother and father, David Citroen. Unfortunately, Sarah was suffering from breast cancer and passed away in November 1930 at the age 64. It was only just over a year later that the unimaginable happened: Doris' mother became ill and soon passed away in October 1932 of cancer of the lung and breast. She died at the age of 43, like her husband. So, Doris, still a teenager at the age of 17, had lost her father and mother and was now left to look after her aging grandfather and his large household, which was no easy task! To make matters worse, her grandfather, David Citroen, with the best of intention, insisted that she go on a couple of cruises, which he loved but Doris loathed. Just over two years later, in January 1935, her grandfather passed away from anaemia and chronic kidney disease at the age of 74.

It was natural for Doris to move in with her brother Jack, who now lived in London, and work for the Ford Motor Company. Together they purchased a nice flat in Hampstead, London at Hillfield Court. It was while she was in London that she was introduced to a good friend of Jack's, Frank Bamford. They were immediately attracted to each other and after a while Frank proposed and Dorrie accepted. They married in 1938.

Dorrie before being presented to Queen Mary in 1937

It was around 1937 that Dorrie was presented to Queen Mary, the widow of George V, before George VI became king. Dorrie's future mother-in-law, Dolly Bamford, thought it important that this presentation take place, so she and Dolly's daughter, Patricia Bamford, were presented at the same time.

World War II broke out in September 1939 with the German invasion of Poland. Many men immediately volunteered to fight the Nazis, and Jack was no exception. He joined the RAF and was killed over Libya, just one month away from his 30th birthday. Naturally, she was devastated and now had only one close relative left on the Holloway side, her cousin Zisla Holloway (Cissie).

Up until Frank became ill, Dorrie ran the household at Yesselcote and brought up five children while he handled the business. However, everything changed in 1960.

After the reorganization of Morris & Co (Kidderminster) Ltd. was completed and Frank had passed away, Dorrie became Madam Chairman and Managing Director of the company at the age of 45. With five children ranging in age from 12 to 20, four of whom were still at boarding school, and with no husband for support, she certainly had her work cut out.

She had to win over the senior management team, many of whom felt that they should be playing a larger role. Arthur Bamford, Frank's younger brother, a manufacturer's carpet representive in London, also thought he should be directly involved with the company, not to mention the 300 employees all concerned about their future employment. There were the day-to-day decisions that had to be made in order to keep a successful company running, which she did, with the help of her senior management team and advisors. The company flourished. The following article was published in the Kidderminister Shuttle in October of 1967.

Woman who met the Challenge

Christine Williams talks to a widow with 5 children who took over her husband's firm

"Making the right decision whether in the kitchen or boardroom is basically a matter of common sense." This is the view of Mrs. Doris Bamford, Chairman and Managing Director of Morris and Company (Kidderminster) Limited.

Mrs. Bamford took over the firm in 1960 after the death of her husband Mr. C. F. K. Bamford. And the woman whose business activity was confined to discussions with her husband, now captains a carpet firm employing nearly 300 people.

Left with five children aged between 12 nd 20, Mrs. Bamford was at a time in life when most women look forward to more relaxation.

New Career

Indstead, she took up the challenge of building an entirely new career. "I have never regretted my decision," she told me. "Even had I not taken on this position, I would have had to do something other than dusting the house and digging the garden."

Absorbing the technical side of her work as she went along, Mrs. Bamford has brought the woman's viewpoint to bear on carpet design. "After all," she said "it's usually a woman who chooses the carpets!"

Before her marriage Mrs. Bamford studied art in London. Her knowledge of design and colour has been invaluable in the carpet company.

For Norway

A design adapted from one of her own skirts has brought the company an £8,000 order. It was selected by a Norwegian architect for the floor of a new supermarket in Fredrikstad,

Helped by cooperative children and understanding colleagues, Mrs. Bamford found it possible to combine successfully the roles of mother and businesswoman.

A Benefit

"During term time there was no problem as the children were at boarding schools, but in the holidays I always tried to devote part of the afternoon to the family," she said.

Far from thinking her children suffered as a result of her absorbing career, Mrs. Bamford thought they had benefited by having a mother whose world was not confined by domestic doings.

"As a person I am far more interesting because of my caareer. I find my work both stimulating and enjoyable," she said.

About women bosses Mrs. Bamford said: "I have found it is simply not true that men dislike working for women. Men discuss their problem with me and probably feel that they'll have a more sympathetic reaction because I am a woman."

Sons, too

Wrapped up in her work, she said that she was always carpet conscious, even when visiting friends. "I get round shoulders at looking at the floor," she laughed.

Mrs. Bamford's eldest son David (27), is now a director of the company and 24-year-old John is a junior executive. The grandmother of three became serious when we discussed the trade situation. Credit restrictions have meant a decline in the carpet trade, especially noticable after a boom year in 1965.

During the last month, however, trade improved and as part of an expansion programme the company will open a new warehouse tomorrow.

Expansion is also planned in the export field. "We are improving our export trade but import taxes make it difficult to compete abroad," said Mrs. Bamford.

There is not much time for other interests in her full life, but she enjoys travelling whenever she has the opportunity.

In 1964, the family sold a minority of its stock to the general public, making it a public quoted company on the Birmingham Stock Exchange. It is believed that Dorrie Bamford was one of the first, if not the first, female Chairman of a British public company.

It was also in 1964 that the facory needed to replace the large chimney for the works boilers. Always on the lookout for a promotional opportunity and having missed the opportunity to lay the foundation brick, someone came up with the idea of laying the last brick in the chimney. Dorrie bravely agreed to the task, and it was reported in the Kidderminster Times in September 1964.

She Laid the LAST Brick!

You've heard of people laying the foundation stone or the first brick. But have you ever heard of anyone laying ceremoniously the last brick of building?

Standing on one plank on a small scaffold, Mrs. Doris Bamford, chairman and managing director of Morris & Co. Ltd. Laid the last brick on the firm's new 77 feet high boiler stack.

Mrs. Bamford was hoisted up inside of the stack by two executives of the firm which had carried out the contract. There was only three feet of room so one heanded her the brick and the other gave her the trowel and mortar to put the finishing touches to the chimney.

The stack rises seven or eight feet above the Hoobrook viaduct so the job was definitely one for a person with a head for heights.

Mrs. Bamford's comment: "It was a wonderful aerial view but the next time it will definitely be the foundation stone!"

Four years after Morris & Co. became a public company, an unsolictited offer was made by Youghal Carpets of Cork, Ireland for a controlling interest in the company. The offer was exceptionlly good, so the Board of Directors accepted. Youghal was basically a yarn-spinning and dyeing company who wished to expand by vertical integrtion, so carpet and rug manufactoring was a good fit. Unfortunately, poor management of the company and their rapid expansion resulted in continuing losses, and the company eventually filed for protection under the bankruptcy laws. Happily, by this time, most of the family shares in the company had been sold.

Five years after Frank died, Dorrie met Andrew Speed at a dinner party, and they became close companions. They went on many holidays together and spent a great deal of time together. At one point, there was talk of marriage, but it was not enthusiastically received. However they looked after each other until he died at the age of 93 in 1991.

Besides her love of travel, Dorrie was a keen artist and loved using watercolours. There are many 'original Dorries' spread throughout the family! She also loved to entertain, giving numerous dinner parties. In her earlier years, she enjoyed playing tennis until her knees began troubling her but she continued to enjoy the game and attended many matches at Wimbledon. She lived a long life, passing away peacefully in 2011, at the age of 96. She spent her last moments at home, a house called "Little Holloway" located in the village of Chaddesley Corbett.

ARTHUR INGRAM BAMFORD

Unfortunately, very little detail is known about Arthur's life. Born in 1923 at Pentre Celyn Hall, North Wales he was the fourth child of Major Charles and Dolly Bamford. He was educated at Wrekin College, Shropshire. After leaving school around 1940, he went into the army like his father. Whether he was conscripted or volunteered is not known, but it was likely the latter, as he joined the newly formed Special Air Services (SAS) after officer's training school. He was sure to have pleased his father.

The SAS is a special force of the British army founded in 1941. It was an unorthodox idea and plan by Lieutenant David Sterling of the Scots Guards. His idea was for small teams of parachute-trained soldiers to operate behind enemy lines to gain intelligence, destroy enemy aircraft and attack their supply and reinforcement routes.[52]

As a 2nd Lieutenant in the SAS, he would have command over a small group of men and was involved with the invasion of Italy in 1943. It is believed that during the invasion, he was commanded to carry out an order that he believed would have meant certain death to all in his command. However, he saw a different way to carry out the same objective and commanded his men accordingly. The objective was achieved without any loss of life. Despite this, disobeying an order from a superior officer, especially during wartime, is an offense and makes the offender liable to being court-martialled. That is what happened.

Arthur put up a good defence but was ultimately found guilty and was stripped of his officer rank. However, he appealed the ruling and ultimately was found to have acted in good conscience, completing his mission without loss of life. His rank was reinstated but for reasons unknown, Arthur rejected the restoration of rank, preferring to stay as

---

52. History of the Special Air Service — en.m.wikipedia.org

a regular soldier. He may have regretted this decision when it became time to receive his pension, but like all 21-year-olds, he was not thinking of his pension. It is quite possible that the stress of the court-martial and appeal put a great deal of stress on the family and may have contributed to his father dying from a heart attack in 1944.

Little else is known about Arthur's military career other that he served in what then was called Palestine after the war ended from 1945 to 1947.

53

After an honourable discharge, he worked in London as a carpet sales representative with Hughes and North. One of the companies he represented was Morris & Co., his brother Frank's company.

In September 1959, Arthur married Peta M. Anderson in Ashford, Kent. Peta was a stage actress, and it was probable that she didn't spend much time at home. Unfortunately, the marriage didn't last, and they divorced in the mid-1960s. Later he met and married Barbara Heaton in March 1970 in Bexley, London. There were no children from either marriage.

---

53. Nationalarchives.gov.uk

Later in life, Arthur's lifetime of smoking caught up with him. He suffered from Buerger's disease (or something similar) and emphysema. One leg eventually became gangrene and had to be removed. This was particularly difficult for a man in his 80s, and he eventually passed away on in 2007, age 84, on Barbara's 69th birthday.

The Kreitmairs

According to Dorothy Stephens (née Bamford), her mother, 'Dolly' Kreitmair, "was related to a von Kritmeyer of Bavaria, probably Munic(h) whose statute was in the square — but bombed in the 1939 war, possibly a Count or Baron."

Research found the following information.

WIGULÄUS VON KREITTMAYR[54]

(b.14 December1705 — d. 27 October 1790)
German legal scientist, electoral Bavarian Real Secret Chancellor

Literature, Weblinks and Footnotes regarding Wiguläus von Kreittmayr are listed in Appendix XI.

---

54. The whole history including pictures of Wiguläus Von Kreittmayr is taken from de.m.wikipedia.org and translated by Google Translate

Wiguläus of Kreittmayr
(Oil painting by the Bavarian Academy of Sciences), photo: BadW

Words in *italics* added.

Wiguläus Xaverius Aloysius von Kreittmayr was a Bavarian legal scientist, electoral Bavarian real secret chancellor, conference minister and supreme Lehenprobst. He was born in Friedberg (*Bavaria*) near Augsburg and was the son of Franz Xaver Wiguläus Kreittmayr and Maria Barbara Degen (or Däg), Franz also was in the Electoral Court of Bavaria. Wiguläus carried the titles of Ritter and Elder von Kreittmayr. (*Elder was, until 1919, the lowest rank of nobility in Austria-Hungary and Germany. The rank was just beneath a ritter (a hereditary knight), but above untitled nobles who used only the nobility particle von before their surname. It was mostly given to civil servants and military officers.*)

Wiguläus of Kreittmayr
(Copper stitch in the possession of the State Graphic Collections)

Wiguläus Kreittmayr married Sophie von Heppenstein in 1745. She and her two sons died early. In a second marriage, he married Maria Romana von Frönau (a widow) from Niederbayerische Offenstetten, with whom he had two sons and a daughter.

Kreittmayr was described as extremely diligent and of calm, open and straightforward character. In his youth, he attended the Jesuit Gymnasium[55] in Munich (now the Wilhelmsgymnasium in Munich) until 1721. He learned Latin as well as French and Italian, "that he could still memorize long passages from the works of Horace, Vergil

---
55. A Gymnasium is a five year high school

and Ovid". [2] Later he studied philosophy at the University of Salzburg, jurisprudence in Ingolstadt, history in Leyden and Utrecht and worked at the courtroom in Wetzlar. [2] [3] The court council was at that time the highest in the country. It was said by the Bavarian Elector, Max Emanuel that the 20 year old Kreittmayr was at "the beginning of a brilliant career". [2] On 15 May 1741 (aged 36) he was elevated to the Knights of the Holy Roman Empire by the imperial vicars and electors Karl Albrecht of Bavaria and Karl Philipp von der Pfalz as court vicariate and court judge in Augsburg and in 1742 he was appointed a real councillor of the lands. On July 6, 1745, he was promoted and appointed Bavarian court council chancellor and to the secret council. In 1749 he became a secret council-chancellor and conference minister, and finally, in 1758, a real secret Chancellor and Supreme Lehens-Advocate.

As "spiritus rector of justice in Bavaria", Kreittmayr strongly influenced the government policy of Elector Maximilian III Joseph and contributed to the consolidation of the Bavarian state from his position. [4] In 1759 he was appointed honorary

Image of the monument of Wiguläus von Kreittmayr on the back of a Bavarian 2-thaler coin from 1845

member of the Bavarian Academy of Sciences. [5] His bust took place at the Hall of Fame in Munich and his monument on the Maximiliansplatz in Munich (on the site of the Schiller monument today) but was not rebuilt after the Second World War. *Apparently, it was destroyed by the Allied bombing of Munich.* There had been opposition in the Munich city council (to replace the statute), as he was accused of lack of discrimination in the adoption of torture and the death penalty in his code of law. However his statute in Offenstetten still stands.

Wiguläus von Kreittmayr
Monument in front of the Schloss Offenstetten, district of Kelheim
Sculptor: Alexander Fischer

Commemorative plaque for Kreittmayr at Haus Burgstraße 6 in Munich, the house where he died. The house is located not far from the Marienplatz.

This undoubtedly was the gentleman that Dorothy Stevens was referring to in her notes. He would have held the title of Baron even though not directly referred to in the article. However, it has been extremely difficult to find the direct connection. Even with the help of a German genealogist (Margarete Handl of Waltenhofen, Germany) a direct connection could not be proven. The problem is that in Germany, their records of that era are entirely church records; there were no census records. As she points out, Munich has 58 parishes and about 30 of the 58 have church books before 1820, the birth date of Karl Joseph Benedikt Kreitmayr.

On his marriage certificate, Dorothy's great-grandfather, Charles (Karl) named his father as Benedict Kreitmair, a lawyer, the same profession as many of the relatives of Wiguläus von Kreittmayr. Benedict Kreitmair would have been the English spelling of his name and was probably Benedikt Kreitmayr in Germany. Given that Charles was born in 1820, Benedikt would have been born around 1790, give or take five years. Dorothy mistakenly thought that her great-grandfather's name was Maximilian, so that could have been Benedikt's father or some other relation — a brother, a distant cousin, or uncle.

There are several possibilities of a connection to Wiguläus von Kreittmayr. He had one brother and eight sisters, seven of whom became nuns. His brother, Joseph Benno, had six daughters and a son, Franziscus, who became a priest. One possibility is that one of the unmarried girls had an illegitimate child carrying the last name Kreittmayr, as could have Franziscus.

Wiguläus himself had three sons, one by his marriage to his first wife, Sophie von Heppenheim, who died giving birth to Bernard, born in 1749. He was a lieutenant in the German army in Wien and was killed in 1781, unmarried. With his second wife, Maria Romana von Frönau auf Offenstetten, he had two sons and a daughter. His first son, Johann, had no children with his wife but did have an illegitimate child, Johann Nepomuk, in 1810. He was later legitimized and inherited the family castle in Offenstetten, as well as the family fortune. His second son, Ignaz Franz Kaspar, had two sons born around 1790. However, neither son married and, incredibly, both sons died in duels, one in 1818 and the other 1820. It is possible that the latter son to die could be Benedikt, the father of Charles (Karl).

Another possibility, and maybe the most plausible, is that Wiguläus' uncle was David Kreittmayr, born in 1675, with his older brother, Franz, being Wiguläus' father. David had two sons and a daughter, the elder son was only seven months old when he died. His second son, Franz Joseph Anton Adam, was born 23 December 1706. Regrettably, he moved out of the parish and no further facts could be found.

KARL JOSEPH BENEDIKT KREITMAYR

Karl was born in 1820 in Munich, Bavaria. At a fairly young age after he had finished studying law at the Ludwig Maximilian University of Munich, he made the decision to leave Germany for England. At that time, many Germans were leaving to settle in other countries, some for religious freedom, others for political reasons and some to avoid conscription. Europe was in turmoil in the 1840s. The potato blight of 1845-1846 brought widespread misery, and an economic depression added to the misery. There were many uprisings, mainly by the poor and liberal-minded students, many of which were successful and brought about many reforms[56]. Whatever Karl's reason was for leaving, he decided to settle in the Liverpool area of England. There he changed his name by deed pole to Charles Joseph Benedict Kreitmair.

Charles (it is assumed that he wished to be known by that name) came from an upper-class German family. It was natural that Charles was looking for a suitably wife of social standing, and he found her: Ellen Scott Lamb was born in 1826, and — according to Dorothy Stephens in a written family tree — was related to the Duke of Buccleugh family. The family name of the Duke of Buccleugh is Scott, so it is quite probable that Ellen's mother or grandmother was a Scott, as Scott was Ellen Lamb's second name.

Charles and Ellen set up home first in Birkenhead and later in Childer Thornton, in the Wirral, Cheshire. He was 30 years old and Ellen was 24 years old when they had their first child, Charles Henry Benedict, in 1850 but he only lived four years. Of the six children they had, only one was to marry, and that was Francis Joseph Benedict, their third son. The second son, Frederick Albert Benedict (Fred) lived until he was 24 years old, when he died of consumption (TB). Their fourth child, Louisa Caroline, died at the age of 23, also of consumption. Charles and Ellen had twins in 1857, Charles Albert Benedict and

---

56. Information from Wikipedia.org

DESCENDANTS OF CHARLES JOSEPH BENEDICT KREITMAIR

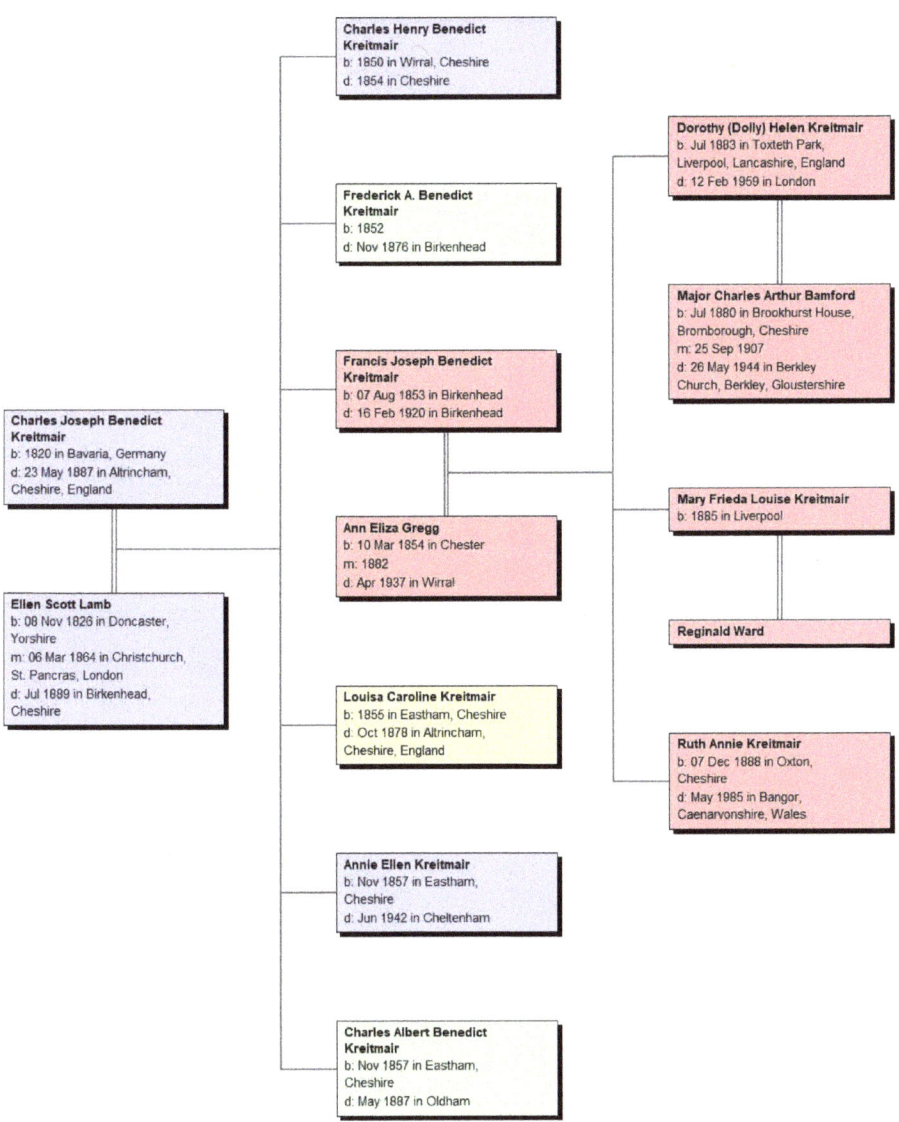

Annie Ellen. Albert only lived until he was 30 years old before dying from consumption — the scourge of the time — and Annie, who was known as Mig, died in Cheltenham in 1942 at age 85, unmarried.

Charles and Ellen were married in 1864 at Christchurch, St. Pancras, London. Since this date is after the birth of their six children it is probable that they had a civil wedding sometime before the birth of their first child.

Charles had a niece, Wilhelmine Hamlein, born in 1844, who was possibly a daughter of Maximilian. She used to visit Charles in Cheshire.

It is remarkable to think that Charles left Germany as a young, well-educated man with a law degree and set up home in England. He had to learn a new language and find something suitable to do, as it was not practical for him to practise law. Presumably, he came to this decision because he would have to receive a new degree in English law, in a language not his own. He decided on a career as a merchant, probably in cotton. Charles passed away two years before his wife in Altrincham Cheshire in May 1887 at the age of 67.

FRANCIS JOSEPH BENEDICT KREITMAIR

Francis was born in Birkenhead in 1853, the third son of Charles and Ellen, and presumably grew up there. In his late 20s, he met and married Ann Eliza Gregg, a young woman from Chester, in 1882, when she was 28 years old. Her father, Robert Gregg was Sheriff of Chester from 1869-1870, serving the usual one-year term. Interestingly, the sheriff's chain that was donated to the city of Chester was first worn by Robert Gregg.

A sheriff in the United Kingdom is a ceremonial position in a city or county awarded to a person of distinction for a period of one year in recognition of their achievements. In ceremonies the sheriff will wear a sheriff's hat, gown and chain. "The Chester sheriff's chain was presented by Alfred W Butt in memory of his father, Alderman Francis Butt, on the occasion of the opening of the Town Hall in 1869. The badge bears the arms known as the arms of the Sheriff, 'a chevron between three garbs' and is surrounded by an earl's coronet supported by a lion and a wolf."[57]

Francis and Annie had three children, all girls: Dorothy Helen (Dolly) b. 1883, in Toxeth Park, Liverpool; Mary Frieda Louise (Frieda) b. 1885, also in Toxeth Park; and Ruth Anne b. 1888 in Oxton, Cheshire, part of Birkenhead.

Francis had no intention of following many previous Kreitmairs into the legal business. He decided on a career in cotton after his father's involvement in the industry. It is not known where he served his apprenticeship, but eventually he set up his own firm, F. Kreitmair & Co., in Orleans House in Liverpool close to the Cotton Exchange. Liverpool was a major centre for cotton brokering and merchandising,

---

57. Sheriffchester.co.uk

DESCENDANTS OF FRANCIS JOSEPH BENEDICT KREITMAIR

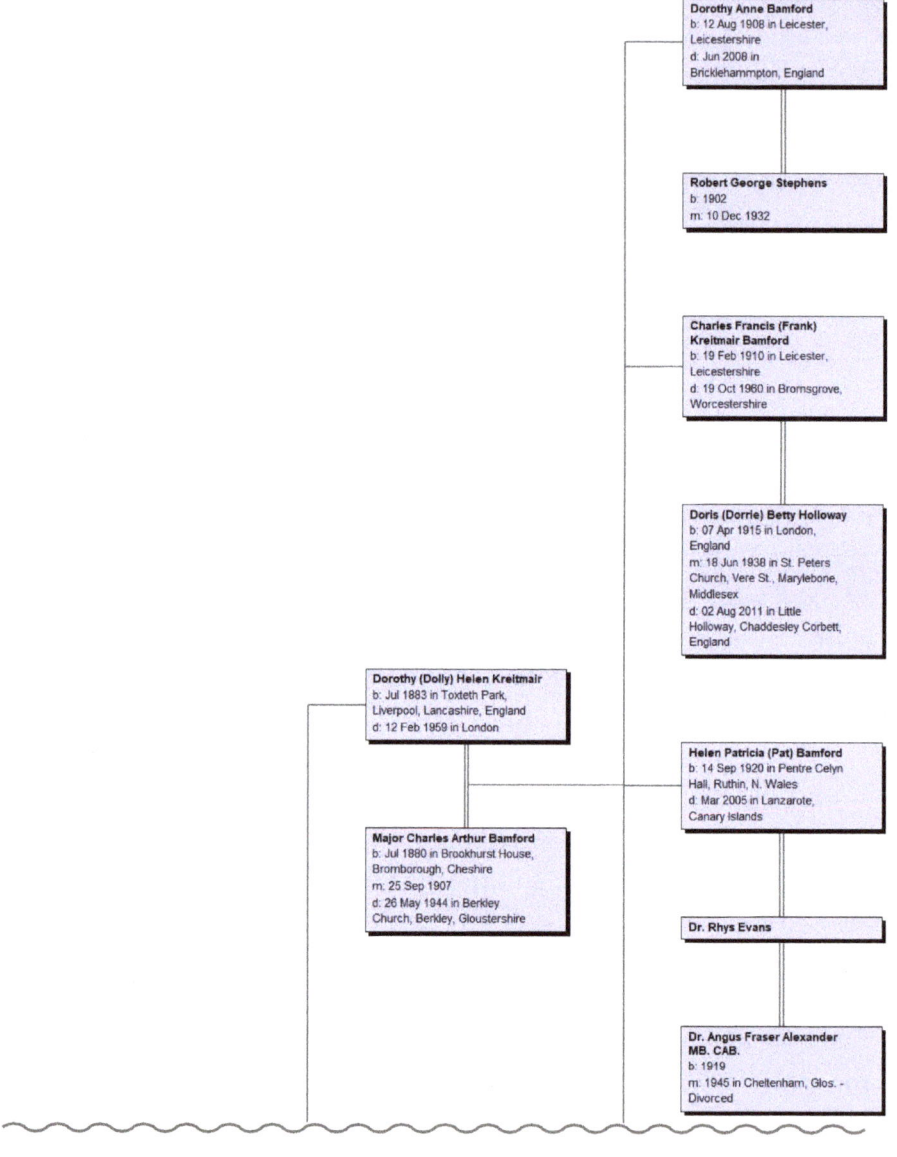

The Kreitmairs

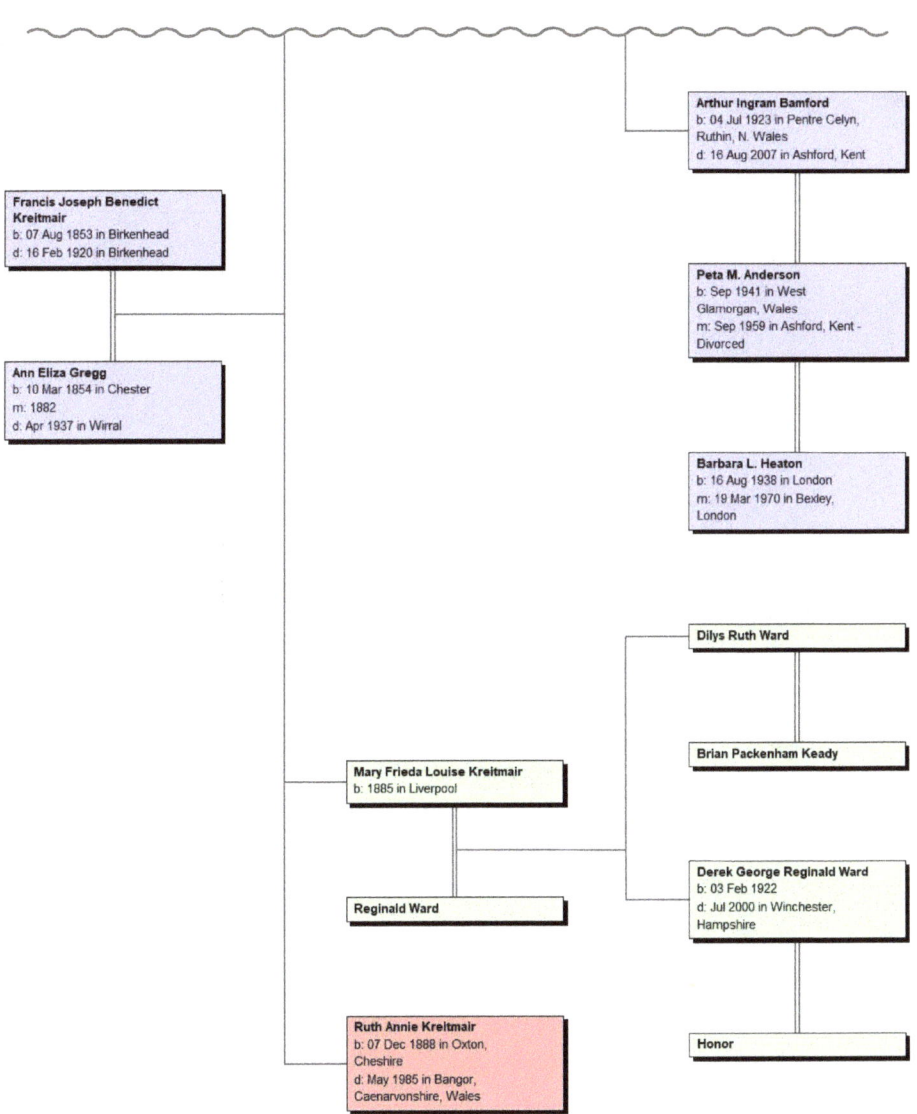

and Orleans House was home to many cotton brokers. In his advertisement, he states that he will give special attention to cotton futures.

Orleans House, 17 Edmund St. Liverpool, now houses luxury apartments.[58]

With a successful business, Francis was able to move his family into a larger house, known as Firdene in Noctorum. Regrettably the house has been demolished to make way for five reasonably sized homes on a road known as Firdene Close.

With no son and heir, unfortunately the Kreitmair line died out. The story continues with 'Dolly' Kreitmair, who married Charles Arthur Bamford (see page 94); Frieda, who married Reginald Ward and went to live in Ireland; and Ruth, who never married but was known to have 'enjoyed her life' in North Wales, dying at the age of 96.

---

58. Photo from http://cityresidential.co.uk/

The Holloways

Holloway is a name of ancient Anglo-Saxon origin and comes from a family who once lived as inhabitants at the hollow-way, or holy way. Holloway is a topographic surname, which was given to a person who resided near a physical feature such as a hill, stream, church or type of tree[59].

JOHN ALEXANDER HOLLOWAY

The Holloway family is an important part of the Bamford family tree, as Dorrie Bamford was a Holloway before marrying Frank Bamford. Unfortunately, there is little information about the Holloways, and the known family lines have ceased to exist. The earliest known Holloway is John Alexander Holloway, who was born in 1840 and married Helen Balfour Miller, from Strand London, at the age 23 in 1868.

John and Helen had three children: Lily, William Claude, and Sydney Charles.

From all appearances, they were reasonably well off. Both John and Helen lived in Westminster, a fashionable part of London, and both of the boys became engineers. It appears that John Alexander, the father,

---

59. www.houseofnames.com

DESCENDANTS OF JOHN ALEXANDER HOLLOWAY

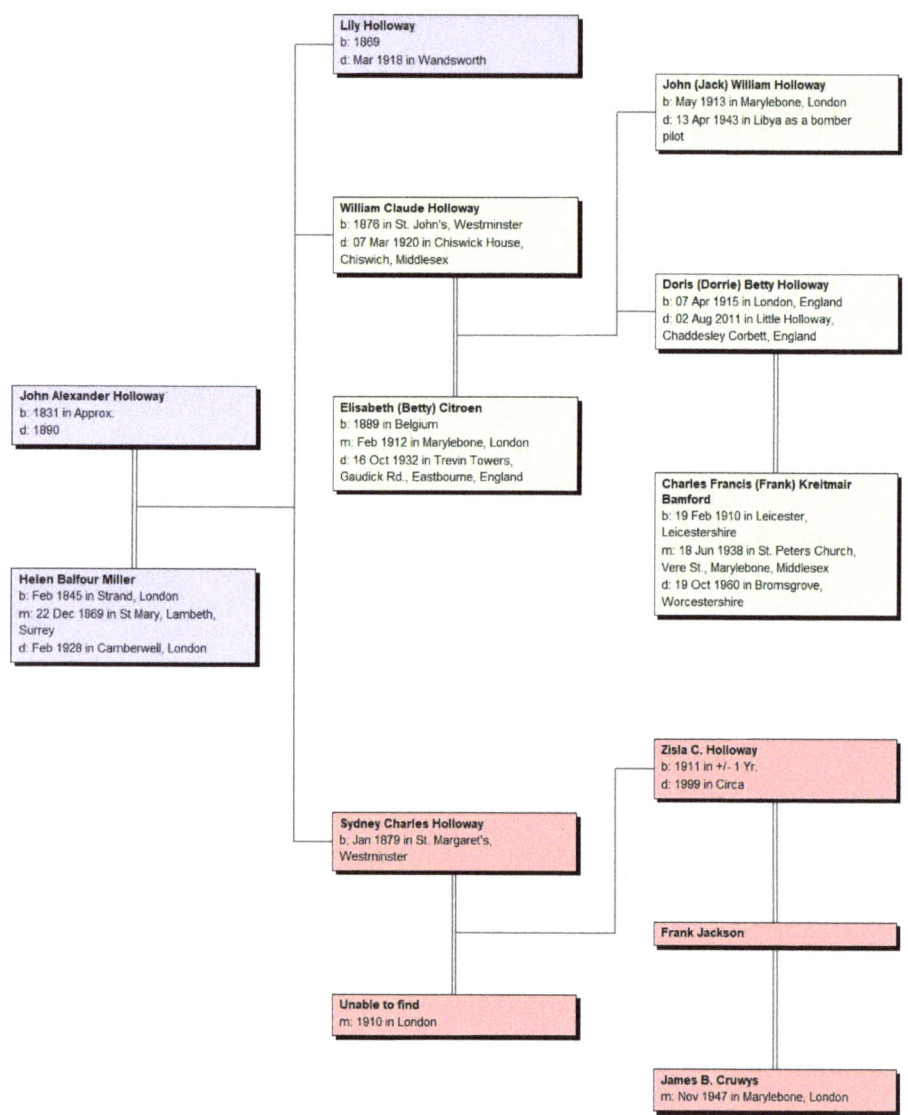

passed away before 1901, as he is not mentioned in that census. In the 1901 and the 1911 census, the rest of the family were living in 15 Old Queens St., Westminster. Also in the 1911 census, both of the brothers were listed as an employer in the motor industry, a fledging industry at that time. In fact, they were both working at the Minerva Company, a Belgium car and motorcycle engine manufacturer. William used to race the early Minervas and drove in the 1905 Tourist Trophy (TT) in the Isle of Man. They were employed by Mr. David Citroen, who manufactured the Minerva car in England under license (see page 160).

WILLIAM CLAUDE HOLLOWAY

In February 1912, William Claude married Elisabeth (Betty) Citroen, David Citroen's daughter. What a beautiful couple they made!

They settled down at 35 Grove End Rd. in St. John's Woods, London. In May of 1913, just over a year later, John (Jack) William was born; two years later, in April 1915, Doris Betty arrived. It is assumed that just before her birth, William was distracted from family life. Somewhere he contracted syphilis, a sexually transmitted disease.

Syphilis is a persistent, highly infectious disease that can have devastating consequences. It is caused by a spiral-shaped bacterium that can live almost anywhere in the body and spreads rapidly. It progresses through four distinct stages — primary, secondary, latent, and tertiary — each of which can last for several years. Serious health complications are common and can be fatal in late-stage syphilis which can occur after three years. At this stage the bacteria reactivate, multiply, and spread throughout the body — damaging the heart, eyes, brain, nervous system, bones, and joints — and a degenerative central nervous system disease can produce dementia, tremors, loss of muscle coordination, paralysis, and blindness. Damage is irreversible.[60]

Today, the disease is easily cured with the administration of antibiotics but not so when William contracted the disease. He was probably given mercurial ointments and injections, which did him no good. As he entered the tertiary stage, he was in poor condition and was admitted to Chiswick House, a mental institution for the wealthy. It was there he died in 1920. The probate notice states:

> Holloway, William Claude of 8 Upper Hamilton Terrace, St. Johns Wood, Middlesex died 7 March 1920 at Chiswick House, Chiswick, Middlesex. Probate London 6 May to Sidney Charles Holloway engineer. Effects £7043 7s 5d.

Chiswick House as it is today[61]
Previously it had two wings housing the wards and nursing care facilities

---

60. Syphilis information from healthcommunities.com
61. Photo from en.m.wikipedia.com

After William went into nursing care, Betty and the two children decided to move into a more manageable house and purchased 8 Hamilton Place, where they lived for several years. In 1928, at the age of 13, Doris went to an all-girls boarding school, Queenswood in Eastbourne, close to where her grandparents lived. Jack was also away at boarding school. So, it was not surprising that when Betty heard that her mother was unwell and, as Betty was living in an empty house in London, she decided to move in with her parents at Trevin Towers in Eastbourne to look after them. Unfortunately, Sarah, her mother had breast cancer and died in November 1930.

When Doris went to her school, Queenswood in Eastbourne, for her first term, she went by train and met Mary who, like her, was on her way to the same school. There they became the very best of friends and when they left, they promised to stay in touch by writing to each other every week. This they managed to do, wherever in the world they were, for 70+ years, until Mary became ill and passed away. An amazing accomplishment and friendship.

When Betty moved to Eastbourne, Jack was finishing his last year at public school and decided to stay in London, where he joined the Ford Motor Company.

8 Hamilton Terrace

SYDNEY CHARLES HOLLOWAY

There is little information about Sydney Charles Holloway, William Holloway's brother. It is known that he was born in 1879 in Westminster, London and, like his brother, trained as an engineer. He married before his elder brother in 1910 and had one daughter, Zisla. Cissie, as she was known, was married twice, first to James Cruwys in 1947 and, after he died, to Frank Jackson. Cissie was a large lady and "always fun to be around", particularly in her earlier years. As Dorrie's closest living relative, her family saw Cissie fairly often, especially on special occasions. She was asked, later in life, if she would record any information that she could remember about the Holloway family. The following is an exact transcript:

> As regards to the Holloway family, around about the 1860s, Cissie's and Dorrie's great-grandfather, the Earl of Balfour, was concerned with building railways in India. Their grandmother's maiden name was Balfour. The Balfour's had Irish blood.
>
> William and Sydney Holloway were engineers and built a car in a garage at the top of a hill when cars were first invented. They drove the car from the top to the bottom of the hill where it fell to pieces! They then had to carry the car piece by piece to the top of the hill again.
>
> On another occasion whilst they were out, all the forward gears failed, and they had to return the whole way in reverse gear.
>
> Both William and Sydney worked at the Minerva Motor company, England which was run by David Citroen who in the early days was seen driving behind a man with a red flag.
>
> Sydney Holloway taught Warwick Wright of the Wright Brothers to drive a car. Both William and Sydney were great motorcyclists and raced at Brooklands.

Warwick Wright was not from the aviator's family, as they had no siblings named Warwick, and neither of Orville or Wilbur were married. He was possibly a first cousin, and there was a Warwick Wright who worked with William and Sydney at Minerva Motors.

Brooklands motor circuit in Surrey, England was the first purposely built banked motor race circuit in the world. The track was opened in 1907.

As previously mentioned, Helen Balfour Miller, born in 1845, married John Alexander Holloway. With a middle name of Balfour, it is probable that her mother was a Balfour before she married. Helen Balfour Holloway (née Miller) was Cissie's and Dorrie's grandmother, so Cissie's note is correct in that fact.

A great deal of research could not uncover a connection to the Balfour family. It is true that James Balfour, 1775-1845, made an immense fortune in India but not building railways in India. His son, James Maitland Balfour, 1820-1856, added to the family fortune as a director of the North British Railway, which earned him a fortune in his own right.[62] His son, Arthur James Balfour, 1848-1930, became Prime Minister from 1902-1905 and became the 1st Earl of Balfour. So, all parts of Cissie's information are true but not in one generation! Like the connection of Ellen Scott Kreitmair née Lamb's connection to the Duke of Buccleugh's family, being able to substantiate a connection of Helen Balfour Holloway's to the Earl of Balfour has proved difficult. It is most unlikely that Dorothy Stephens or Cissie Jackson would make up stories, but it is possible that family lore changed a little with each generation. It is also possible, of course, that the connection is through an illegitimate child.

---

62. Wikipedia

JOHN (JACK) WILLIAM HOLLOWAY

The only son of William and Betty Holloway, Jack was born in May of 1913. He was probably born at home, 35 Grove End Rd. in St John's Wood, London. Although it is not known exactly when his father, William, was committed to Chiswick House, it is likely that he hardly knew his father, who died when he was just six years old. Jack's schooling was at Oundle, a well-regarded boarding school paid for by his grandfather, David Citroen.

After completing school, Jack joined the Ford Motor Company in London. Like his father and grandfather, he was interested in automobiles and felt he could work his way up the company. However, after the death of his grandfather, Jack learned that there was a clause in his Will that concerned his three grandsons only. Clause 19 (in Appendix VIII) stated,

> … if any one of my grandsons shall desire to purchase a share or partnership in the profession of a Stockbroker Solicitor Surveyor Chartered or Incorporated Accountant or to qualify for practicing any such professions such grandson shall be at liberty…to appoint in his own favour from the said trust funds set apart for his benefit such a capital sum or sums as may be necessary…

Two grandsons enacted this clause: Jack decided to make a career as a chartered accountant, and Donald left his stockbroking career to study law. However, on 1 September 1939, Germany invaded Poland, and two days later Britain and France declared war on Germany. World War II had begun.

Like many men at that time, Jack volunteered to fight for his country and decided on the RAF Volunteer Reserve. There he learned to fly, training on the de Havilland Tiger Moth and after his first solo flight on the North American Harvard[63]. After his final tests and examinations he earned his 'Pilot's Wings', and held the rank of flying officer. As he was older than most volunteers and enlistees, he was given the job of training new pilots. However, in 1942 when the war was looking bleak, he asked to be transferred to the front. His wish was granted, and he was assigned to the RAF 70th Squadron, which at that time was stationed in Abu Sueir in Egypt.

It was there that he was to fly Wellington bombers to support the ground troops during and after Battles of El Alamein. On the 13 April 1943, he and his crew were sent on another bombing raid over Libya, but this time he was not to return. His plane encountered unusually heavy ground fire, and his plane was hit so badly that he crashed in Libya. He and all of his crew were killed.

64

---

63. Information extracted from www.rafmuseum.org.uk
64. Image from aircrewremembered.com

Wellington bomber[65]

Alamein Memorial at the entrance of cemetery[66]

---

65. Image from https://i.ytimg.com/vi/yTQIUEa4cqA/maxresdefault.jpg
66. Image from the Commonwealth War Graves Commission website

Jack with his crew are memorialized at the Alamein Memorial at the entrance of the Alamein cemetery in El Alamein, Egypt. Jack's name is in column 268. The memorial also commemorates the 11,866 Commonwealth forces who died in World War II.

Like many men (and women) who fought in World War I and World War II, he sacrificed his life to preserve our freedom. By all accounts, Jack was a caring, intelligent, and well-like person, impressing all those who came into contact with him. For the family, it was a truly heart-breaking event.

The Citroens

The surname Citroen was originally Limoenman, Dutch for lime man or one who sells limes, as in a fruitier. In the early 19th century Barend Roelof Limoenman (1808-1895), son of Roelof Limoenman (1781-1814), changed his surname from Limoenman to Citroen, which is Dutch for lemon. This was obviously done after his father's death — he was only six when his father died — and, according to A. J. Ayer in his book "Part of my Life", was done "at the request of his wife's parents who were socially superior to him....and (the name) more genteel[67]".

The Citroen family are an important part of the Bamford family history, as David Citroen was Doris Bamford's grandfather, her mother being Elisabeth Citroen. But more on them later.

BAREND ROELOF CITROEN

Barend Citroen married Jeannette Roosenboom in 1831 and had 14 children! They all lived relatively long lives except Eva, the last child, who was born in 1851 and died the same year. Barend and his family lived in Amsterdam. He started his working life as a goldsmith but later went into the retail side of the jewellery business.

---

67. Part of My Life, A.J. Freddie Ayer, page 15

DESCENDANTS OF BAREND BARUCH ROELOF RAPHAEL CITROEN

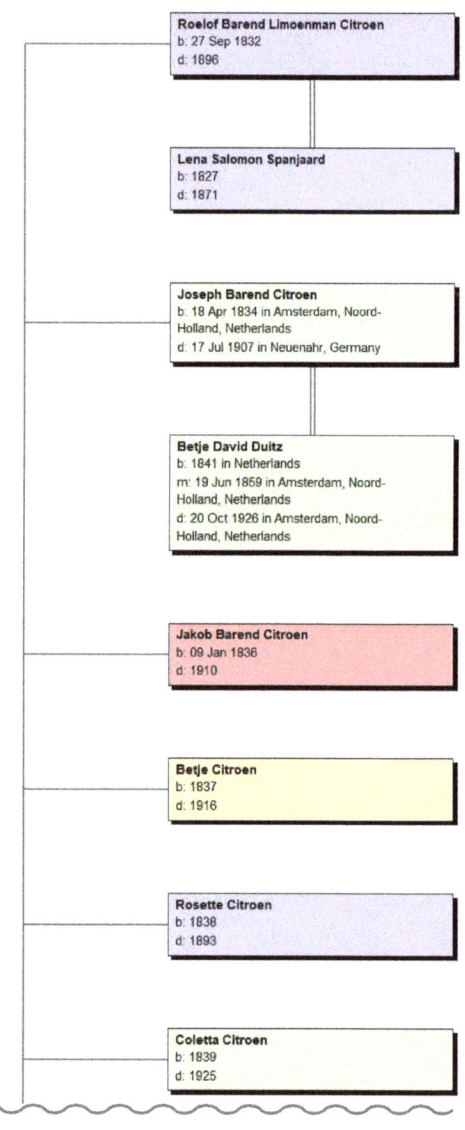

The Citroens

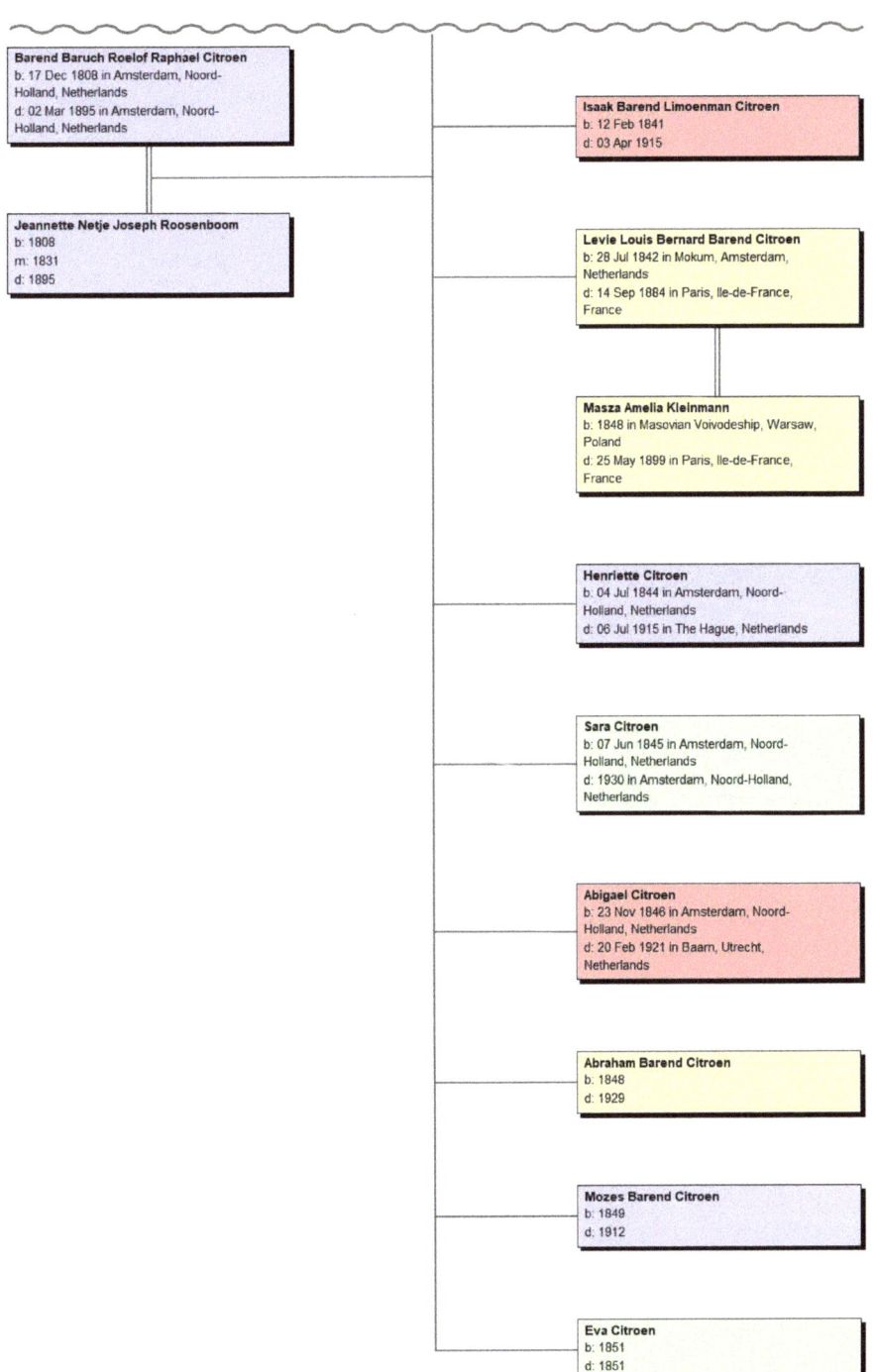

The following information is taken from the website of Schaap + Citroen, a high-end jeweller in Amsterdam.

> "When the 19-year-old Barend Roelof Citroen completed his training as a goldsmith in 1827, he opened the doors to his jewellery store at the Jodenbreestraat in Amsterdam. Some years later, Citroen moved his shop to the Nieuwendijk, which was the main shopping street in Amsterdam at the time.
>
> Barend's eldest son — Roelof — opened his own store in one of the most important shopping streets in the centre of Amsterdam, the Kalverstraat, in 1859. He used to sell precious metal objects as well as jewellery and watches.
>
> After the Second World War, the Dutch firm Roelof Citroen was awarded the title: 'Purveyor for the Royal Family'[68]."

---

[68]. www.schaapcitroen.nl.

JOSEPH BAREND CITROEN

Barend's second son Joseph Citroen (1834-1907), it is believed, went into the wholesale diamond business in Amsterdam. He married Betje David Duitz on 19 June 1859 in Amsterdam and immediately started a family. Dorus Joseph Citroen was born in 1860 and was later to be known as David. He was the first of eight children: six boys and one girl, Clara, and a stillborn. All the children, including Clara, carried their father's first name, Joseph.

For reasons unknown, Joseph's father Barend, together with some of Barend's sons, left Amsterdam for Paris and started dealing in diamonds there. This left Roelof and Joseph in Amsterdam to carry on with their successful jewellery business on the Kalverstraat and diamond trading business respectively.

It is believed that Joseph's eldest son David decided to follow in his father's footsteps and become a diamond dealer, although Freddie Ayer wrote in his book that he started out as a fruit trader in Antwerp. He travelled a great deal, including South Africa and London, and it was while David was on a trip to London that he met the daughter of a diamond dealer, Sarah Rozelaar, who was five years younger than him. She was a Dutch girl of Jewish religion who was born and lived in Highbury, London. David was 27 years old and Sarah 22 years old when they married in The Netherlands in 1887. David was well educated and was able to speak, English, French and German fluently, as well as his native tongue, Dutch. He also had the uncanny ability of adding a column of pounds, shillings, and pence all at once, with there being 12 pennies to a shilling and 20 shillings to the pound. Thank God for decimalisation in 1971.

Sarah was probably already pregnant when they married, as their first daughter, Reine David, was born in June 1887 in Antwerp, Belgium, where they had set up home. At that time Antwerp was, and still is, considered the centre of the diamond dealing and cutting industry.

DESCENDANTS OF JOSEPH BAREND CITROEN

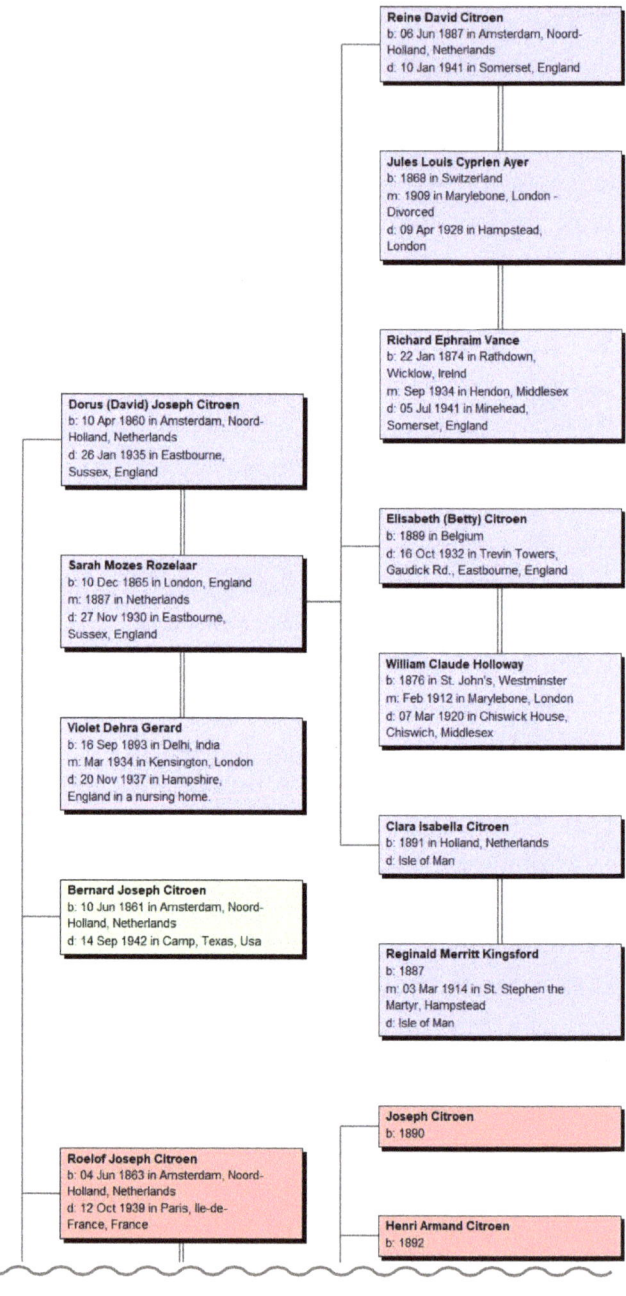

The Citroens

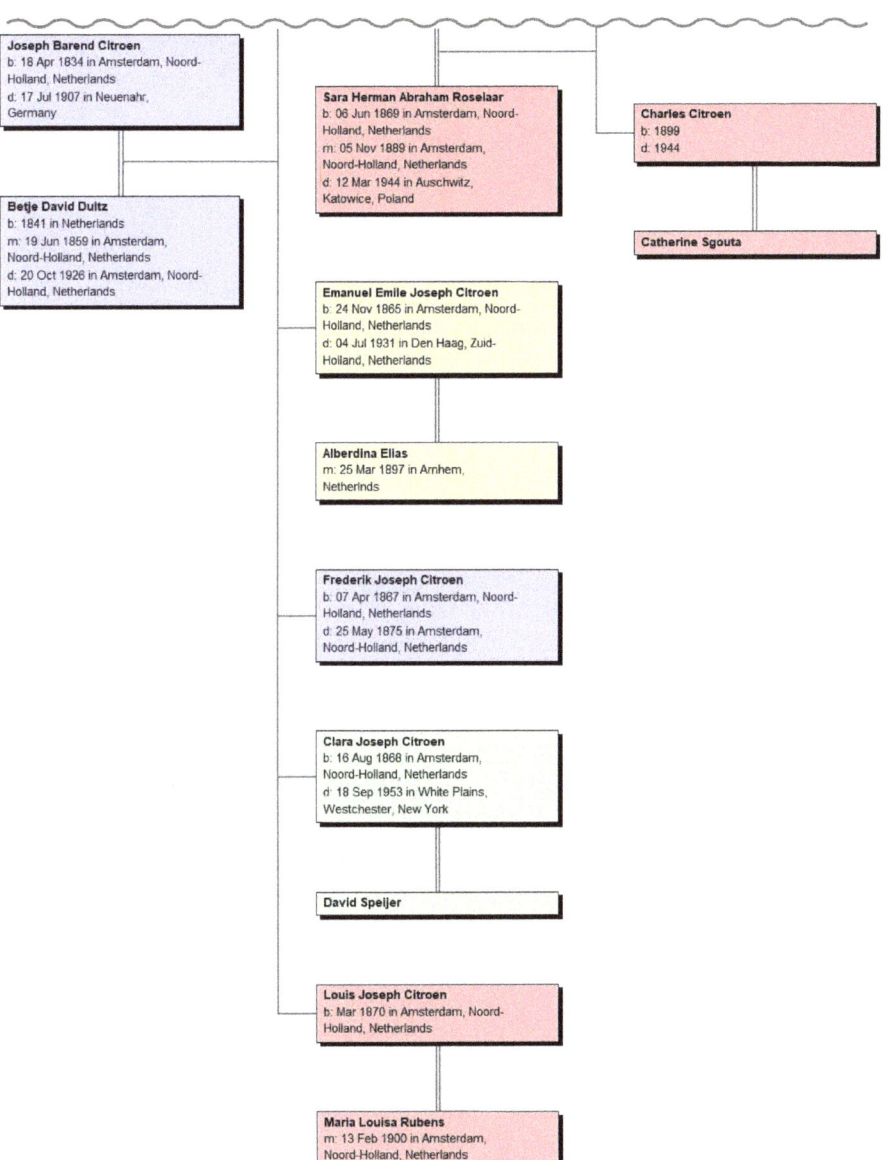

David Citroen with granddaughter, Doris, and Sarah Rozelaar

Two years later, David and Sarah had a second child, Elisabeth David, who was also born in Antwerp, Belgium in 1889.

When Sarah became pregnant for the third time, David, with two healthy daughters, was now hoping for a son. It was not to be, as Clara Isabella was born in Amsterdam in 1891. Whether the Citroens had moved to Amsterdam or were just visiting is not known.

Sometime in the mid to late 1890s David decided to move his family to London. A new type of antisemitism had begun to develop in Europe known as racial antisemitism.[69] His in-laws lived in London, and he wanted to bring his family up in a more secure environment. He decided to leave the Jewish faith and became atheist and insisted his daughters marry gentiles. David first moved into home on Green Lanes in Highbury, London, which was very familiar to Sarah, as she had grown up in that area. Interestingly, there were many of foreign

---

69. Wikipedia, antisemitism in Europe

descent living on Green Lanes. On the 1901 census, he was listed as a diamond broker and a company director. Around 1902 or 1903, David and Sarah purchased a house 'Melrose' in Shoot-up Hill, Cricklewood, London. In the late 1910s he bought a country estate in Essendon, keeping his London home close to his business.

MINERVA MOTORS

Excerpts from Motor Sport, December 1962 'Fragments on the forgotten makes No. 20: The Minerva'[71] and Grace's Guide to British Industrial History[72].

MINERVA — Roman goddess of Wisdom, War, Art, Schools and Commerce.

While living in Belgium, David Citroen came across Sylvain de Jong, a Dutchman living in Antwerp, Belgium. De Jong and his brother started a bicycle company in 1883, and at the end of the 19th century, they designed light weight clip-on engines for bicycles, which proved very successful. These engines were exported all over Europe and Australia. David struck a deal with Sylvain, making David the sole importer of the engines into the United Kingdom. He started business at 45 Holborn Viaduct, London in 1902 and soon realized that advertising was an important business practice to get this new product known, as were motor shows. The larger of the two cycle engines available was

---

70. Photo from en.m.wikipedia.org
71. en.m.wikipedia.com
72. gracesguide.co.uk

known as the Minerva, as was de Jong's company. So, David registered a new British company Minerva Motors in 1901.

An example of a 1903 advertisement[73]

---

73. Illustration from Gracesguide.co.uk

A Minervette with who is thought to be David Citroen and his three daughters: Reine, Betty and Clara. 'Driver' unknown, possibly a niece or friend of Clara[74].

Sylvain de Jong's company, NV Minerva Motors Company in Berchem (Antwerp) produced their first car, the small 1-cylinder, 5-h.p. Minervette in 1904 with a £105 price tag in England.

With the clip-on cycle engines selling well and the Minervette car now available David took a stand at the Stanley Motor Show.

Both Sylvain and David Citroen could see the benfit of motor racing and entered road races in Europe. When the French Werner brothers — competitors of Minerva — sought publicity and pronounced their car to be the winner of a race from Paris to Bordeaux and back again, it was all too much for David. He took out this advertisement to protest and promote his cars. In the stop press section of the advertisement it

---

74. Photo from pinterest.com

states, "Following our great victory in the Spanish Races, we have just received a telegram from Moscow announcing that the MINERVA has won EVERY EVENT in the Russian Spring Races".

Ad for the 1904 Motor Show[75]

---

75. Illustration from Gracesguide.co.uk

76.

Following up on their European victories, David Citroen entered two 16-h.p. cars in the first Tourist Trophy race in the Isle of Man in September 1905. His drivers were Ernest Arnott and William Holloway,

---

76. Illustration from Gracesguide.co.uk

his future son-in-law, two engineers at his company. The race was held in the Isle of Man because the Motor Car Act in the United Kingdom placed a speed limit of 20 mph on all roads. The four laps of the 52-mile circuit was won by John Napier in an Arrol-Johnson at an average speed of 33.90 mph.

Minerva Motors continued racing, advertising, and attending motor shows with some success. In fact, Charles S. Rolls (of later Rolls Royce fame) was a Minerva dealer in England. Minerva Motors continued to import cars, motor cycles, and motorcycle engines into the United Kingdom. They supplied their well-known engines to many of the leading British motorcycle manufacturers, including Triumph, when the industry was in their adolescent stage.

Leon Molon drives his 3.3 litre Minerva to third place in the 1914 TT held on the Isle of Man[77]

---

77. Photo from uniquecarsandparts.com

The company adopted the Knight double sleeve-valve engine before the First World War, and a team of these cars, emitting the usual smoke-haze, finished second, third and fifth in the 1914 T.T., driven respectively by C. Rieken, L. Molon and C. Porporato.

Both William Claude Holloway and Sydney Charles Holloway worked at Minerva Motors, and both of them continued to race motorcycles and William, cars. At that time, David Citroen was the Chairman, William the Managing Director and Sydney the Works Manager.

When World War I commenced, car production in Antwerp ceased, and the English company began manufacturing shells and fuses. Sylvain de Jong and his engineers headed to Amsterdam, where they kept on developing parts and added armour to existing cars to convert them into armoured cars. The Antwerp factory survived the German invasion, machine tools having been shipped to Holland when war broke out, and two Minerva chassis had been saved by hauling them up into one of the factory chimneys.

In England, after the Great War, a move was made to Charlotte Street, W.1 and then to Chenies Street, off the Tottenham Court Road, where William Holloway and his brother Sydney built Minerva House some years before the war, complete with a statute of Minerva.

When William became ill and had to stop work, Sydney was promoted to managing director. Also on the board was Reginald Kingsford, another son-in –law of David's.

New cars began to arrive by 1919, with the new shapely radiator replacing the flat radiator of the pre-war Minervas. Two models were available: the 20-h.p. 4-cylinder and 30-h.p. 6-cylinder. The cars were highly regarded and were purchased by royalty and the rich and famous. Some famous owners of Minervas are listed in Appendix X.

The six-cylinder model was a well-designed and magnificently built car that was endowed with some of the most beautiful coachwork in the world. Some of the coachwork was made by all the leading specialists in such work, although Minerva also made their own bodies.

Perhaps the peak year was 1925, when the delivery drivers were each bringing in a car or chassis a day from Harwich and imports from Antwerp were unloaded at Parkeston Quay. Apart from cars, commercial vehicle chassis were also imported, where they were made into lorries or coaches. The Royal Arsenal Co-operative Society had a fleet of Minerva hire and funeral cars.

1923 Minerva Type AB 3.4 litre Fully Convertible Salamanca[78]

---

78. Photo from Bonhams.com

A Minerva charabanc advertisement[79]

---

79. Illustration from Gracesguide.co.uk

In 1927, Minerva Motors Ltd. became a public company, trading as Minerva Motors (England) Ltd. All the shares sold out quickly. The prospectus quoted profits for the year ending mid-1923 as £41,985, rising to £89,432 in 1924/25 and dropping to £50,855 for 1926/27[80]. After becoming a public company, David Citroen stepped away from the company while Sydney Holloway stayed on as Managing Director. The company expanded satisfactorily and, having outgrown the Tottenham Court Road premises, added an additional service station in Park Royal, London. Minerva Road is there to this day.

In October 1929, the Great Crash occurred when the New York Stock Exchange collapsed, wiping out billions of dollars of value. The world markets quickly followed, and hard times ensued for most. The market for luxury cars fell dramatically, and the "Buy British" campaign worsened the situation for Minerva.

With the economic crisis of the 1930s, the company filed for bankruptcy in 1936 and finally stopped trading in October 1938. David Citroen, fortunately, did not see the demise of his company, as he had passed away in 1935.

The remains of the company were taken over by another Belgian constructor named Imperia, who placed the name Minerva on their vehicles for export to England and France. In the meantime, Sydney Holloway started his own motor business behind the Ladies Carlton Club in Halkin Street, but with the outbreak of World War II in 1939, not much could be expected.

---

80. £50,000 in 1926 is worth £2,784,645 in 2017

DESCENDANTS OF DORUS (DAVID) JOSEPH CITROEN

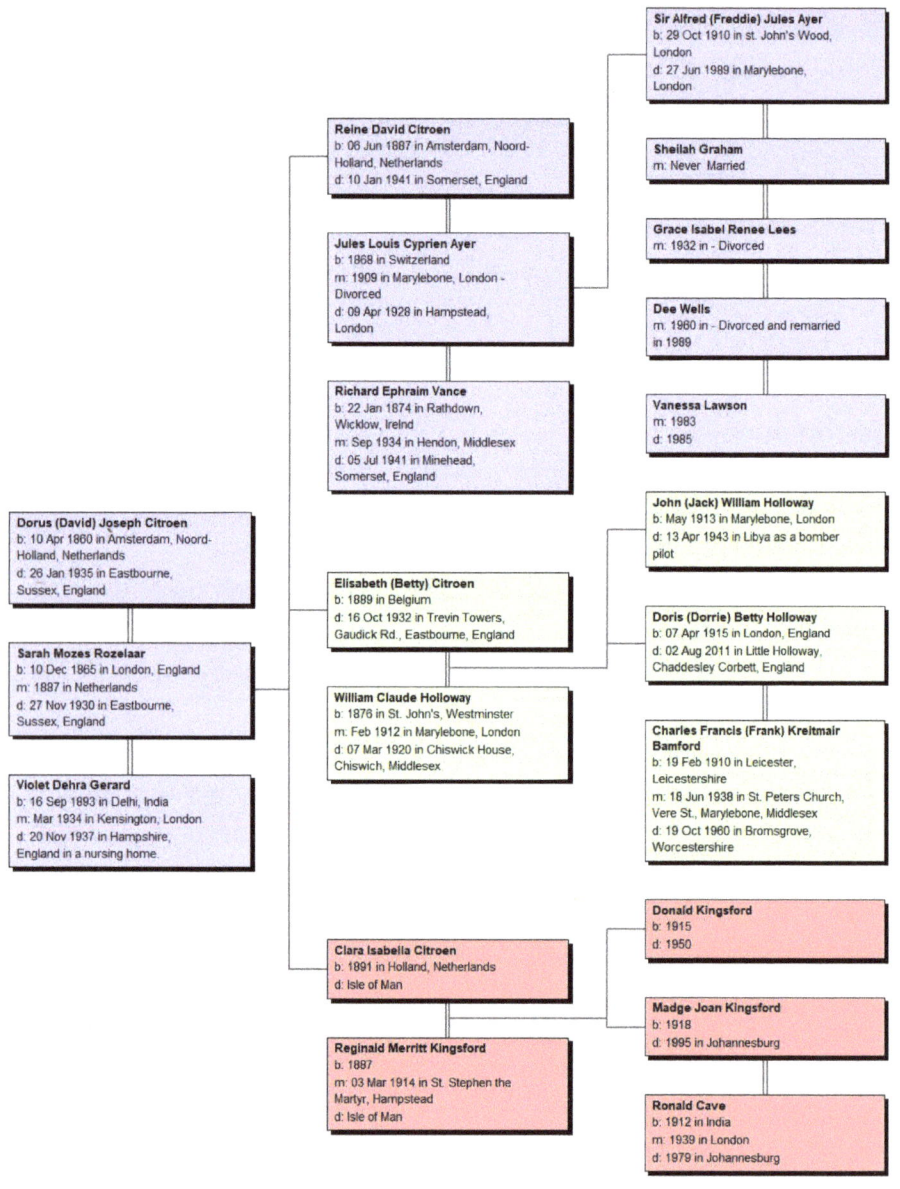

DAVID CITROEN

Having started Minerva Motors and moved his family to 'Melrose' in Cricklewood, David decided that he would like to become a British citizen and also give that benefit to his three daughters, none of whom were of age. His wife, Sarah, already had British citizenship. David had to have lived in England for at least five years in the previous eight years before he could become a British subject, which he did in January 1904. Reine was 16 years old, Elisabeth 15 years old, and Clara 13 years old.

The three girls all married at the age of 23. Reine married a Swiss, Jules L. C. Ayer, and they had one child, Alfred Jules, in 1910. He was known as Freddie and was highly intelligent. He studied philosophy at Christ Church, Oxford and then in Vienna. While a research student and lecturer at Christ Church in 1936, he wrote the much-acclaimed book entitled "Language, Truth and Logic". During the Second World War, Freddie was a Special Operations Executive[81] and a MI6 agent[82]. After the war, he was Grote Professor of Mind and Logic at University College London, where he transformed a run-down department into a contender with Oxford and Cambridge.[83] He then returned to Oxford to become Wykenham Professor of Logic at New College. Freddie often appeared on radio and television. Unusual for an academic, he was a keen sportsman (an ardent supporter of 'Spurs') and somewhat of a socialite. In 1970, he was knighted by Queen Elizabeth. During his life, he married four times, twice to the same woman — Dee Wells.

Freddie had two children, Valerie and Julian, by his first marriage to Renee Lees and another son, Nicholas, by Dee Wells, his second and fourth wife. However, he also had an illegitimate daughter, Wendy, by

---

81. There is an interesting series on Netflix — Churchill's Secret Agents — about the training of SOEs
82. MI5 is the British security service, there to catch foreign spies, while MI6 is the British foreign intelligence service, our spies! The Guardian > notesandqueries > query
83. The Independent, Obituary

Sheilah Graham, a famous British-born Hollywood gossip columnist. Wendy was brought up by Sheila and Trevor Westbrook, Sheila's second husband, and carried the last name Westbrook[84].

In A.J. (Freddie) Ayer's book "Part of My Life", he reveals some interesting facts regarding David Citroen, his grandfather. To quote:

> "For some years after I was born, my grandfather had an estate at Essendon in Hertfordshire…When war broke out, my grandfather was suspected of being a German spy, because of his guttural accent; he responded by calling a meeting of his neighbours to vindicate himself, which he did triumphantly. Having worked in the Ministry of Munitions under Winston Churchill, an experience which left him with an abiding contempt for Civil Servants, he was offered a Knighthood which my grandmother persuaded him to refuse, on the grounds that it would make them look ridiculous. He sold his estate in Essendon and bought a luxurious London House in Hamilton Terrace (No.44) with a billiard room and large garden[85]".

Since David Citroen had no sons, he must have been delighted to have three son-in laws and five grandchildren. Elisabeth fell for William Holloway, the dashing race car driver and managing director of Minerva Motors, and they were married in 1912.

It must have been a bitter blow to everyone when William contracted syphilis and was later committed to Chiswick House. (See page 140)

---

84. One of the Family, Wendy W. Fairey, her memoir
85. Part of My Life, A.J. Ayer, page 20

William Holloway with son Jack and daughter Doris, 1915

His third daughter, Clara, married Reginald Kingsford in 1914. Their two children were Donald (1915-1950) and Madge (1918-1995). Unfortunately, Donald took his own life when he was unable to secure a job in the diplomatic corps. Unbeknown to him a letter was in the mail offering a job opportunity. Madge married Ronald Cave in 1939 and settled in Johannesburg, South Africa.

David Citroen became a wealthy man in his life. Around 1925, he purchased Trevin Towers in Eastbourne, a large Victorian home built for James John Hissey, a travel writer, in 1894.[86] It was a particularly large

---

86. historicengland.org.uk

house for just David and his wife Sarah, but no doubt they had plenty of live-in staff to help run the property. One of the attractions of the property was the large 'motor house' and stables with living quarters, which had been added sometime in the early 1900s. It was probably there where his chauffeur, Harold John Goodman, lived. The motor car that the chauffeur drove was undoubtedly a Minerva and possibly the 'Fully Convertible Salamanca' pictured on page 167. Inside the house, there was a lot of oak panelling, carvings, and a large inglenook fireplace. The property today is owned by the University of Brighton and the extensive grounds, including a grass tennis court, have been mostly built upon. One of David Citroen's hobbies was collecting antiques. Whenever he travelled somewhere, he was sure to bring something home, so the large house was well-furnished and full of objets d'art. When he had no more room, he sold much of it and started again!

Trevin Towers from the southeast

The stables, 'motor house' and attached accommodation

The Holloway story reveals that Sarah Citroen developed breast cancer around 1929 and died the following year, probably surrounded by her three daughters and David. For David, it must have been a crushing blow, but he had his daughter, Elisabeth Holloway, and granddaughter, Doris living with him at Trevin Towers, which must have given him a great deal of comfort. He took to cruising and went to the West Indies (Caribbean) several times in two years. Then disaster struck again when Elisabeth fell ill and subsequently died of lung and breast cancer in October 1932 at the age of 43. One can only imagine what he was feeling.

But Doris, at the age of 17, did what she could, both running the household and completing her schooling. However, after the death of Sarah, David contacted a woman he knew named Dehra who lived in Johannesburg, South Africa.

To quote again from Freddie Ayer's book, "Part of my Life",

"My grandfather was a patriarch, but not a domestic tyrant. My grandmother had a strong character of her own and usually had her own way in the house. There had been a crisis in their marriage when a young girl called Dehra came to Essendon as a companion for their youngest daughter (Clara), after the two elder daughters had got married. I think it unlikely that my grandfather had an affair with her, but he paid her such attention that my grandmother declared that either she or Dehra must leave the house. It was Dehra who left. My grandfather was far too deeply attached to his family kingdom to sacrifice it for love[87]".

Violet Dehra Hadfield, known as Dehra, was married in 1922 to Gerald Hadfield. At some point, the Hadfield's and their two children, Dehra and Jack, moved to Johannesburg, where Gerald worked as an accountant. However, in early 1932, Dehra received word from David that Elisabeth was unwell. The two had been in contact with each other for some time, probably after his wife Sarah had died. In an unhappy marriage, she decided to leave Gerald in June and went to England with her two young children. She stayed with a good friend by the name of Constance Beaumont in Broadclyst in Devon. After Elisabeth died in October of that year, David again wrote to Dehra, inviting her to come and live at Trevin Towers, which she did. She filed for divorce and when it was final, David and Dehra married in a civil ceremony in Kensington, London in March 1934. The children, who up until that time were living at Trevin Towers, returned at some time in 1934 to live with their father, who passed away in Johannesburg in 1959.

Obviously, David enjoyed the company of Dehra but not Doris, who thought she was meddling and after her grandfather for his money. She was probably correct on both counts. Nevertheless, he was now 74 years old, and the marriage didn't last a year, as David passed away in January 1935.

---

87. Part of My Life, A.J. Ayer, page 32-33

In David Citroen's Will (Appendix VIII), which he made one month before he died, he was very specific as to what each of his relatives were to receive. Dehra did well, although she probably thought that she deserved more. She received a lump sum of £2,000 and an annuity of £100 a month (worth about £1,750 today.) Despite this, Dehra had a mean streak. Each grandchild was allowed to choose one object from David's collection. Doris chose a matching pair of Dresden figurines, and Dehra insisted that that counted as two items, so Doris had to give one back. However, when the remaining estate went to auction, Doris went to try and buy the other half of the pair. The auctioneer, hearing the story, brought his hammer down as soon as Doris made her first bid!

An interesting clause in David's Will is clause 20, which states, "that no Grandchild of mine who shall marry his or her first cousin shall take any interest under my Will…." So, did Jack have an interest in Madge or Donald an interest in Doris? Freddie was certainly a ladies' man, so maybe it was he who triggered this unusual clause. Whatever the reason, it never had to be enacted.

David Citroen was close to his brother Roelof, who lived in Paris, and bequeathed him £1,000 and Roelof's granddaughter, Micheline, £500. Roelof married Sara Roselaar, whose christian and surname were the same as David's first wife, although a slightly different spelling. Roelof died in 1939, but his wife suffered at the hands of the Nazis in World War II. After the German invasion of Paris, she was rounded up with most others of the Jewish faith and transported to the death camp Auschwitz in Poland, where she was murdered at the age of 74. It is probable that many others of the Citroen family living in Paris at that time suffered the same fate.

DESCENDANTS OF LEVIE LOUIS BERNARD BAREND CITROEN

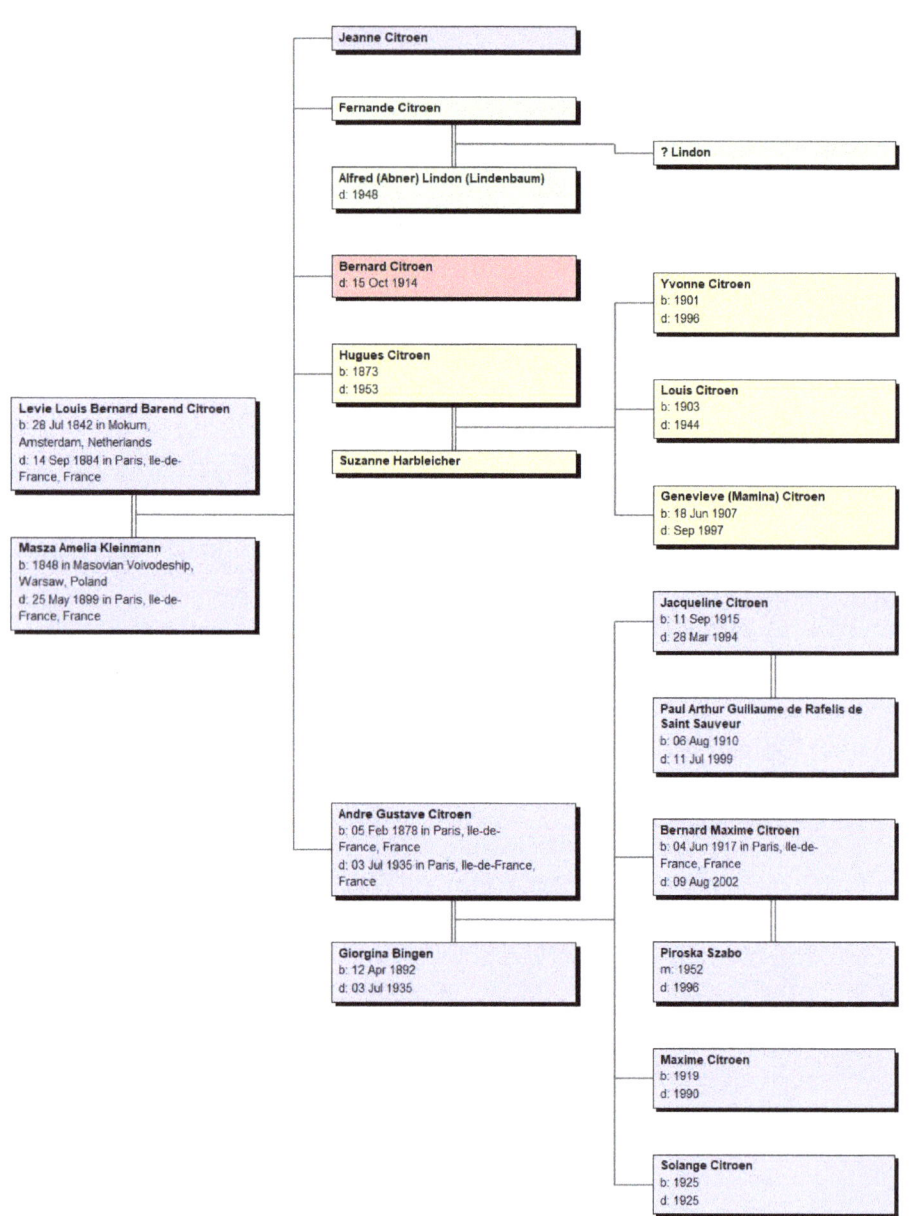

ANOTHER MOTOR CAR CONNECTION[88]

David Citroen had numerous first cousins, as his father, Joseph Barend Citroen, was the second of 14 children. It is almost certain he did not know all of his first cousins, but he undoubtedly knew André Gustave Citroën (1878-1935), the fifth and last child of the Dutch Jewish diamond merchant, Levie Citroen, and Mazra Kleinmann of Warsaw, Poland.

André-Gustave Citroën[89]

---

88. Much of the information in this chapter was extracted from the Newworldencyclopedia.org
89. Image from dyler.com

The Citroen family moved to Paris from Amsterdam in 1873. Upon arrival, the diaeresis was added to the name, changing Citroen to Citroën. André was only six years old when, after a failure in a business venture in a South African diamond mine, his father committed suicide.

André studied engineering at the prestigious École Polytechnique in Paris, but after his mother passed away, his grades plummeted, and he was unable to secure a job in an engineering firm, so he joined the French Army.

With the loss of his mother, André decided to reconnect with her family in Poland. While he was there, he visited a cotton mill and became fascinated by the wooden gears used to drive cotton mills. Citroën studied them and realised that the gears not only ran quietly but also were able to transmit considerable loads without damage to the gears. He felt that steel gears would improve efficiency, and when he returned to Paris, he secured the patent rights to a steel herring-bone type gear invented by a now anonymous Russian. In 1904, he and two friends set up a small workshop to produce his own pattern of double-helical gearwheels and Citroën was soon a recognized name in French engineering.

To increase production, André began to improve the manufacturing process, always wanting to use the latest machinery. This not only involved engineering techniques but also production control. He thought that maintaining good worker relations was imperative. For example, he was in favour of worker benefits and later pioneered maternity leave for his women workers. He established dental and medical facilities, built a worker's gymnasium, and provided a crèche.

In 1908, André Citroën took leave from his own company to assist the Mors Car Company increase their production. Their cars were large and expensive, but by applying his production techniques, he increased the Mors production from 125 cars to 1,200 cars per year, making them much less expensive.

A 22'+ double helical gearwheel[90]

By 1910, André's gears were in great demand, and his annual turnover was over a million francs. The company continued to expand and became a public company in 1913.

During World War I, André helped the French army dramatically increase the number of munitions they were able to produce in a day

---

90. Image from en.m.wikipedia.org

in a factory that the army provided him. With the end of the war, Citroën needed to switch the factory to peace time production, as he was anxious to continue using the already "fully equipped precision manufacturing plant"[91].

André's earlier experience with the Mors Company and a chance meeting with Henry Ford led him to believe that that the future lay in automobile manufacturing, even though he was not a car enthusiast. So, in 1919, he founded the Citroën automobile company by converting his existing munitions factory. It is almost certain that the double chevron of his gears formed the basis for the Citroën car emblem.

Citroën emblems from 1919 to present[92]

---

91. A Brief History of André Citroën and the 5CV Citroën Model
92. Image from carlogosfree.com

Unlike his cousin David, André's aim was to mass-produce a small, inexpensive automobile. His engineering and entrepreneurial abilities in the auto industry earned him the title of Ford of France, which he enjoyed as an admirer of Henry Ford. Not only was André an amazing engineer, he was also a great promoter of his products: he once had his name and logo illuminated on the Eiffel Tower[93]. His company was the first to allow prospective buyers to test drive the cars; and he opened his own insurance company and offered low rates to Citroën buyers. New Citroën factories were constructed, and his firm became one of the largest auto-manufacturing companies in France.

André didn't always make a good impression in the media, however. He was somewhat lavish with his money, spending a great deal on clothes and was a heavy gambler. When his finances were drained, he would take money out of the company. During the Great Depression, he did not cut back and pushed hard to introduce the Traction Avant, or 'front wheel drive', the only mass-produced front-wheel-drive car of its time. He invested a great deal of money in buying out patents and investing in new ideas. The Traction Avant was innovative in many ways, but design and engineering costs were huge.

In the early 1930s, his creditors became increasingly alarmed at the financial state of the Citroën Car Company, and André was promising that the new Traction Avant was going to resolve all the issues. However, when he finally put on a demonstration of the vehicle for his creditors, the transmission failed dashing all hopes of his creditors. The French government stepped in and declared the company bankrupt. The Michelin tyre company, being the largest creditor, took over the company and André Citroën was forced to step aside by French law. André became very despondent and lost the will to live and, in July 1935, he died.

---

93. A Brief History of Citroën, Citroën Car Company

1934 Citroën Traction Avant 11CV — front wheel drive with independent suspension, hydraulic brakes and an all-steel monocoque body[94]

The Traction Avant went into full production in 1934 and was hugely successful until 1957 when the last car rolled off the assembly line. Dorrie Bamford owned a Traction Avant for many years and continued to have had two more Citroëns after that.

In Paris, there is now a Quai André Citroën and a Parc André Citroën, and in 1998 André, was inducted into the Automotive Hall of Fame in Dearborn, Michigan.

---

94. Image from en.m.wikipedia.org

Bamford Family Timeline

(Direct ancestors and important dates in **bold** type)

1891 — Samuel Bamford born

1813 — Samuel Bamford married Mary Jones (b. 1881)

1814 — Hannah Bamford born (Samuel and Mary)

1816 — Samuel Bamford Jr. born (Samuel and Mary)

1818 — Eliza Bamford born (Samuel and Mary)

1818 — Charles Bamford born (Samuel and Mary)

1820 — Mary Bamford born (Samuel and Mary)

1823 — Edwin Bamford born (Samuel and Mary)

1826 — Louisa Bamford born (Samuel and Mary)

1841 — Samuel Jr. married Theresa Selina Ladbury

1845 — Charles and Edwin form Bamford Brothers

— Charles married Eleanor Smith

1846 — Mary Bamford died (Samuel Sr.'s wife)

1848 — Charles Smith Bamford born (Charles and Eleanor)

1848 — Samuel Sr. married Ann Moore

1850 — Eleanor Bamford born (Charles and Eleanor)

1851 — Eleanor died (1 year old)

1852 — Eleanor died (Charles' wife)

1853 — Charles married Hannah Clifford Yerl

1853 — Edwin married Elizabeth Evason

1854 — Samuel Bamford born and died (Charles and Hannah)

1855 — Hannah Maria born (Charles and Hannah)

1857 — Arthur John Jones Bamford born (Charles and Hannah)

1859 — Samuel Bamford Sr. died

1862 — Albert Edward born (Charles and Hannah)

1862 — Charles Bamford 1st trip to the U.S.A.

1865 — Charles Bamford family moves to the U.S.A

1868 — Albert Edward Bamford died (aged 5)

1868 — Eleanor Caroline born (Charles and Hannah)

1870 — Edwin moves to Raby Hall, Raby Mere, Cheshire

— Charles buys Llanrhaiadr Hall, Ruthin, North Wales

1871 — Charles Smith Bamford died (age 22)

1872 — Bamford Brothers acquires

156 West Street, Manhattan N.Y.
Meat packing facility on 42nd Street N.Y.
10 Matthew Street, Liverpool
16 Button Street, Liverpool
Zinc mine in Pennsylvania

1878 — Charles Bamford family moves back to the U.K.

— Hannah Maria Bamford married Thomas P. Williams (b. 1847)

1879 — Arthur J. J. Bamford married Anne Nash (b. 1855)

— Charles acquires Brookhurst, Bromborough, Cheshire

1880 — **Charles Arthur Bamford born** (Arthur and Anne)

1881 — Mary Hannah Bamford born and died (Arthur and Anne)

1885 — Charles purchases Misterton Hall and estate in Leicestershire

1886 — Edwin Scott Bamford born (Arthur and Anne)

1886 — Hannah Clifford Bamford died (Charles' wife)

1887 — Bamford Brothers partnership dissolved

— Bamford, Nash and Bamford formed

1888 — Anne Nash Bamford born (Arthur and Anne)

1889 — Arthur J. J. Bamford elected to Liverpool council

1890 — Eleanor Caroline Bamford married Samuel James Waring (b. 1860)

— **Charles Bamford died**

1894 — **Arthur John Jones Bamford died**

— Edwin Bamford died

1906 — Anne Bamford married Captain, The Honourable Harold Hawke (b. 1867)

— Anne Bamford sells the Bamford zinc mine in Pennsylvania

1907 — Charles Arthur Bamford married Dorothy Helen Kreitmair (b. 1883)

— Charles Arthur Bamford sells Brookhurst, Bromborough, Cheshire

1908 — Dorothy Anne Bamford born (Charles and Dorothy)

1910 — **Charles Francis Kreitmair Bamford born** (Charles and Dorothy)

1911 — Anne Nash Bamford married Sidney Carlton Jones (b. 1875)

1913 — Ann Hawke died intestate

1913 — E. Scott Bamford married Louisa Mary Lottie Smith (Lulu) (b. 1883)

1915 — Captain E. Scott Bamford killed

1920 — Helen Patricia (Pat) Bamford born (Charles and Dorothy)

1923 — Arthur Ingram Bamford born (Charles and Dorothy)

1932 — Dorothy Anne Bamford married Robert (Bob) George Stephens (b. 1902)

1937 — Helen Patricia Bamford and Doris B. Holloway presented to Queen Mary

1938 — Charles Francis Kreitmair Bamford married Doris Betty Holloway (b.1915)

— C. F. K. (Frank) Bamford purchased Morris & Co.

1940 — David Charles Bamford born (Frank and Doris [Dorrie])

1942 — Jayne Elisabeth Bamford born (Frank and Dorrie)

1943 — John William Bamford born (Frank and Dorrie)

1944 — Major Charles Arthur Bamford died

1945 — Helen Patricia (Pat) Bamford married Dr. Angus Alexander Fraser (b.1919)

1946 — Peter Frank Bamford born (Frank and Dorrie)

1948 — Anita Betty Bamford born (Frank and Dorrie)

1959 — Dorothy Helen Bamford died (Charles Arthur's wife)

— Arthur Ingram Bamford married Peta M. Anderson (b. 1941)

1960 — Charles Francis Kreitmair Bamford (Frank) died

1963 — David Charles Bamford married Joanna Isabel Horton (b. 1941)

1964 — Jayne Elisabeth Bamford married Peter Nigel Gray (b. 1939)

1964 — Morris & Co (Kidderminster) Ltd. became a public company

1968 — Morris & Co (Kidderminster) Ltd. sold to Youghal Carpets, Ireland

1969 — Christopher (Kit) Charles Kreitmair Bamford born (David and Joanna)

1970 — Peter Frank Bamford married Suzanna Adriana van Alten (b. 1947)

— John William Bamford married Kay Amanda James (b. 1944)

— Arthur Ingram Bamford married Barbara L. Heaton (b. 1938)

1972 — Carl Francis Bamford born (John and Kay)

1972 — Anita Betty Bamford married James Alan Tangye (b. 1945)

1993 — Carl Francis Bamford married Marcia Boden (b. 1965)

1996 — Charles Edward Bamford born (Carl and Marcia)

2007 — Arthur Ingram Bamford died

2011 — Doris Betty Bamford died (Frank's wife)

Postscript

The ancestors of Frank and Dorrie were truly amazing. Some came from nothing and made huge fortunes while others were related to dukes, earls, and barons. If the connection with the Duke of Buccleugh can be made, then the family would be related to Charles II through his firstborn son, James Crofts (later Scott), Duke of Monmouth and 1st Duke of Buccleugh. Some family members were offered knighthoods; one accepted and one rejected.

Even though the "family" owned large homes and estates and employed many to help them, they were not shielded from the scourges of their day. Childhood deaths were common, regardless of one's status in life. For example, Charles Bamford lost both Eleanor and Samuel Bamford at a very young age, Albert Bamford at five years old, and Charles Bamford at 23 years of age. Had Charles (the elder) lived four years longer, he would have seen his fourth son die at the age of 37.

Most of Frank and Dorrie's direct ancestors, including Frank, were entrepreneurs, a trait that continues today with all six of their grandsons carrying on their own successful businesses. Those ancestors who decided not to run their own business became officers in the British army.

There remain many unanswered questions. Did Arthur J. J. or Anne sell their ownership of the lead and silver mines in Illinois and Nevada respectively after Charles' death? Was the 99-year lease on the property in Chicago renewed and who holds the title to that land? Then there were the shares in the two banks and an insurance company that Charles had a major investment in. Were these handled appropriately by Arthur J. J. or Anne? Could any one or all of these assets still be in the "family"?

Then there are the uncertainties of whether Frank and Dorrie were related to the Earl of Balfour and Baron Wiguläus von Kreittmayr. Both of these lines need a great deal of research to be proven one way or the other.

For those so interested, the churches of St Dyfnog's in Llanrhaiadr, St. Barnabas in Bromborough and St. Leonard's in Misterton are all well worth a visit. Each of these churches were patronised by the Bamford family and each contain a number of plaques regarding the family or their donations to the church. Also, the family gravestones of Charles Bamford and Arthur J. J. Bamford are in desperate need of attention. (At the time of writing Charles, Hannah and little Mary's gravestone has been cleared of vegetation but still needs attention.) Although the Parochial Church Council is responsible for the maintenance and care of a church yard (although in some instances where the churchyard has been closed for burials, this responsibility has been assigned to the local authority) the kin or heirs at law of the deceased own the monument or memorial stone and are the persons primarily responsible for its repair.

There are several blank pages at the end of this book so that one can add additional family information, charts and notes. Pictures are also important, and as the saying goes, "are worth a thousand words". Although seemingly mundane at present, it no doubt will be of great interest to future generations of your family.

So, the lineage of the Bamford family continues. It is hoped that the descendants of Frank and Dorrie will enjoy learning about their ancestors and can emulate their business acumen and learn from their mistakes. This is what all great families do and the Bamfords should be no exception.

Additional family trees not previously displayed

DESCENDANTS OF HANNAH MARIA BAMFORD

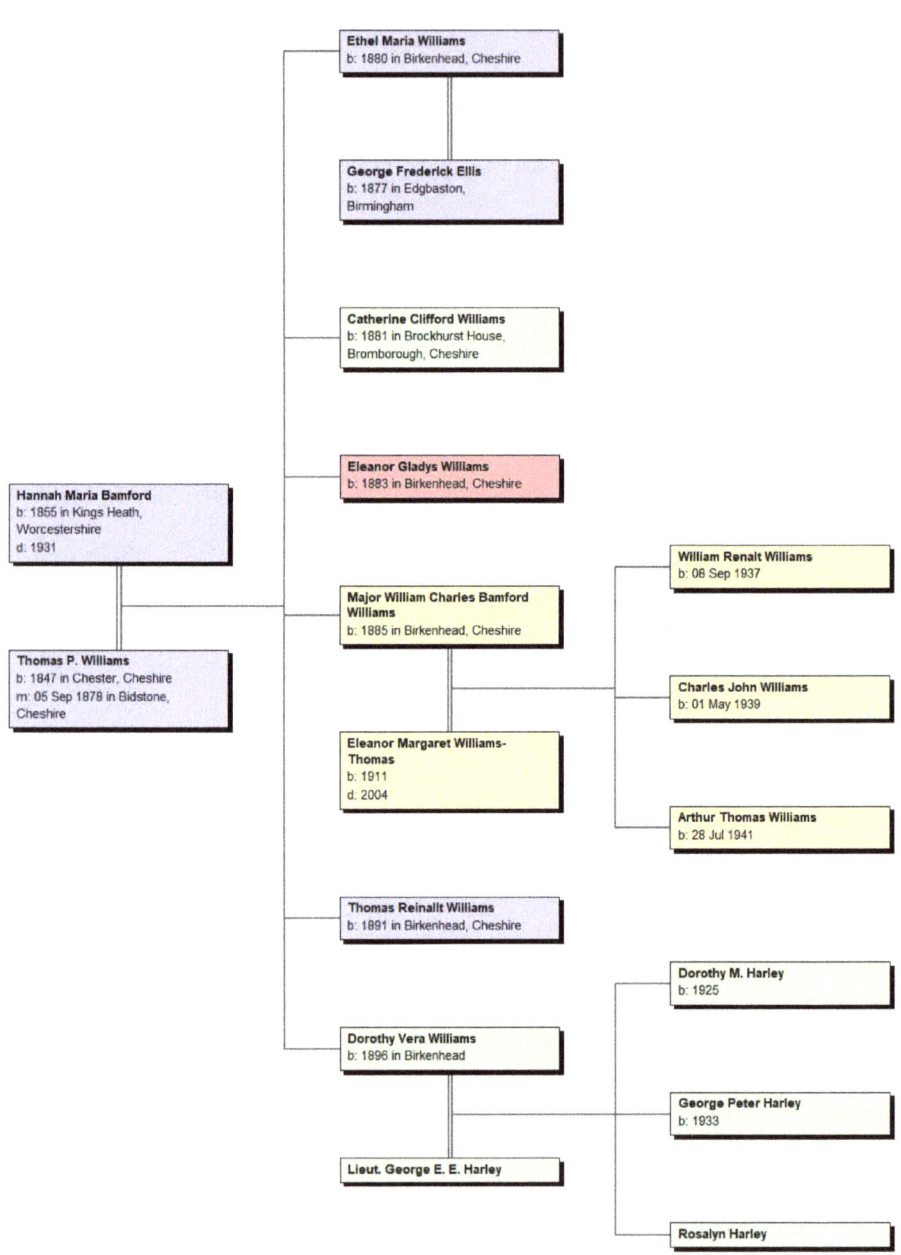

Additional family trees not previously displayed

DESCENDANTS OF ELEANOR CAROLINE BAMFORD

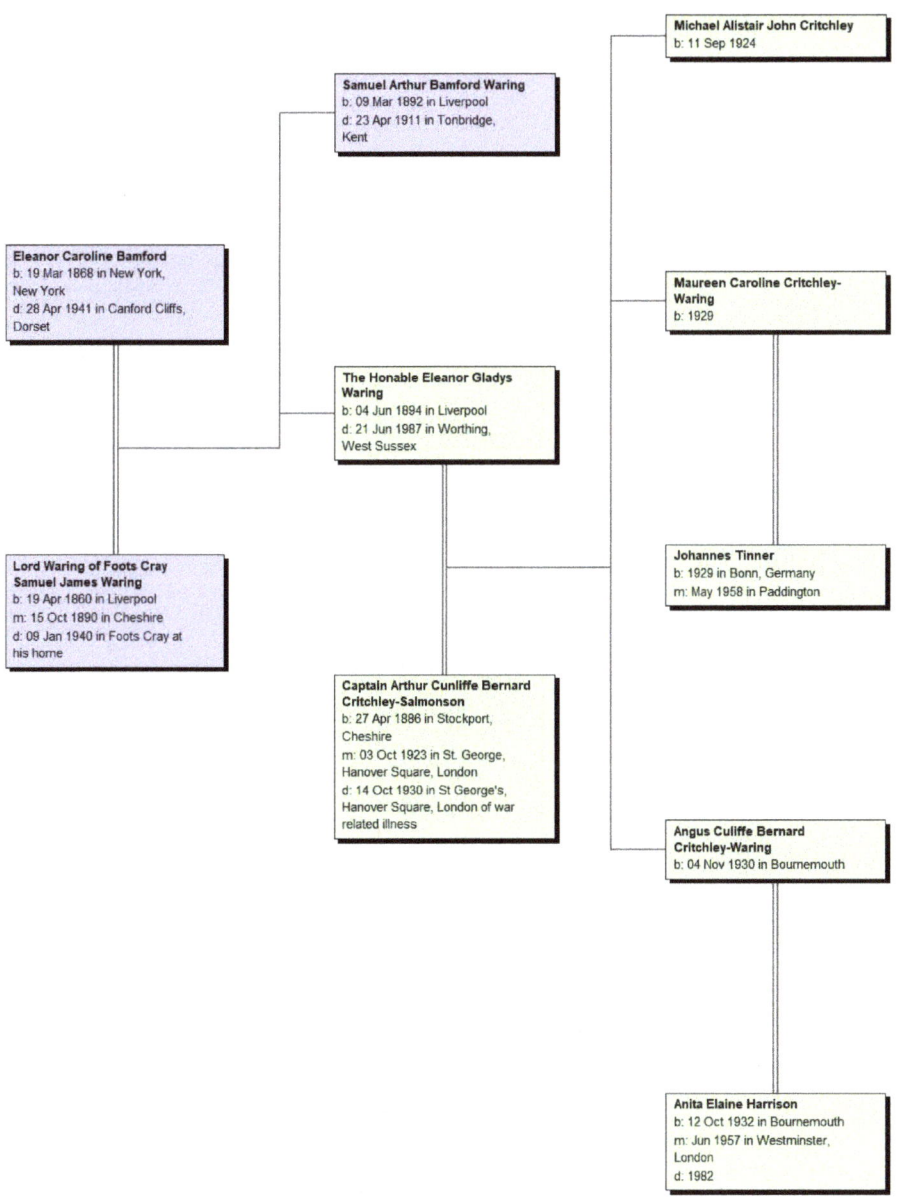

DESCENDANTS OF DOROTHY ANNE BAMFORD

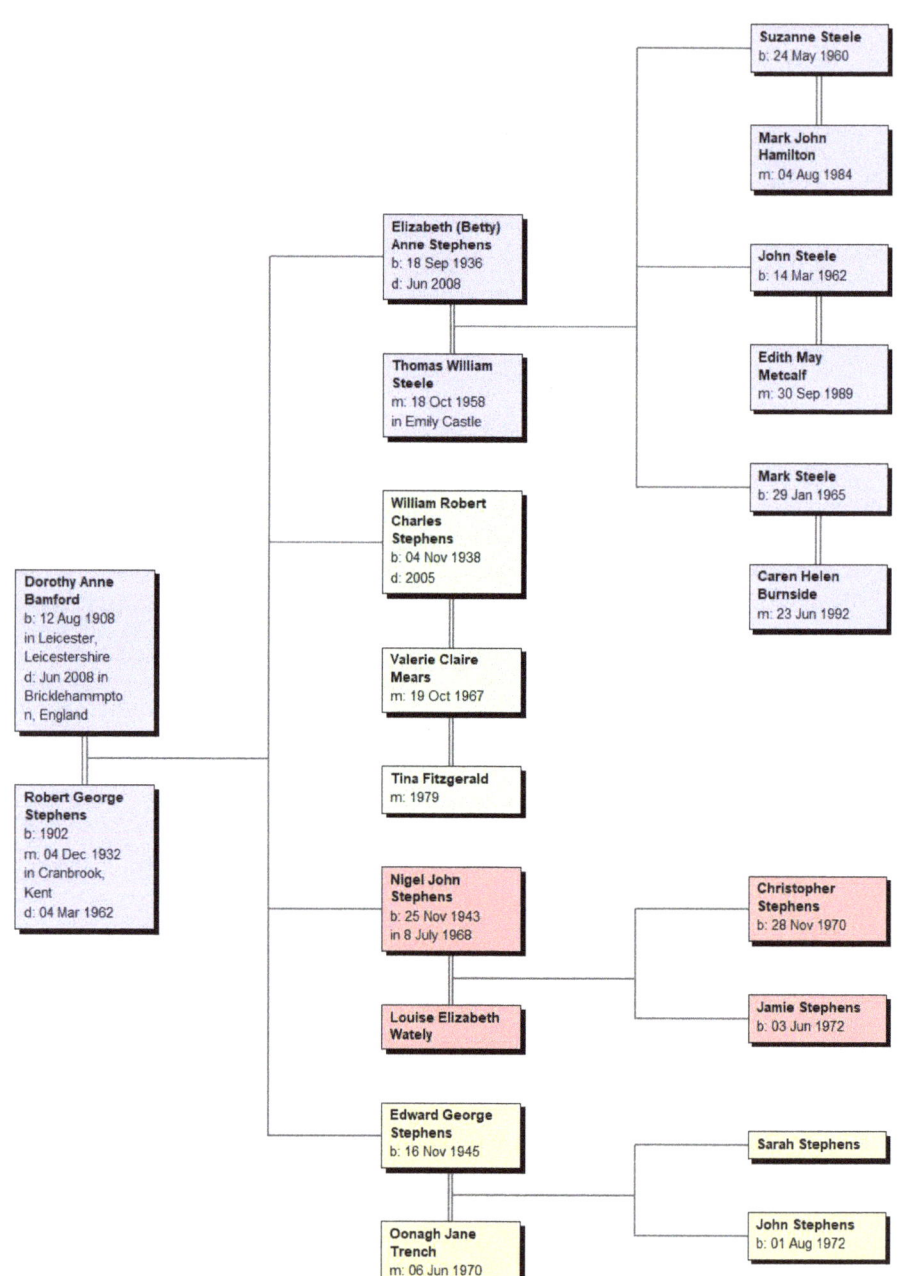

DESCENDANTS OF HELEN PATRICIA BAMFORD

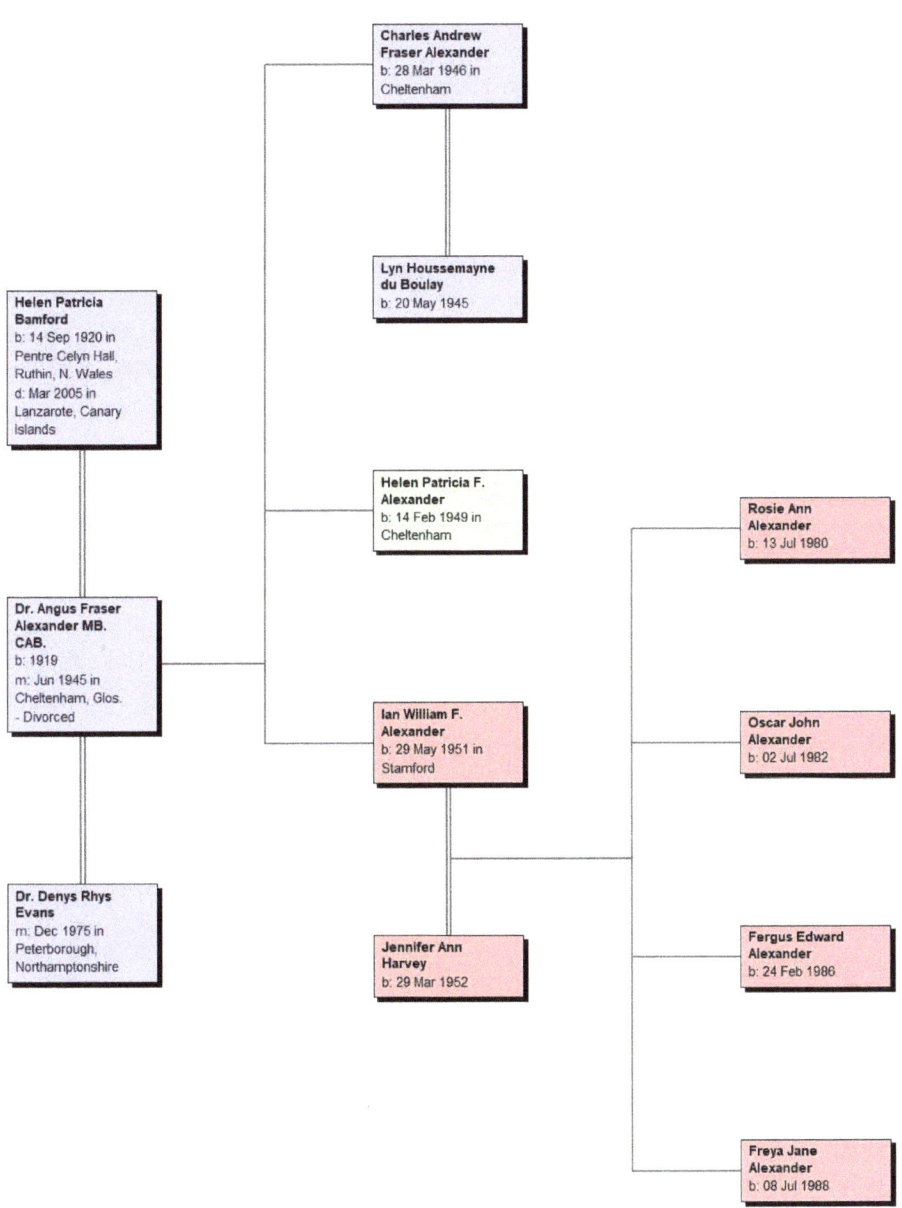

DESCENDANTS OF DAVID CHARLES BAMFORD

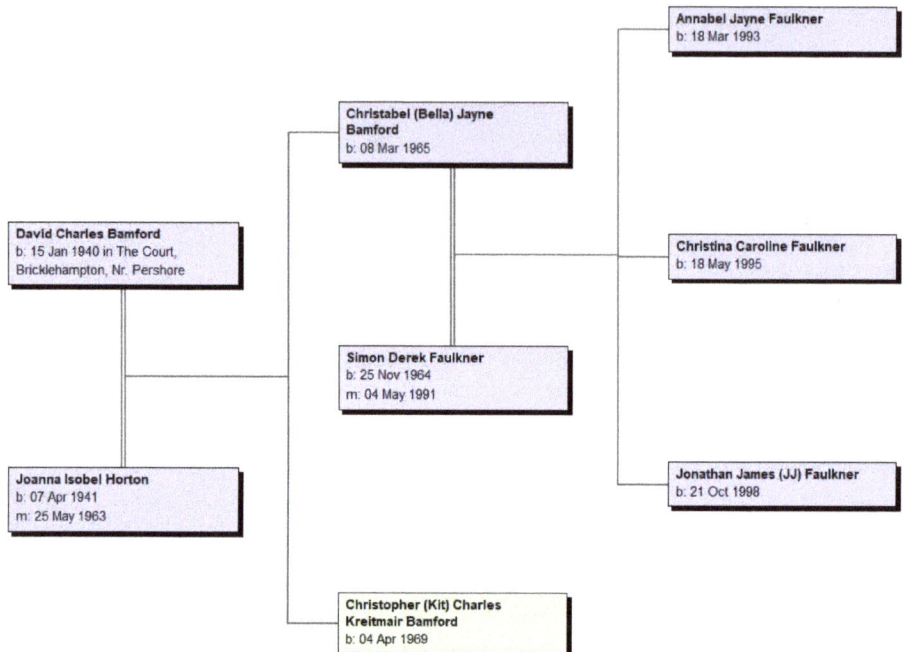

Additional family trees not previously displayed **199**

DESCENDANTS OF JAYNE ELISABETH BAMFORD

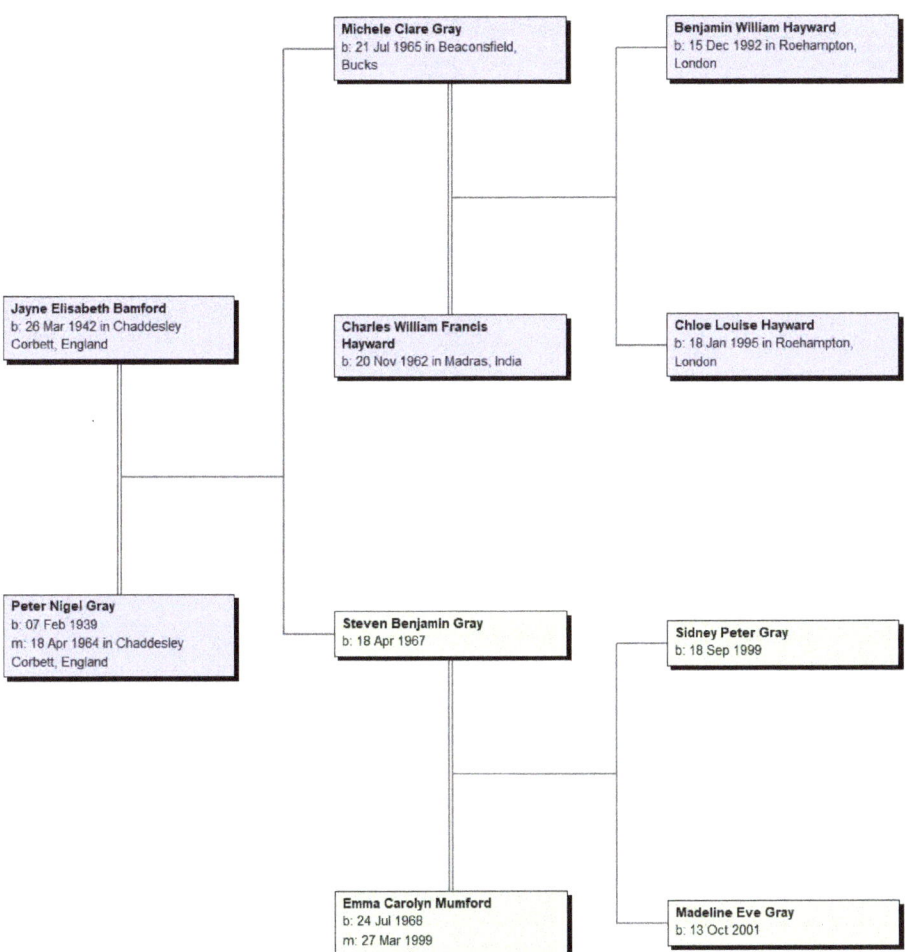

DESCENDANTS OF JOHN WILLIAM BAMFORD

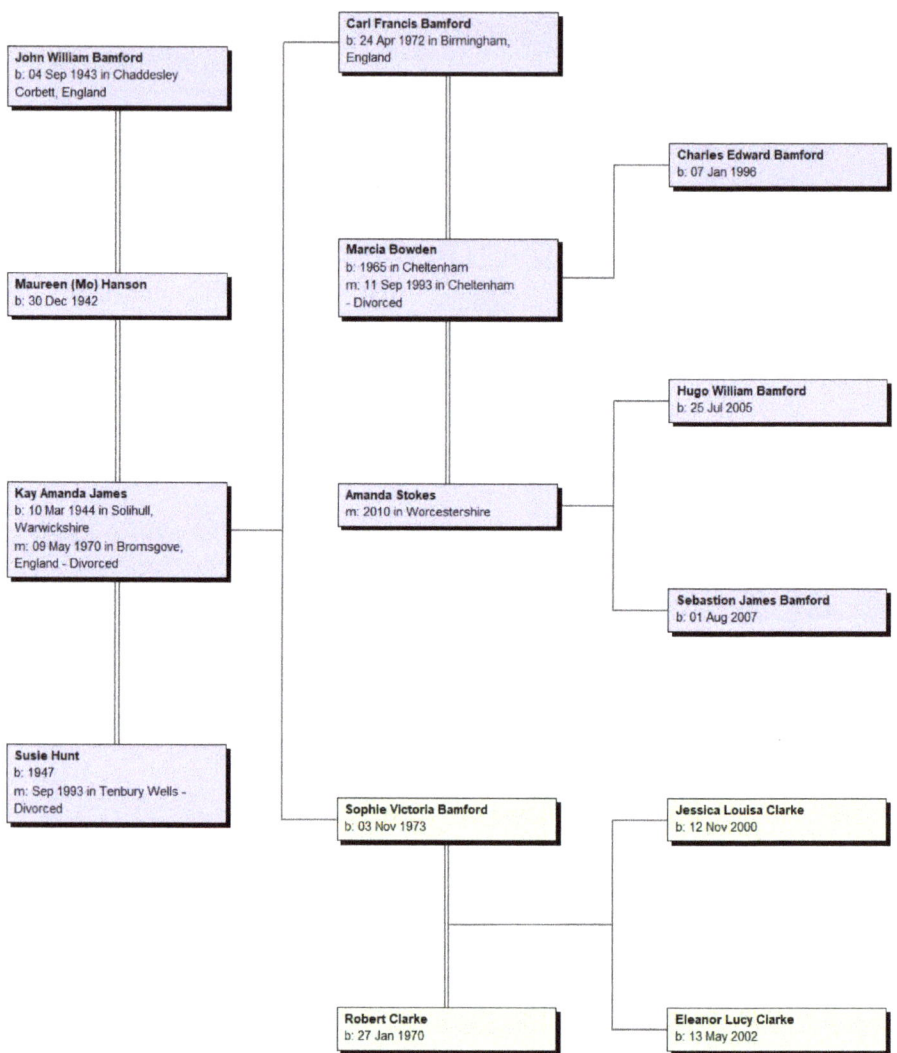

Additional family trees not previously displayed

DESCENDANTS OF PETER FRANK BAMFORD

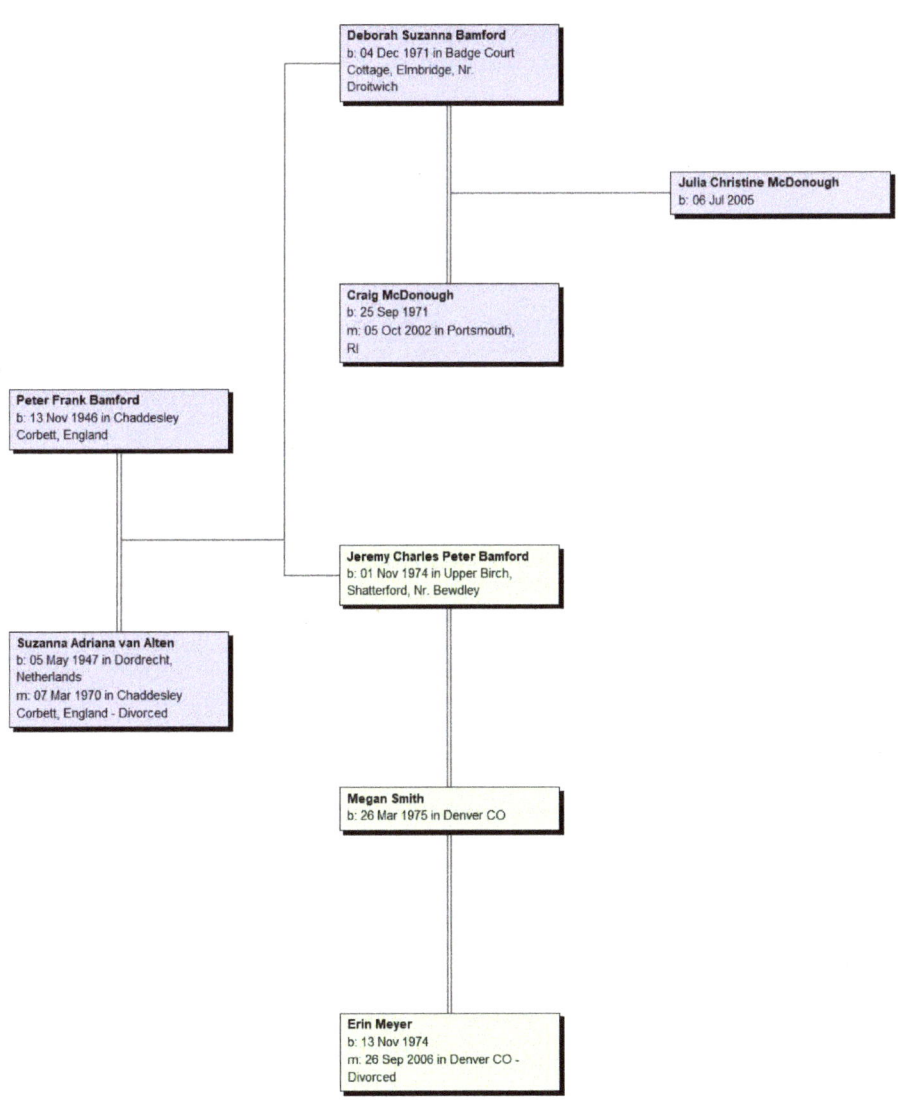

DESCENDANTS OF ANITA BETTY (NEENIE) BAMFORD

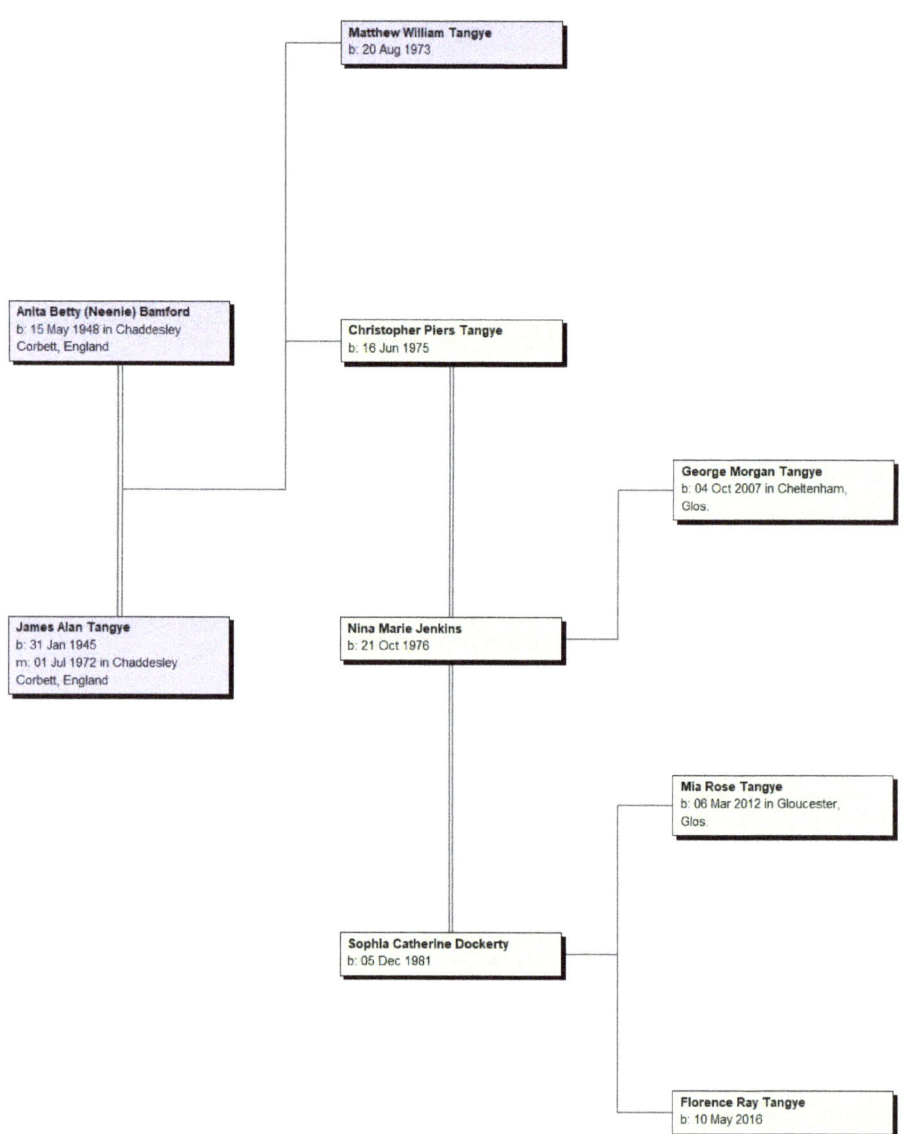

DESCENDANTS OF MADGE JOAN KINGSFORD

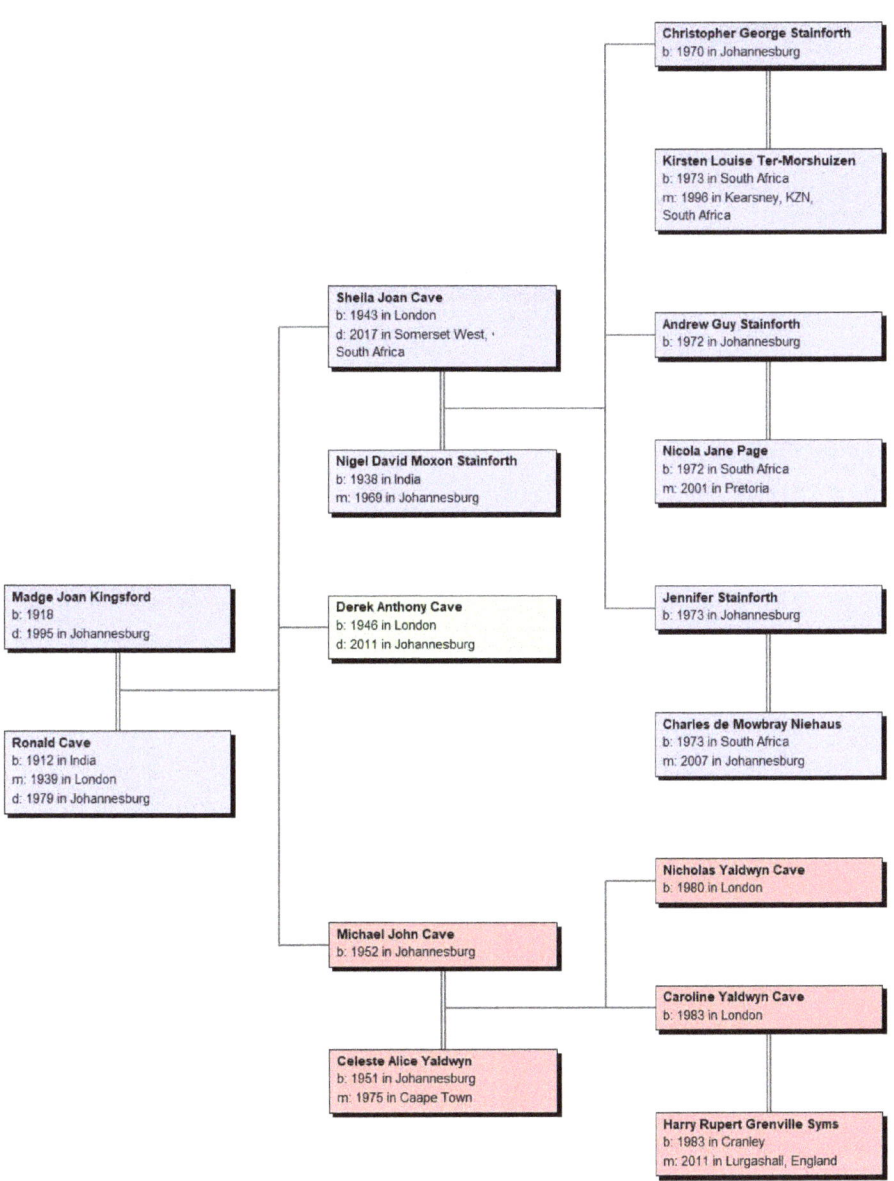

DESCENDANTS OF ALFRED (FREDDIE) JULES AYER

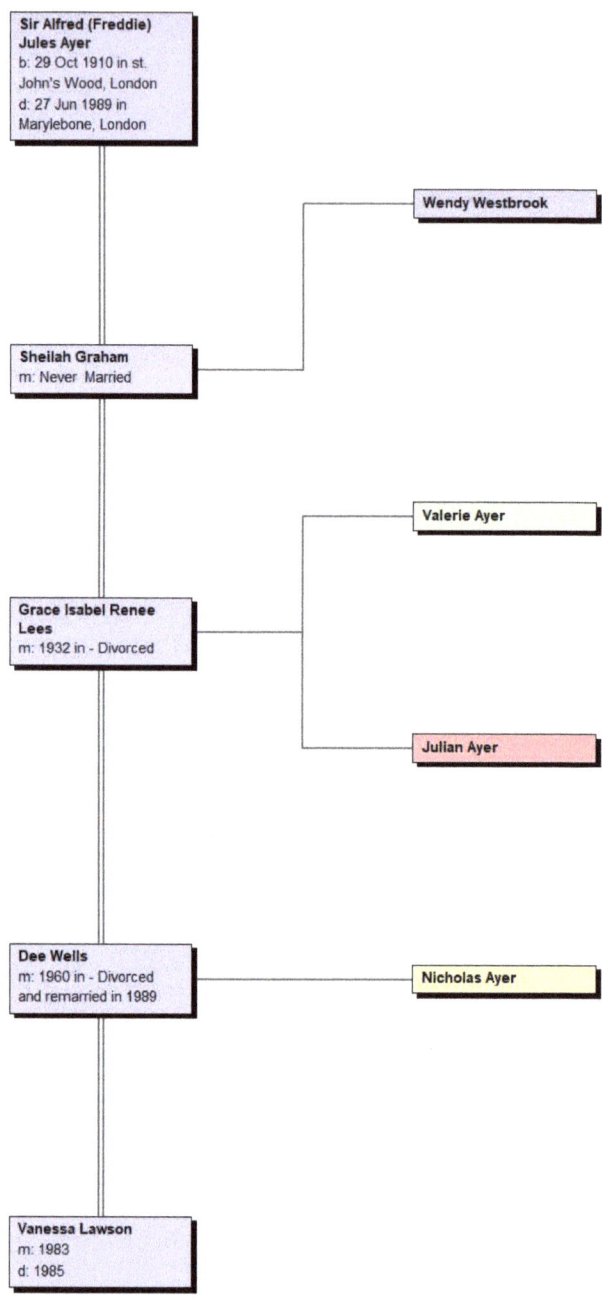

Appendix I

Will of Samuel Bamford the Elder

(Punctuation added)

This is the last Will and Testament of me Samuel Bamford the Elder of Wednesbury in the County of Stafford Gentleman, as follows, (that is to say) First I direct all my just debts personal and testamentary expenses to be paid by my Executors hereinafter named out of my general personal estate.

I bequeath the Bed Chair in my own private use and also my Iron Safe unto my Son Charles Bamford absolutely.

I bequeath my Bureau Bedstead to my Grandson Charles Smith Bamford absolutely.

I bequeath all the remainder of my household goods and furniture, plate, linen, china, and other household effects and all my ready money and securities for money and also the several sums of forty pounds and fifty pounds charged upon parts of my real estate hereinafter devised and all other my personal estate (except what I have specifically bequeathed as aforesaid) to my Sons Charles Bamford and Edwin Bamford, their executors administrators and assigns. Upon trust that the said Charles and Edwin Bamford the survivors of them or the executors or administrators of such survivor (all and every of whom are comprehended within the terms hereinafter used of "Trustees and Trustee" and "Trustees or Trustee" shall within six Calendar Months from my decease call in and sell and convert into money such part of my said personal estate as shall not consist of money, and collect, get in and receive my ready money and securities for money including the said several sums charged upon parts of my real estate as hereinafter particularly mentioned and to stand possessed of the proceeds to arise from such sale, conversion, calling in and receipt of my said general personal estate In Trust (after payment of my said debts and funeral and testamentary expenses as aforesaid) to apply any sum requisite to complete the discharge of a sum of four hundred pounds owned on a mortgage of the messuage and premises hereinafter devised to my said Son Edwin Bamford and then In Trust divide the residue of the said trust monies (after the deductions hereinafter authorised) unto and equally amongst my Children Hannah, Charles, Edwin and Samuel equally as tenants in common. But if any or either of my said four children shall die in my lifetime having lawful issue then I give and bequeath the share or shares of him, her or them so dying of and in the said trust monies unto such issue shares and share alike such issue taking the share or shares his or their parent or parents would have been entitled to if living at my decease.

I give and devise all that my messuage[95] or Public House in Wednesbury aforesaid called "The Old Royal Exchange" with the outbuildings and appurtenances thereto belonging now occupied by George Wooliscroft And also all my messuage or dwelling house adjoining the Public House with the outbuildings and appurtenances thereto belonging now in the occupation of Frederick Warrender unto my said Son Charles Bamford for and during his life. And from and after his decease I give and devise the same messuages and hereditaments to my said Grandson Charles Smith Bamford his heirs and assigns for ever but in case my said

---

95. A dwelling house and its adjacent buildings

Grandson shall die in the lifetime of my said Son Charles and shall not have attained his age of twenty one years or having attained that age shall die without issue then I devise the same unto my said son Charles Bamford his heirs and assigns for ever Subject nevertheless to the payment of my Trustees within three calendar months from my decease the sum of forty pounds. And I hereby charge and make chargeable the same messuages and premises with the payment of that sum accordingly in aid of my general personal estate.

I give and devise unto my said Trust or Trustees all that my Messuage or Tenement with the outbuildings, yard and appurtenances thereto belonging situate in High Street in Wednesbury aforesaid and now in the occupation of Thomas Price. Upon trust as soon as conveniently may be after my decease to sell and dispose of the said hereditaments and premises either by public auction or private contract and for the best price that can be obtained for the same with powers to vary or rescind any contract for sale and out of the proceeds arising from such sale after payment of all expenses incurred thereon in the first place pay off and discharge the existing mortgage debt of two hundred pounds and interest now affecting the same property and then to deduct and pay over to my said Son Charles Bamford a sum of two hundred and twenty one pounds being the amount he has advanced to or for my said Son Samuel Bamford at different times and also deduct all such sums as I shall have paid from the twenty third day of January One thousand eight hundred and fifty one up to the time of my decease by way of interest to the mortgagee in respect of the said mortgage of two hundred pounds and then apply the aggregate amount of such interest towards paying off and discharging the said sum of four hundred pounds owing on mortgage of the messuages and hereditaments herein after devised as aforesaid and then to pay the balance of the said purchase money (if any) to my said son Samuel Bamford.

I give and devise all that my messuage or dwelling house with the outbuildings, yard and appurtenances thereto belonging situate in High Street in Wednesbury aforesaid and now in the occupation of William

Morris unto my said Son Edwin Bamford his heirs and assigns forever Subject nevertheless to the payment to my said Trustees within three calendar months from my decease of the sum of fifty pounds. And I hereby charge and make chargeable the said messuage and premises so devised to my said Son Edwin with the payment of the said sum of fifty pounds in further aid of my said general personal estate.

I give and devise All that my messuage or dwelling house with the outbuildings yard and appurtenances thereto belonging situate in High Street in Wednesbury aforesaid and now in the occupation of Edward Ellis to my said Daughter Hannah for her life subject to the same being kept by her in a state of tenantable repair and after her decease I give and devise the same messuage and buildings yard and appurtenances unto all and every the children of my said Daughter Hannah who shall be living at the time of her decease, share and shares alike as tenants in common and the issue of such of her children as shall be then dead such issue respectively to have and take such share only equally amongst as tenants in common as their respective parents would have been entitled to them if living and to their respective heirs and assigns forever of the children of my said Daughter Hannah and their issue accordingly. But in case there shall be no children or issue of children of my said Daughter Hannah living at the time of her decease I give and devise the said last mentioned messuage, outbuildings, yard and appurtenances unto such of my three Sons Charles Edwin and Samuel as shall be living at the time of the decease of my said Daughter Hannah share and share alike as tenants in common and the issue of such of them my said three sons as shall be then dead such issue respectively to have and take such share only amongst them equally as tenants in common as their respective parents would have been entitled to if then living and to the respective heirs and assigns of my said three last mentioned children and their issue accordingly.

I give and devise all that my messuage or tenement with the outbuildings and appurtenances thereto belonging situate in the High Street in Wednesbury aforesaid adjoining to the said Royal Exchange so devised to my said Son Charles as aforesaid and now in the occupation of Benjamin Kendrick with the use of one of the privies in the said yard now used jointly with the tenant of the said house now occupied by the said Frederick Warrender, unto my Daughter Eliza, Wife of Charles Burton of Wolverhampton in the County of Stafford, Cattle Dealer, for her life for her own separate use subject to the same being kept by her in a state of tenable repair And after her decease I give and devise the said last mentioned messuage outbuildings and appurtenances unto her Daughter Hannah Burton her heirs and assigns but in case the said Hannah Burton shall die under the age of 21 years the I devise the same hereditaments and premises unto Ann Burton Sister of the said Hannah her heirs and assigns for ever.

I give and devise all that my messuage or tenement with the outbuildings and appurtenances thereto belonging situate in High Street in Wednesbury aforesaid now in the occupancy of John Jones unto my Daughter Louisa Bamford for her life for her own separate use and benefit subject to the same being kept by her in a state of tenantable repair and after her decease I give and devise the said last mentioned messuage outbuildings and appurtenances unto all and every the children (if any) of my said Daughter Louisa who shall be living at the time of her decease share and share alike as tenants in common and the issue of such of her children as shall then be dead such issue respectively to have and take such share only equally amongst them as tenants in common as their respective parents would have been entitled to if then living and to the respective heirs and assigns forever of the children of my said last mentioned Daughter and their issue respectively. But in case there be no children or issue of children of my said Daughter Louisa at the time of her decease then I give and devise the said last mentioned messuage outbuildings and appurtenances unto such of my four Children Hannah, Charles, Edwin and Samuel as shall be living at the time of the decease of my said Daughter Louisa share and share alike as tenants in common and the issue of them my said four last mentioned children as shall be then dead such issue respectively to have and take such share only equally amongst them as tenants in common as their respective parents would have been entitled to if then living and to the respective heirs and assigns of my said four last mentioned children and their issue accordingly.

I give and devise all that my messuage or tenement wherein I now reside with all the outbuildings yard and appurtenances there to belonging situate in Sansome Lane in Wednesbury in Wednesbury aforesaid unto my Wife Ann Bamford for and during such part of the remainder of her life as she shall choose to occupy the same. But I will and direct that my said wife will not permit either of her present Sons by a former husband to reside with her at any time for more than one week at any one time except in the case of illness of either Sons or their mother and that she at all times keep the said messuage and premises in tenantable repair and as to the said last mentioned Messuage or Tenement outbuildings yard and appurtenances from and after the decease of my Wife or from and after the period she shall cease to occupy the same whichever shall first happen I give and devise the same messuage and premises unto my Daughter Mary the Wife of Edwin Steers for her natural life for her own separate use and benefit subject to the same being kept by herein a tenantable repair. And after her decease I give and devise the said last mentioned messuage outbuildings and appurtenances unto all and every the Children (if any) of my said daughter Mary who shall be living at the time of her decease share and share alike as tenants in common and the issue of such of her children as shall be then dead such issues respectively to have and take such share only equally among them as tenants in common as their respective parents would have been entitled if then living and to the respective heirs and assigns forever of the children of my said last mentioned Daughter and their issue respectively. But in case there be no children of my said Daughter Mary living at the time of her decease then I give and devise the said last mentioned messuage, outbuildings and appurtenances unto such of my said four children Hannah, Charles, Edwin, and Samuel as shall be living at the time of the decease of may said Daughter Mary share and share alike as tenants in common and the issue of them my said four last mentioned Children as shall be then dead such issue respectively to have and take such share only equally amongst them as tenants in common as their respective parents would have been entitled to if then living and to the respective heirs and assigns of my said four last mentioned Children and their issue accordingly.

I give and devise unto my said Trustees their heirs and assigns All those my to messuages outbuildings and appurtenances sometime since erected by me situated in Sansome Lane, Wednesbury aforesaid now in the occupations of Joseph Neale and the widow Kendrick And also that plot of land situated in Earps Lane, Wednesbury aforesaid purchased by me from John Kendrick and others. Upon trust as soon as conveniently maybe after my decease to sell the said messuages and plot of land either by public auction or private contract and for the best price or prices that can be obtained for the same and when sold to convey and assure the same unto the purchaser or purchasers hereof and out of the proceeds of such sale in the first place to retain such sum of money as maybe necessary to make up the sum of four hundred pounds after receipt of the before mentioned sums of forty pounds and fifty pounds and the amount which shall have been paid for interest as foresaid and then pay off and discharge the said mortgage of four hundred pounds now existing on the said messuage and premises herein before devised to my said son Edwin and then apply the balance (if any) in further aid of my general personal estate.

Provided always and I do hereby direct that my Trustees and Executors shall respectively be accountable for such monies as they shall respectively actually receive and not the one for the other of them but either of them for his own acts receipts and defaults only. And that they shall not be accountable for any Banker, Broker or other person with whom the said trust monies shall be deposited nor for any loss which may happen in the execution of the trusts hereinbefore contained unless the same shall be occasioned by their own wilful neglect or default. And it shall be lawful for my said trustees and trustee to deduct and retain and to allow each other all reasonable costs, charges and expenses which maybe incurred in the execution of the said trusts and in relation thereto. And that the receipts of the said trustees and trustee for the time being shall be good and sufficient discharges for all moneys payable to them or him under this my Will.

I devise all estates vested in me as trustee or mortgagee unto the said Charles Bamford and Edwin Bamford their heirs and assigns upon the trusts and subject to the equities affecting the same respectively. And I appoint the said Charles Bamford and Edwin Bamford Executors of this my Will.

In witness whereof I have hereunto set my hand this fourteenth day of December in the year of our Lord One thousand eight hundred and fifty eight — Samuel Bamford Sen. — Signed by the said testator as his last Will and Testament in the presence of us, present at the same time, who in his presence, at his request, and in the presence of each other, have subscribed our own names as Witnesses — Henry Jackson, Solicitor, Westbromwich — R. J. W. Pitt, his Clerk.

Appendix II

Will of Charles Bamford

This is the last will of me Charles Bamford of Brookhurst, Bromborough in the county of Chester, Provision Merchant, which I make this twenty fifth day of January one thousand eight hundred and eighty three.

I appoint my wife Hannah Clifford Bamford my son Arthur John Jones Bamford and my son in law Thomas Williams the Executors of this my will.

I give my grand piano made by Broadwood to my daughter Eleanor Caroline Bamford absolutely for her separate use.

I give the oil painting of myself to my daughter Hannah Maria Williams absolutely.

I give to my said wife for her own use absolutely the sum of two hundred pounds and all the money named to me by ticket No. 73 of the New York Produce Exchange Gratuity Fund namely ten thousand dollars and all my horses, carriages, conveyances, cows, live and dead stock on my farm and all my farming implements and all money at my credit in the Denbigh Branch of the North & South Walls Bank and all wines and spirits and consumable stores which may be in my house at Brookhurst at the time of my decease.

I devise and bequeath all my land, messuage & hereditaments at Brookhurst aforesaid, which were conveyed to me by an indenture dated the 6th day September 1878, to the use of my said wife & after her decease to the use of my son Arthur John Jones Bamford during his life and after his decease **To the use** of my grandson Charles Arthur Bamford (son of said Arthur John Jones Bamford) his heirs and assigns.

I bequeath to my Executors all the furniture, plate, pictures, linen and household effects in and about Brookhurst aforesaid **In Trust** to allow my said wife to have the use and enjoyment thereof during her life and after her decease **In Trust** to allow my son Arthur John Jones Bamford during his life to have the use and enjoyment of the said premises and after his death to hold in trust for my said grandson Charles Arthur Bamford absolutely.

I devise all my messuages, lands, farms and hereditaments in situate in the Parishes of Llanrhaiadr-ya-Gimmerch and LLanyuys in the county of Denbigh which were conveyed to me by an indenture dated the 21st day of December 1882 **To the use** of my said Executors **In Trust** to pay the net rents and profits thereof to my wife during her life and after decease to pay one equal moiety of the said net rents and profits to my daughter Hannah Maria Williams during her life for her separate use without power of anticipation and after her decease the trustees of my wife shall stand seised of one equal moiety of the said premises in trust for all the children or any child of the said Hannah Maria Williams who being sons or a son shall attain the age of 21 years & being daughters or a daughter that attains that age or marry & if more than one in equal parts & after the death of my wife the trustees of her will shall pay the other moiety of the rents and profits to my daughter Eleanor Caroline Bamford during her life for her separate use without power of anticipation and after her decease the trustees of her will shall stand seised of the remaining moiety of the said premises **In Trust** for all of her children or any child who being sons or a son shall attain the age of 21 years or being daughters or a daughter shall attain that age or marry and if more than one in equal shares and if no child of the said Eleanor Caroline Bamford shall attain a vested interest in the said moiety the same shall be held **In Trust** for the said Charles Arthur Bamford absolutely.

I devise all my farms and premises called Rhiwlas Llcha situate in the Parish of LLanrhaiadr-ya-Gimmerch in the county of Denbigh which were conveyed to me on indenture dated the 29th day of September 1882 **To the use** of said executors **In Trust** to pay the net rents and profits thereof to my daughter said Hannah Maria Williams during her life for her separate use without power of anticipation and after her decease to hold the said premises **In Trust** for all her children or any child who being sons or a son shall attain the age of 21 years or being daughters or a daughter shall attain that age or marry and if more than one in equal shares. I devise all my farm and premises called Bhiwbebyll situate in the Parishes of Llangwynfan & LLndydyreoog in the County of Denbigh conveyed to me by an indenture dated the 29th day of September and all my hereditaments call Lyddyn Merchant situate in the same parishes conveyed to me by an indenture dated the 18th day of November 1882 **To the use** of my said Executors **In Trust** to pay the net rents and profits thereof to my daughter the said Eleanor Caroline Bamford during her life for her separate use without power of authentication and after her decease to hold the said premises **In Trust** for all her children of any her child who being sons or a son should attain the age of 21 years or being daughters or a daughters should attain that age or marry & if more than one in equal shares & if there be no such child then **In Trust** for my grandson Charles Arthur Bamford absolutely.

I devise and bequeath to my said son Arthur John Jones Bamford for his own use absolutely all my undivided half share in the business carried on at 22 to 26 Cheapside, Liverpool under the filing of Bamford Brothers & all my property & interest therein at the time of my death

& all my -------- of the sum of fifteen thousand pounds but --------
___tgage by said firm on premises in Matthew Street and Harrington Street Liverpool & all money standing to my credit at the Bank of Liverpool at the time of my death and all my half share and interest in the zinc, lead & silver smelting works with the farms, houses & appurtenances hereto belonging known as "Bamford Brothers Smelting Works" situate in East Hemfield Township, Lancaster County, State of Pennsylvania. Also my half share & interest of the shop store and premises No. 156 West Street, New York now in the occupation of A. Bennett & Co. at a rent of two thousand six hundred dollars per annum. Also all my farms containing about two hundred & thirty one acres & nineteen one hundredth of an acre together with the works, engines & machinery known as the Apple River & Galena Lead Mining property situate at Apple River in Davies County in the State of Illinois also a sum of one hundred and ten pounds owing to me from Henry Jackson on the security of a promissory note, also five hundred shares in the Union Bank of Birmingham on certificate No. 38, ten shares in the same bank on certificate No. 1031, ten shares in the same bank on certificate No. 1113, fifteen shares in the same bank on certificate No. 1114, fifteen shares in the same bank on certificate No. 1115, twenty shares in the same bank on certificate No. 1116, twenty shares in the same bank on certificate No. 1120, five shares in the same bank on certificate No. 1121 & five shares in the same bank on certificate No. 1122 making in all six hundred shares in said Union Bank of Birmingham also sixty five shares in the Bank of Liverpool on certificate No. 6685 and forty shares in the same bank on certificate No. 6689 & thirty five shares in the same bank on certificate No. 6678 & twenty one shares in the same bank on certificate No. 6677 making in all one hundred and sixty one shares in the Bank of Liverpool & all my interest in the Silver mines in Nevada in partnership with the Joel A Sperry of Newhaven Connecticut for which I paid ten thousand dollars & all my half share of the Insurance fund now deposited at the Union Bank of Birmingham in the name of Bamford Brothers.

I give to my Executors my thirty five shares in the Bank of Liverpool on certificate No. 6679 in trust to pay the dividends thereon to my brother Samuel Bamford during his life and after his death the said shares shall be **In Trust** for my son Arthur John Jones Bamford for his own use absolutely.

I give to my Executors my thirty five shares in the Bank of Liverpool on certificate No. 6680 **In Trust** to pay the dividends thereon to my sister Hannah Bamford during her life and after her death the said shares shall be **In Trust** for my daughter Hannah Maria Williams for her separate use.

I give to my Executors my thirty five shares in the Bank of Liverpool on certificate No. 6681 **In Trust** to pay the dividends thereon unto my wife's sister, Mary Ann Gretton during her life that all the _____ after her decease the said shares shall be in trust for my daughter Eleanor Caroline Bamford for her separate use.

I direct devises, legacies & bequests hereinbefore made shall be free of legal and succession duty.

I devise & bequeath all the residue of my estate, real and personal unto & to the use of my Executors in trust to sell the said real estate and call in and convert into money the said personal estate & out of the money to arise from such sale calling in and conversion to pay any debts, funeral & testamentary expenses & all legacy & succession duties payable under my will & to *hand* possessed of the remainder of such money **In Trust** for my son Arthur John Jones Bamford for his own use absolutely.

If the said residue of my estate shall not be sufficient to pay the said legal & possession duties, I direct that any that any deficiency shall be made good by my said son Arthur John Jones out of his interest under this my will.

I direct that the said Hannah Clifford Bamford, Arthur John Jones Bamford & Thomas Williams or the survivors or survivor of them or the heirs, executors or administrators of the survivor, their or his assigns or other trustees or trustee for the time being of this my will, shall be alluded and taken to be the trustees or trustee of my will for the purposes of the Settled Land Act 1882.

And I direct that the power of appointing a new trustee or trustees of this my will, shall be exercisable by the trustees or trustee for the time being of my will, or the executors or executor & administrators or administrator of the last surviving or continuing trustee or by the last retiring trustee & upon any such appointment, the number of trustees may be maintained, increased or diminished.

In witness whereof, I, the said Charles Bamford, have to this my last will, contained on this & the preceding sheets of paper, set my hand the day and year first before written.

Charles Bamford

The writing contained on this & the preceding sheets of paper was signed by the said testator as and for his last will and testament in the presence of us, the under signed, present at the same time who at his request in his presence & in the presence of each other have hereunto subscribed our names as witnesses.

B. E. James
Solicitor, Liverpool

W. Harris
Articled Clerk
With Messrs. Pemberton, Sampson & James, Solicitors, Liverpool

December 29th, 1890 — Testator died.
At Chester on the 21st of February 1891. Probate of the will was granted to Arthur John Jones Bamford and Thomas Williams the surviving executors.

Gross value of personal estate £60,273 — 3 — 8

Be it known that at the date hereunder written the last will and testament of Charles Bamford, late of Brookhurst, Bromborough in the County of Chester, Provision Merchant, deceased, who died on the 29th day of December 1890 at Brookhurst aforesaid and who at the time of his death had a fixed place of abode at Brookhurst aforesaid within the District of the County of Chester, was proved and registered in the District of Probate Registry of Her Majesty's High Court of Justice at Chester and that administration of the personal estate of the said deceased was granted t by the aforesaid Court to Arthur John Jones Bamford of Brynmofydd LLanhaiadr, in the County of Denbigh, Esquire, the son of the said deceased and Thomas Williams of Voilas, Bidson Road, Birkenhead in the County of Chester, Esquire, the surviving executors named in the said will they having been first sworn, will faithfully to administer the same.

Dated the 21st day of February 1891

Appendix III

Will of Arthur John Jones Bamford

This is the last will and testament of me Arthur John Jones Bamford of Old Croft, Rhyl in the county of Flint Esquire. I hereby revoke all former Wills and Testamentary dispositions heretofore made by me and I declare this to be my last Will and Testament. I appoint my Wife Anne Bamford the sole Executrix of this my Will. I desire my just debts and funeral and testamentary expenses to be paid as soon as conveniently maybe after my decease. I hereby devise all my real estate and personal estate whatsoever and wheresoever situate, subject to the payment of my debts and funeral and testamentary expenses as aforesaid, unto my said Wife Anne Bamford absolutely. In witness hereof I have to this Will set my hand this 21st day of August 1894.

Arthur J. J. Bamford

Signed by the said Testator as and for this last Will and Testament in the presence of us, present the same time who at his bequest in his presence and in the presence of each other have hereunto subscribed our names as witnesses.

J. Parry Jones
Solicitor, Denbigh

Edward Parry
Graig Brewery House, Denbigh
Solicitors clerk

Testator died November 3rd 1894 at Old Croft, Rhyl
Will proved at the Asaph District Registry 25th February 1895 by
Anne Bamford. Widow Relist of dec. the Sole Executor
Duty on the Real Estate £143-2-6
Gross Personal Estate £17,355-3-2
Net   - do -   Nil
Registrar's fees £3-2-0

Appendix IV

Will of Edwin Bamford

(Handwritten copy of Will in the hands of the State of Pennsylvania, dated 9th day of January 1905, punctuation added)

I Edwin Bamford of Raby Hall, Bromborough in the county of Chester, Merchant, hereby revoke all former testamentary dispositions and declare this to be my last Will.

I appoint my friend John Broker and my sons Alfred Charles and Henry Samuel my trustees and executors of this my Will.

I give to the said John Broker a legacy of two hundred and fifty pounds, free of duty.

I give to the said John Broker and to my sons Alfred Charles and Henry Samuel all my cash and ready money in my house or place of business or standing to my credit at my Bank and also all the share and interest which shall belong to me at my death in the capital stock in trade, profits and assets except goodwill, machinery plant and trade utensils whether accrued or accruing of the business of Provision Merchants now carried on by me and my said sons Alfred Charles and Henry Samuel in co-partnership under the plate of Bamford Brothers or which shall at my death be carried on by any other person or persons in succession to the said firm. I trust to collect, call in and convert into money such parts thereof as shall not consist of money and out of the moneys produced or forming part of such share and interest and the said cash and ready money in exoneration of all other all other my real and personal estate to pay for my funeral and testamentary expenses and debts including all debts or sums of money which shall at my death be secured by way of mortgage charge or lien on my real or household estates or any part thereof in exoneration of the same real or household estates.

My trustees shall stand possessed of the residue of the said moneys mentioned in the last preceding clause upon trust to pay there out the sum of one hundred thousand pounds to my said sons Alfred Charles and Henry Samuel in equal shares. I also give to my said sons Alfred Charles and Henry Samuel my share and interest in the Goodwill (if any), machinery plant trade utensils of the said business.

I also give to my said sons Alfred Charles and Henry Samuel in equal shares the use and enjoyment of the house, lands and buildings known as Raby Hall together with all articles of domestic or household use or ornaments including horses, carriages, harness and stable furniture belonging to or used in connection therewith for the period of twelve calendar months from my decease then keeping the same in good and tenantable repair and insured against loss or damage by fire and also paying all rents rates tare and performing all covenants in respect thereof and I declare that in case either of my said sons Alfred Charles and Henry Samuel shall die in my lifetime the survivor of them shall be entitled to the same use and enjoyment during the period aforesaid on the same conditions.

And I also give to my said sons Alfred Charles and Henry Samuel in equal shares all my warehouses, lands and hereditaments known as The Phoenix Warehouses situate in Mathew Street and Harrington Street, Liverpool charged in exoneration of my other real estate and personal estate with the annuity of two hundred and sixty pounds hereinafter bequeathed to my said son William Evason, but if either of them the said Alfred Charles and Henry Samuel shall die in my lifetime without leaving issue who shall survive him and me, I give the hereditaments charged as aforesaid to the other of them absolutely and if both of them die without leaving such issue as aforesaid, then the same hereditaments charges aforesaid shall sink into my residuary estate.

I give to my son William Evason during his life an annuity of two hundred and sixty pounds commencing from my death and to be payable in equal weekly sums of five pounds and the first payment thereof to be made as soon as may be after my death. And I declare that the same shall be charged exclusively on and payable out of my Phoenix Warehouses herein before devised to my sons Alfred Charles and Henry Samuel in equal shares in exoneration of all other my real and personal estate and effects and I declare that if my said son William Evason shall at my death be an undischarged bankrupt or shall assign the said sum of five pounds a week or any part thereof or if any other event shall happen in my lifetime or after my death whereby if such sums belonged to him absolutely he would be deprived of the personal enjoyment thereof or any part thereof, then the gift hereby made shall cease as if he were dead.

I give to my trustees the sum of twenty thousand pounds with interest thereon until payment at the rate of four pounds per cent per annum to be charged exclusively upon and raisable and payable out of the lands and hereditaments in the County of Leicester hereinafter devised to my daughter Eliza Ann Colt.

And also I give to my trustees all my five thousand pounds consolidated ordinary stock of the Lancashire and Yorkshire Railway Company and also all my eighty three shares in the Birmingham and Midland Bank Limited and also all my one hundred and twenty shares in the Bank of Liverpool Limited In Trust as to all the said moneys stock and shares for my son Edwin absolutely and in case he shall die in my lifetime then In Trust for the child or children of my said son Edwin who shall survive me and attain the age of twenty one years and if more than one in equal shares and in case there be no such child who shall attain the age of twenty one years then the same shall, subject to the powers hereby or by law conferred on my trustees, fall into and form part of my residuary estate. And I declare that my trustees shall have power to raise the said loan of twenty thousand pounds together with the costs of raising the same by sale or mortgage.

I devise to my trustees all my land and hereditaments situate in the ___*perral?* Parishes of Ashby Magna and Peatling Parva in the County of Leicester and in the Lordships or *libities?* or Parishes of Dunton-Bassett and Corby in the said County and elsewhere in the County of Leicester according to the tenure thereof respectively, charged in exoneration of all other my real and personal estate and effects with the payment of the said legacy of twenty thousand pounds and interest for the same at the rate of four pounds per cent per annum from my decease until payment upon trust for my said daughter Eliza Ann Colt wife of Arthur MacKenzie Colt absolutely and in case she shall die in my lifetime leaving a child or children who shall survive her and me then In Trust to pay the income thereof to the said Arthur MacKenzie Colt during his life but so long only as such child or all such children if more than one shall be under the age of twenty one years, the said Arthur MacKenzie Colt properly educating and such child or children during their respective minorities. And if and when any such child or children shall at my death be the age of twenty one years or shall afterwards attain that age then my trustees shall during the remainder of the life of said Arthur MacKenzie Colt from time to time divide the said income into twice as many equal parts as there shall be children of the said Eliza Ann Colt for the time being living and shall pay one such part to each such adult child, his or her executor administrators and assigns and shall pay the remainder of the said income to the said Arthur MacKenzie Colt be properly maintaining and educating thereof any minor children of said Eliza Ann Colt and subject to the trusts aforesaid and to the power of Maintenance hereby or by law conferred on my trustees my trustees shall hold the said trust property comprised in this clause and the income thereof In Trust for the chid or children of my said Daughter Eliza Ann Colt who shall survive me and before or after my death attain the age of twenty one years and if more than one in equal shares And I also declare that in case my said daughter Eliza Ann Colt shall die in my lifetime without bearing a child who shall survive me and attain the age of twenty one years, then my trustees shall hold the same property In Trust to pay the whole income thereof to my said son in law Arthur MacKenzie Colt during his life be properly maintaining and educating thereof the minor children of any of my said daughter Eliza Ann Colt for the time being and from and after his death then the said property and the income thereof charged as aforesaid and subject and subject to the said power conferred on my trustees shall fall into and form part of my residuary estate but I declare that my trustees shall not be concerned to see that said Arthur Mackenzie Colt maintains and educates the said children or be liable in respect of any default of the said Arthur MacKenzie Colt in that regard.

I devise the Advowson and perpetual right of nomination[96] of the Vicarage of Ashby Magna in the County of Leicester unto and to the use of my daughter Eliza Ann, her heirs and assigns. And in case she shall die in my lifetime, I devise the same to my trustees to hold the same until the youngest child for the time being of my daughter Eliza Ann shall attain the age of twenty one years upon trust from time to time as occasion shall require to present to the said Vicarage such qualified Parson as my trustee for the time being shall elect. And when as so soon as the youngest child for the time being of my said daughter Eliza Ann shall attain the age of twenty one years then upon trust for the child or children of my said daughter Eliza Ann who shall be __*ring*? when such youngest child shall attain the said age of twenty one years and if more than one in equal shares.

---

96. Writers wording as Will wording undecipherable

I devise to my trustees all my lands and hereditaments situate in the Parish of Bilton with Harrogate in the County of York known as The Dragon Estate and all other my lands and hereditaments in the said county of York and also all my lands and hereditaments situate in the Parish of Harbury in the county of Warwick and in the Parish of Wednesbury in the county of Stafford and all other my lands and hereditaments in the said counties of Warwick and Stafford and all my lands and hereditaments situate at Tranmere in the County of Chester and my leasehold lands and hereditaments situate at Booth in the County of Lancaster but subject as to the said last mentioned lands and hereditaments to the yearly rent of twenty seven pounds, ten shillings and to the agreements covenants and conditions affecting the same) and also the house, lands and buildings now occupied by me and known as Raby Hall together with all articles of domestic or household use or ornament including horses, cattle, carriages, harness and stable furniture belonging to or and in connection therewith and subject nevertheless to the use and enjoyment of the said Raby Hall premises and personal effects herein before given to my said sons Alfred Charles and Henry Samuel and also subject to the lessees covenants and conditions effecting the same but free as to the whole of the said lands and hereditaments mentioned in this clause from any lien for the unpaid purchase money thereof (if any) and also all my five hundred shares in the Liverpool Mortgage Insurance Company Limited and also all my estate and interest in any real, leasehold or personal property in the United States of America *reprove?* trust for my daughter Emma Jane Cunliffe, wife of Walter Cunliffe absolutely and in case she shall die in my lifetime, then my trustees shall hold the said property comprised in this clause and the income thereof upon the like trusts and with and subject to the like powers conferred on my trustees and conditions in favour of the children and the said husband of my daughter Emma Jane Cunliffe as are herein before declared or contained of and concerning the said property in the County of Leicester in favour of the children and husband of my said daughter Eliza Ann Colt respectively and with the like ultimate destination to the residue as is herewith before contained concerning the said last mentioned property.

I declare that my trustees may after the death of the parents of any minor children entitled to any share or interest under this my Will apply the whole or any part at their discretion of any income to which any such minor shall or if of full age would for the time being be entitled in possession under the trusts or disposition contained in this my Will for or towards the maintenance education or benefit of such minor and shall during such minority accumulate the remainder, if any, of the same income at compound interest by investing the same and resulting income of such reinvestments in augmentation of the fund or share from which the same income shall have proceeded but with the power to apply as aforesaid any such accumulations in any subsequent year as if the same were income of that year.

I give and devise to my trustees all my real and personal estate whatsoever and wheresoever not hereby otherwise disposed of In Trust for my said children Edwin Bamford, Eliza Ann Colt and Emma Jane Cunliffe in equal shares and in case any one or more of them shall die in my lifetime, then the share of him or her as dying shall be held by my trustees upon the same for the like trusts and with and subject to the same or the like powers and conditions as are herein before declared or contained of and concerning the respective properties herein before devised and bequeathed in trust for him or her respectively or such of the same trusts powers and conditions as shall be applicable and as that the ultimate destination to residue shall take effect in regard to the share of residue of my child as dying in forms of the survivor s or survivor at my death of my last mentioned children. In Witness thereof, I have signed my name at the end of this my will contained in this and the preceding five sheets of paper this thirtieth day of December, One thousand eight hundred and ninety three.

(Signed)   Edwin Bamford

Signed by the before named Edwin Bamford as his last will in the presence of us who being present at the same time who in his presence and in the presence of each other have here unto subscribed our names as witnesses.

(Signed)   Tho. Bellringer   Solicitor, Liverpool
           Mary E. Hamer   Housekeeper, Raby Hall

Be it known that at the date hereunder written the last Will and Testament of Edwin Bamford of Raby Hall near Bromborough in the County of Chester, Provision Merchant deceased, who died on the 3rd day of April 1894 at Raby Hall aforesaid and who at the time of his death had a fixed place of abode at Raby Hall aforesaid within the district of the County of Chester was proved and registered in the District Probate Register of Her Majesty's High Court of Justice at Chester and that administration of the personal estate of the said deceased was granted by the aforesaid Court to John Broker of The Park, Eccles, near Manchester in the county of Lancaster, Provision Merchant, and Alfred Charles Bamford of Raby Hall aforesaid, Provision Merchant and Henry Samuel Bamford of Raby Hall aforesaid, Provision Merchant, the Sons. The executors named in the said Will, they having been first sworn, will and faithfully to administer the same.

Dated the 18th day of April 1894
Gross value of personal estate £113,738 — 1 — 7
Extracted by Bellringer & Cunliffe of Liverpool

Appendix V

The Honourable Anne Hawke — Letters of Administration

This the document that delivers the entire estate of Anne Hawke (previously Bamford) to Harold Brooke Hawke.

In His Majesty's High Court of Justice
The Principal Probate Registry

Be it known that The Honourable Anne Hawke of Bathafarn Hall, Ruthin in the County of Denbigh, died on the 6th day of August 1912 at Bathafarn hall aforesaid intestate.

And be it further known that that at the date hereunder written Letters of Administration of all the Estate which by law devolves to and vests in the personal representative of the said intestate were granted by His Majesty's High Court of Justice at the Principal Probate Registry thereof to the Honourable Harold Brooke Hawke, the lawful husband of the said intestate.

And it is hereby certified that an Affidavit for Inland Revenue has been delivered wherein it is shown that the gross value of the said Estate within the United Kingdom (exclusive of what the said deceased may have been possessed of or entitled to as a Trustee not beneficially) amounts to £4412-13-3.

And it is further certified that it appears by a receipt signed by an Inland Revenue Officer on the said affidavit that £2-2-3 on the amount of Estate Duty and Interest on said duty has been paid.

Dated the 23rd June 1913

W. Indewick
Registrar

Appendix VI

Honourable Harold Brooke Hawke – Letters of Administration

This the document that delivers the entire estate of Harold Brooke Hawke to his brother Martin Bladen Hawke, exactly six months to the day after Harold had officially gained possession of the Bamford estate.

In His Majesty's High Court of Justice
The Principal Probate Registry

Be it known that The Honourable Anne Hawke of Bathafarn Hall, Ruthin in the County of Denbigh, died on the 6th day of August 1912 at Bathafarn Hall aforesaid intestate.

And in the month of June 1913 Letters of Administration of all the Estate which by law devolves and vests in the personal representative of said intestate were granted at The Principal Probate Registry to the Honourable Harold Brooke Hawke her lawful husband on the 20th day of June 1913 leaving part thereof unadministered. That the said intestate did not die possessed of any real estate.

And Be It Further Known that at the date hereunder written Letters of Administration of all the unadministered Estate which by law devolves to and vests in the personal representative of the said intestate were granted in His Majesty's High Court of Justice at the Principal Probate Registry thereof to the Right Honourable Martin Bladen Baron Hawke the administrator of the Estate of the said Honourable Harold Brooke Hawke deceased. And it is hereby certified that an Affidavit for Inland Revenue has been delivered wherein it is shown that the gross value of said Estate within the United Kingdom (exclusive of what the said deceased may have been possessed of or entitled to as a Trustee and not beneficially) amounts to £1806-2-3.

And it is further certified that it appears by a Certificate proved by an Inland Revenue Officer that £2-2-3 on account of Estate Duty and interest on such Duty has been paid.

Dated 23rd day of December 1913

A. Musgrave
Registrar

Appendix VII

Will of Francis Joseph Benedict Kreitmair

After the first four paragraphs, with the exception of the sale or dissolution of his business, this will is mainly legal jargon to protect trustees and executors

This is the last will and testament of me Francis Joseph Benedict Kreitmair of Firdene, Noctorum in the County of Chester, Cotton Broker and Merchant. I appoint my wife Ann Eliza Kreitmair and Cecil –umbe Smith of the city of Chester Solicitor (hereinafter called my trustees) to be the executors and Trustee of this my will.

I give to my said Wife my motor car and motor accessories and such of the household furniture and effects at or belonging to Firdene aforesaid as all belong to me at my death and also the sum of One thousand pounds which I desire to be paid to her as soon as conveniently may be after my death. I give to each of my Daughters the sum of five hundred pounds to be paid as soon as conveniently may be after my death.

I bequeath to my sister Anne Ellen Kreitmair the sum of Two hundred pounds to be paid as soon as conveniently may be after my death. And I direct that the same legacy shall not be deemed a ---- satisfaction of a debt owing by me to her and I also give to my said Sister such of my late Father's furniture pictures and household effects belonging to me as shall be in her possession at my death.

I bequeath to my Granddaughter Dorothy Anne Bamford the sum of One hundred pounds and to my Grandson Charles Francis Kreitmair Bamford the sum of two hundred and fifty pounds.

I Declare that if any of my legatee shall be under the age of twenty one years his or her legacy may be paid by my trustees at their option and in their absolute and irresponsible discretion to such legatee whose receipt thereof not withstanding he or she may be a Minor shall be sufficient discharge.

I declare that the specific and pecuniary legacies hereinbefore bequeathed shall be paid and delivered to the respective legatees free from Estate Legacy and other if any death duties and such duties shall be deemed part of my testamentary expenses and be paid accordingly.

I Devise and Bequeath all the real and personal estate not hereby or by any Codicil otherwise specifically disposed of and which I can dispose of by Will in any manner I think proper either as beneficially entitled thereto or under any general power unto my Trustees Upon Trust that my Trustees Shall (subject to the directions hereinafter contained with respect to my business) sell the said real estate and call in and sell and convert into money such part of my personal estate as does not consist of money and shall out of the money to arise from the sale and conversion of my said real estate and personal estate and out of my ready money pay my funeral expenses, testamentary expenses and debts and shall also pay the legacies hereby or by any Codicil bequeathed but so that all legacies and the duty on all legacies and annuities bequeathed free of duty shall be paid primarily out of my personal estate and shall invest the residue of the said money in their names in or upon any of the investments hereby authorised with power from my Trustees in their absolute and irresponsible discretion to change such investments for others of a like nature and shall stand possessed of the investments hereinbefore directed to be made or authorised to be retained (excluding any part of my residuary estate remaining unconverted) and the investments for the time being representing the same (hereinafter to be called "the Trust Funds") and of the annual income thereof In Trust to pay to my said Sister an Annuity of Three pounds per week during her life (free of duty) the first payment to be made at the end of one week from my death and subject thereto In Trust to pay the Income of the Trust Funds to my said wife during her life and after her decease.

I Direct that the capital and income of the Trust Funds(subject to the provision herein contained with respect to the said Annuity) be held In Trust for such children of mine living at the death of the survivor of me and my said wife and such issue then living of any child or children of mine then dead as being males shall either before or after the death of such survivor attain the age of twenty one years or being female shall either before or after the same period attain the age or be married, such children and other issue to take as tenants in common in a course of distribution according to the stocks and not to the number of individual objects and so that the issue of a deceased child may take as tenants in common by way of substitution the share only which their parent would, if living, have taken.

I Empower my Trustees with the consent of my said Wife during her life and after her death at their discretion to advance and apply the whole or any part or parts of the capital or estimated value of the capital to which under any disposition herein contained each or any infant shall be entitled or presumptively entitled in or towards his or her advancement, preferment or benefit to pay the same to such infant or to some other person or persons to be so applied without being in any way responsible to see the application thereof.

With respect to the business of a Cotton Broker and Merchant now carried on by me in conjunction with Messieurs William J Bennett and Fitz Zacharias under the name or style of F. Kreitmair & Co., I Empower my Trustees to carry out the provisions of any deed that may have been entered into by me and may be existing at my death with respect thereto and in addition authorise my Trustees in their absolute and irresponsible discretion to sell the said business as a going concern or any part or share parts or shares therein and either with or without the right to use the name or style of F. Kreitmair & Co. and either upon or partly upon credit and without any ----with such security as they think fit and ---- provisions herein contained as to selling upon or partly upon credit and with or without any security shall apply to a sale to the said William J. Bennett and Fritz Zacharias or either of them as well as to anyone else. And for the purpose of the better disposal thereof, I Empower my Trustees in their absolute and irresponsible discretion to continue the said business for so long as they think fit and either under the name or style of F. Kreitmair & Co. or otherwise or to discontinue the same at any time and to wind up the affairs thereof and to sell get in and convert into money the assets thereof with liberty for my Trustees if and so long as they shall continue the said business to employ therein the whole or any part of capital which shall be employed therein at my decease and also such further part (if any) of my estate as they in their absolute and irresponsible discretion shall think proper and with liberty also to my Trustees to employ and dismiss Managers, Agents, Clerks and others and to become and continue to be limited partners in in the said business under the Limited Partnership Act, 1907 or any statutory modification or re-enactment thereof for the time being in force or such term or terms and upon such conditions as they shall in such discretion as aforesaid think fit and to sell and assign their share or shares in such partnership or to dissolve and wind up the affairs thereof. And notwithstanding the specific powers hereinbefore conferred on my Trustees and without prejudice thereto, I authorise my Trustees to deal with my said business as they shall in their absolute and irresponsible discretion consider advisable without being answerable for any loss arising thereby, it being my intention that my Trustees shall have the fullest powers and discretions as to be made of dealing with or conducting my said business and otherwise in relation thereto as if they were the absolute owners thereof.

I Authorise my Trustees to postpone the sale and conversation of my property or any part thereof as so long as they shall think fit and during such period to manage and order all the affairs thereof with the power to grant Leases for such terms and at such rents and generally on such conditions as my Trustees shall deem advantageous. And I declare that the rents, profits and income of my property for the time being remaining unsold and unconverted (including the profits of my said business while carried on by my Trustees and also such profits or income to be derived from any such united partnership as aforesaid) shall after payment of all incidental expenses and outgoings be divided and applied to the person or persons and in the manner to whom and in which the income of the proceeds of such sale and conversion would for the time being be payable or applicable under this my Will if such sale and conversion had been finally made.

I Declare that all monies liable to be invested under this my Will may be invested in any of the public stocks or funds or Government securities of the United Kingdom or India or any Colony or Dependency of the United Kingdom or Province thereof or upon freehold, copyhold, leasehold or chattel real securities in England or Wales (including second or contributory mortgages) or in or upon the shares, stocks, debentures, bonds, mortgages or securities of any Company or Corporation or Body or Authority whether commercial, municipal, county, local or otherwise carrying on business or constituted for any purpose in the United Kingdom.

I Authorise my Trustees at their discretion to provide for the payment of the said Annuity by setting apart and appropriating any part of my estate or any investments for the time being forming part of my estate sufficient at the period of appropriation to answer by means of the income thereof such annuity or by purchasing a life annuity in the names of my Trustees and until such annuity shall be provided for in one or other of the modes aforesaid the same shall be paid out of the income of the Trust Funds but I Declare that when and so soon as each annuity shall have been provided for such provision shall exonerate and liberate the remainder of my estate real and personal from such annuity and all liabilities in respect thereof and that the part of my estate and the investments so appropriated or as much thereof as shall not have been resorted to or applied in payment of the said annuity shall in the death of my said sister revert to and remain part of the Trust Funds.

I Declare that the Executors and Trustees at the time being of this my Will may, instead of acting personally, employ and pay a Solicitor or other person to transact any business or do any act required to be done in connection with the administration of my estate or the trusts powers or provisions herein contained including the receipt and payment of money and that any Executor or Trustee being a Solicitor or other person engaged in any profession or business or his firm may be so employed as being a sole Executor or Trustee may so act and shall be entitled to charge and be paid all professional or other charges for any business or act done or time expended by him or his firm in connection with the Trust including any act which an Executor or Trustee not being a Solicitor or other person engaged as aforesaid could have done personally.

I Declare that my Trustees may exercise or concur in exercising all powers and discretions hereby — by law given to them not withstanding that they ---- either on any of them may have a direct or other personal interest in the mode or result of exercising any such power or discretion.

I revoke all prior Wills.

In Witness whereof I have to this my Will contained in this and the eight preceding pagers of paper set my hand this Nineteenth day of February One thousand nine hundred and thirteen.

Signed by the said Testator Francis Joseph Benedict Kreitmair as and for his last Will and Testament in the presence of us who at his request in his presence and in the presence of each other have hereunto subscribed our names as witnesses:

J. Eustace Jones — Solicitor Chester
Alfred Gresty - his Clerk

In a Codicil he bequeathed Dyllis Ruth Ward, his granddaughter, the sum of One hundred pounds.

Appendix VIII

Will of David Citroen

I David Citroen of Trevin Towers, Meads, Eastbourne hereby Revoke all former testamentary instruments made by me and DECLARE this to be my last Will which I make this twenty ninth day of December One thousand nine hundred and thirty four.

1. I APPOINT NATIONAL PROVINICIAL BANK (hereinafter called "the Bank") to be the EXECUTOR and TRUSTEE of this my Will AND I DECLARE that the Bank may in either such capacity act by its proper Officer or Officers who may employ and pay a Solicitor Broker or any other Agent to transact all or any business required to be done (including the receipt and payment of money) AND I FURTHER DECLARE the Bank may (without being liable to account for any profit thereby made) retain as Bankers on current account or deposit account or advance all moneys necessary or convenient to be retained as aforesaid or advanced in connection with my estate on such terms as the Bank would reasonably make with a customer of the Bank in London under similar circumstances and the Bank shall also be entitled to remuneration (free from duties and as a first charge on my estate) in accordance with the

Scale of Fees arranged by special written agreement between the Bank and me.

2. I DIRECT that my body shall be cremated without any religious ceremony and my ashes dispersed and it is my desire that no flowers or mourning shall be used and my funeral shall be simple and informal.

3. I CONFIRM all Settlements whatsoever which I have made or may hereafter make during my life and I declare and I declare that the provisions hereby made for my Wife and children and other issue are intended to be in addition to and not in satisfaction of those made or covenanted to be made for them respectively in and by such respective Settlements.

4. I GIVE to my Wife Violet Dehra (calling herself Dehra) nee Gerard any three articles of furniture or china or ornaments or pictures or silver not otherwise bequeathed which she shall within one calendar month from my death select and subject to this bequest I give to each of my two daughters Reine Vance (formerly Reine Ayer) and Clara Isabella Kingsford any two articles of furniture or china or ornaments or pictures or silver not otherwise bequeathed which she shall within six weeks of my death select. For the purposes of making the selection my said daughters shall select in order of seniority. Subject to the previous bequests I give to each of my five Grandchildren Alfred Jules Ayer, John William Holloway, Doris Betty Holloway, Donald Kingsford and Madge Joan Kingsford one article of furniture or china or ornaments or pictures or silver not otherwise bequeathed which he or she shall within two calendar months from my death select. My Grandchildren shall be entitled to make their selection notwithstanding any one or more may be under the age of twenty one and shall be capable of giving good discharge to the Bank and shall make their selection in the order named. I give my granddaughter Doris

Betty Holloway the picture of herself as a baby painted by Mrs. *(Mary Lemon)* Waller and the miniature of herself painted by Mrs. Gertrude Massey and frame.

5. I MAKE the following pecuniary bequests vide licet:- to my Wife the sum of Two thousand pounds to be paid to her within one month after my death to each of my surviving daughters Reine Vance and Clara Isabella Kingsford the sum of One Thousand pounds to each of my surviving Grandchildren Alfred Jules Ayer john William Holloway Doris Betty Holloway Donald Kingsford and Madge Joan Kingsford if and when he or she respectively attains the age of Twenty One years or being female marries under that age the sum of One thousand pounds and the receipt of either of my Granddaughters for the same in the event of her marriage under that age shall notwithstanding her minority be sufficient discharge. To my brother Roelof Citroen of 54 Rue Blanche Paris the sum of one thousand pounds but should he predecease me I give the same sum to his Wife Sara Citroen nee Rozelaar and I request them to leave Five hundred pounds out of the said sum to their Granddaughter Micheline Citroen of 26 Rue Boislevent Paris XVI. In the event of both my said Brother and his Wife predeceasing me then I give the said Micheline Citroen the sum of Five hundred pounds if and when she shall attain the age of twenty one years or marry under that age and her receipt for the same shall in the event of her marriage notwithstanding her minority be a sufficient discharge. To my former Secretary and Friend Harry Everett the sum of two thousand pounds. To my Chauffeur Harold John Goodman an amount equal to two years wages provided he shall be in my service at the time of my death and not under notice to leave whether given or received. To Edith Hart an amount an amount equal to one year's wages or an amount equal to two years' wages if she has been in my service for a period of six years or longer provided she shall be in my service at the time of my death and not under

notice to leave whether given or received. To every indoor and outdoor domestic servant not including the said Harold John Goodman and Edith Hart in my service at the time of my death (including Chauffeurs and Gardeners) who shall not be under notice to leave whether given or received (hereinafter called "my domestic servants") the amounts following that is to say:- To each of my domestic servants who has been in my service for a period of two years but less than six years an amount equal to one year's wages and To each of my domestic servants who has been in my service for a period of six years or longer an amount equal to two years wages.

6. I GIVE to my Wife an annuity of One thousand two hundred pounds during her life without power of anticipation to begin from my death and to be payable by equal quarterly payments the first payment thereof to be made at the expiration of three calendar months from my death and so that the said annuity shall not vest absolutely in my wife but shall be held by the Bank upon the statutory protective trusts for the benefit of my wife for the period of her life provided that the Bank shall not be responsible for making payment to my wife after the protective trust in her favor shall have failed or determined unless the Bank had at the time of making such payment express notice of the act or event causing such failure or determination.

7. I have made provision by Settlement during my lifetime for my two surviving daughters which I considered ample but in view of the present uncertainty of the value and income of the investments I give to each of them my said daughter Reine Vance and my said daughter Clara Isabella Kingsford an annuity of Four hundred pounds during their respective lives without power of anticipation to begin from my death and to be payable by equal quarterly payments the first payment thereof to be made at the expiration of three calendar months from my death and so that the said annuities shall not vest absolutely

in my said daughters but shall be held by the Bank upon the statutory protective trusts for the benefit of each such daughter for the period of her life provided that the Bank shall not be responsible for making payment to either of my said daughters after the protective trust in her favour shall have failed or determined unless the Bank had at the time of making such payment express notice of the act or event causing such failure or determination.

8. (i) The Bank shall appropriate and retain a sufficient part of my estate or of the investments representing the same as funds or a Fund (according to the number annuities) for answering by the annual income thereof each annuity hereinbefore given and the expenses incidental to the payment thereof but without prejudice to the powers of sale and investment and transposing investments hereinafter contained and I declare that if the annual income of any appropriated fund at the time of appropriation be sufficient to satisfy the annuity in respect of which the same shall have been appropriated such appropriation shall be a complete satisfaction of the trust or direction hereinafter declared to provide for such annuity and the annuitant shall thereafter have no claim against or right to resort to any part of my estate (other than the fund so appropriated) for the payment of the annuity and further that if the income of the appropriated fund shall at any time prove insufficient for the payment in full of such annuity resort shall be had to the capital thereof from time to time to make good such deficiency and the surplus income (if any) of the said fund from time to time remaining after payment of the annuity shall be applicable as income of my residuary estate.

(ii) As and when any annuity shall cease the fund so appropriated for payment of such annuity or so much thereof as shall not have been applied in payment of the said annuity shall sink into and form part of my residuary estate and until any annuity shall have been provided for in manner aforesaid the same shall be paid out of the income of my residuary estate.

9. I DIRECT that all legacies and annuities bequeathed by this my Will or any Codicil hereto shall be paid and satisfied free of all death duties.

10. I DECLARE that notwithstanding anything to the contrary contained in this my Will my Wife shall in the event of her surviving me be entitled to the personal use occupation and enjoyment free from rent rates and taxes for the period of six calendar months after my death (if she shall desire the same) of my residence "Trevin Towers" aforesaid together with the stables coachhouse garage garden pleasure-grounds and appurtenances thereto belonging or held therewith and the furniture and effects of domestic stable garage or garden use or ornament which at my death shall be in or about belonging to or enjoyed with the same or appropriated thereto she keeping the same insured against loss or damage by fire but without liability for fair wear and tear. The articles so as aforesaid to be selected by my daughters and grandchildren to remain on the premises insured under a comprehensive policy until the six calendar months have expired and subject thereto I DECLARE that the same property effects and premises other than the selected articles shall form part of my residuary real and personal estate and shall pass by the general devise and bequest thereof hereinafter contained.

11. I DEVISE AND BEQUEATH all the real and personal property whatsoever and wheresoever of or to which I shall be seised possessed or entitled at my death or over which I shall then have a general power of appointment or disposition by Will or of which I shall then be tenant in tail in possession except property otherwise disposed of by this my Will or any Codicil hereto Unto the Bank upon the trusts and with and subject to

the powers and provisions hereinafter declared of and concerning the same that is to say:- UPON TRUST that the Bank shall sell call in collect and convert into money the said real and personal property at such time or times and in such manner as the Bank shall think fit (but as to reversionary property not until it falls into the possession unless it shall appear to the Bank that an earlier sale would be beneficial) with power to postpone the sale calling in or conversion of the whole or any part or parts of the said property including leaseholds or other property or a terminable hazardous or wasteful nature during such period as the Bank shall think proper and to retain the same or my part thereof in its present form of investment without being responsible for loss it being my desire that my investments be left undisturbed unless the Bank see special reason to the contrary the time comes to wind up the estate except freehold and leasehold properties partly paid shares and investments that have to be sold for payment of death duties legacies and carrying out the provisions of my Will liabilities and expenses AND I DIRECT that the income of such of the same premises as for the time being shall remain unsold shall as well during the first year after my death as afterwards be applied as if the same were income arising from investments hereinafter authorized to be made of the proceeds of the sale thereof and that no reversionary or other property not actually producing income shall be treated as producing income for the purposes of this my will.

12. THE BANK shall out of the clear moneys to arise from the sale calling in and conversion of or forming part of my said real and personal property and out of my ready money pay my funeral and testamentary expenses (including all estate duty leviable at my death in respect of my estate) and debts and the legacies given by this my will or any Codicil hereto and all death duties and other moneys which under or by virtue of my direction or bequest free of duty contained in this my Will or any Codicil hereto are payable out of my general personal estate and make

provision for the payment of the annuities hereby or by any Codicil hereto bequeathed by me.

13. ANY moneys requiring to be invested shall be invested in name of Bank in or upon any of the investments hereby authorized with power to vary or transpose such investments for or into others of a nature hereby authorized and the Bank shall stand possessed of the said investments hereby authorized to be made or retained (hereinafter called "my residuary trust fund") and of the annual income thereof upon the Trusts hereinafter mentioned.

14. The BANK shall as soon as conveniently may be after my death divide my residuary estate into five equal parts and the Bank shall hold the said five equal parts and the investments for the time being representing the same and all accretions thereto and the income thereof (such five equal parts or the investments representing the same and all accretions thereto being hereinafter respectively generally called "the Alfred Jules Ayer Trust fund" "the John William Holloway Trust Fund" "the Donald Kingsford Trust Fund" "the Doris Betty Holloway Trust Fund" and "the Madge Joan Kingsford Trust Fund" respectively) Upon Trust as to one of each of such Trust Funds for the benefit of each of my five Grandchildren vide licet Alfred Jules Ayer the only child of my daughter Reine Vance John William Holloway the only son of my late daughter Elizabeth (Betty) Holloway Donald Kingsford the only son of my daughter Clara Isabella Kingsford Doris Betty Holloway the only daughter of my late daughter Elizabeth Madge Kingsford the only daughter of my daughter Clara Isabella Kingsford during their respective lives but subject as hereinafter mentioned and so that the same shall not vest absolutely in my said Grandchildren respectively except as to the extent hereinafter mentioned but shall be held by the Bank upon the respective trusts and subject to the powers

and provisions following that is to say: As to the Alfred Jules Ayer Trust Fund

(i) If any act or event shall be done or happen either before or after my death whereby the life interest hereby given to the said Alfred Jules Ayer in the Alfred Jules Ayer Trust Fund or some part thereof would if belonging to him absolutely have become vested in or charged in favour of some other person or persons then the Bank shall hold the income of the Alfred Jules Ayer Trust Fund for his benefit during his life upon the statuary protective trusts subject to the variations hereinafter mentioned.

(ii) If and so often as on any day occurring after the failure or determination of the interest of the said Alfred Jules Ayer in the Alfred Jules Ayer Trust Fund or any part as aforesaid the whole of the said income if hereinafter made payable absolutely to him during the whole of his life would again belong to and be payable to him absolutely alone during the residue of his life for his own absolute use and benefit free from encumbrances then the Bank shall hold the said income accruing after such day Upon the trusts (including the provision determining the trusts in his favour of the same income) upon which the same would for the time being be held if the trusts of such income had not failed or determined.

(iii) The Bank shall not be liable or responsible for paying the said income to the said Alfred Jules Ayer or permitting him to receive the same after the failure or determination during his life of the trust hereinafter declared in his favor unless and until the Bank shall have express notice of the act or event causing such failure or determination.

15. AFTER the death of the said Alfred Jules Ayer The Bank shall stand possessed of the Alfred Jules Ayer Trust Fund and the income thereof In trust for such person or persons for such purpose and in such manner as the said Alfred Jules Ayer shall from time to time by Will or Codicil without transgressing the rule against which such perpetuities appoint And in default of and subject to any such appointment in trust for any Wife of the said Alfred Jules Ayer who shall survive him during her life without power of anticipation and after her death In trust for all or any the children or child of the said Alfred Jules Ayer who being male shall attain the age of twenty one years or being female shall attain that age or marry and if more than one in equal shares and if there shall be only one such child the whole to be in trust for that one child.

16. As to the John William Holloway and Donald Kingsford Trust Funds respectively the Bank shall hold the same Upon the like trusts and subject to the like powers and provisions in favour of my Grandsons the said John William Holloway and Donald Kingsford respectively and their respective Wives and children and otherwise as are hereinafter declared and contained concerning the said Alfred Jules Ayer Trust Fund and income thereof as if such trusts powers and provisions were herein repeated with the substitution of the names of the said John William Holloway and Donald Kingsford respectively for the name of the said Alfred Jules Ayer.

17. As to the Doris Betty Holloway and Madge Joan Kingsford Trust Funds respectively the Bank shall hold the same Upon the like trusts and subject to the like powers and provisions in favour of my Granddaughters Doris Betty Holloway and Madge Joan Kingsford respectively and their respective children and otherwise as are hereinafter declared and contained concerning the said Alfred Jules Ayer Trust Fund and income

thereof as if such trusts powers and provisions were herein repeated with the substitution of the names of the said Doris Betty Holloway and Madge Joan Kingsford respectively for the name of the said Alfred Jules Ayer but omitting the provision of a life interest to the Wife in default of appointment.

18. If and so often as the trusts in respect of any one or more of the said Trust Funds hereinbefore declared shall fail or determine then subject to the trust powers and provisions hereinbefore declared and contained and to the powers by law vested in the Bank shall hold the Trust Fund and all accretions thereto by virtue of this present provision the trusts whereof shall have failed or determined by way of accrue to the Trust Funds or Trust Fund the trusts of which shall for the time being be still subsisting and if more than one in equal shares and so that the share which shall so accrue and be added to the respective Trust Funds or Trust Fund shall be held Upon the Trusts and subject to the powers and provisions herein declared and contained concerning the original Trust Fund to which the same shall be added or as near thereto as circumstances will admit.

19. I DECLARE that (notwithstanding the trusts of the share of any of my grandsons hereinbefore mentioned) if any one of my grandsons shall desire to purchase a share or partnership in the profession of a Stockbroker Solicitor Surveyor Chartered or Incorporated Accountant or to qualify for practicing any such professions such grandson shall be at liberty with the consent of the bank under the hand of the Manager for the time being of the Banks Trustee Department to appoint in his own favour from the said trust funds set apart for his benefit such a capital sum or sums as may be necessary from time to time for such purpose Provided always that the Bank shall be at liberty at its sole discretion to consent or to refuse its consent to or to act upon such appointment.

20. I DECLARE that no Grandchild of mine who shall marry his or her first cousin shall take any interest under my Will save in so far as such interest shall at the time of such marriage have already vested and become receivable and this is to apply to any legacy bequeathed to them by this my Will or ant Codicil hereto and also to the capital and income of every and any Grandchild's share or Trust Fund and I hereby bequeath any and every such interest which shall not have become so vested and receivable as aforesaid and shall be forfeited under the forgoing provision to King Edward's Hospital Fund for London and so that the receipt of the Treasurer for the time being shall be sufficient discharge Provided Always that whilst I rely upon the Bank to carry out these instructions the Bank shall not be liable or responsible for any payment it may have made contrary to this condition so long as it remains ignorant of such marriage.

21. I DECLARE that any sums of money which I may have advanced or paid or may advance or pay to or for the benefit of my Wife or any daughter of mine or her husband or any Grandchild or any sums of money which I may have settled or may settle for the benefit of my Wife or any daughter or issue not be taken into account in any way in the division of my estate

22. THE Bank may in its absolute discretion retain all or any of the investments of my property which shall exist at the time of my death for such time as it shall think fit but subject thereto and to the expression of my wishes contained in clause 11 hereof it is my desire that the Bank shall invest and I give to the Bank power to invest all moneys coming into the hands of the Bank and liable to be invested under any provisions of this my Will in any manner in or upon which trust funds or cash under the control or subject to the order of the Court may for the time being be authorised to be invested (except real securities in Ireland Australian and Indian Securities and Preference shares

of any kind) and in addition the Bank may invest such moneys in or on Debentures Debenture Stock or Rent Charge or Guaranteed Stocks of any Company Incorporated by Special Act or by or under any Public General Act of the Imperial Parliament. In addition to the power herein contained for the Bank to retain investments existing at my death I authorise the Bank to take up new shares or securities offered to them in relation to any such investments.

23. I DIRECT that the income of my residuary Trust Fund however invested shall be treated and applied as income and that no part thereof shall be treated as capital except accumulations of surplus income.

24. SO long as my house Trevin Towers in Eastbourne remains unsold I direct the Bank to give my Chauffeur Harold John Goodman (if still in my service at the time of my death) the opportunity to continue to live with his family in the flat over the Garage provided he accepts the position of caretaker at a wage of not less than three pounds per week and keeps the house clean and the grounds tidy to the satisfaction of the Bank. I further direct the Bank to pay him a percentage of three pounds per hundred on the proceeds of the sale of the house (to ensure him doing his best when an intending purchaser presents himself).

25. The Bank may determine whether any moneys are to be considered as Capital or income and whether any expenses outgoings or other payments ought to be paid out of capital or income and may apportion blended trust funds and determine all questions and matters of doubt arising in the execution of the trusts of this my Will or any Codicil hereto. And every such determination whether made upon a question actually raised or implied in the acts or proceedings of the Bank shall be conclusive and binding on all persons claiming hereunder.

IN WITNESS thereof I have to this my Will set my hand the day and year first above written.

Signed by the said DAVID CITROEN the Testator as and for his last Will and Testament in the presence of us who at his request in his presence
D. CITROEN
and in the presence of each other have hereunto subscribed our names as witnesses

A.E. Hingley   Violet T. Holland
Solicitor   Clerk to Hingley, Roll & Willoughby
Eastbourne   Solicitors, Eastbourne

David Citroen died 28 days later on 26 January 1935

Appendix IX

Lehigh Zinc Iron Company v. Bamford

United States Supreme Court
150 U.S. 665 (1893)

At law. Action by Charles Bamford and Edwin Bamford against the Lehigh Zine & Iron Company to recover rents. There was verdict and judgment for plaintiff, and a motion for a new trial was denied. 33 Fed. 677. Defendant brings error. Affirmed.

Statement by Mr. Justice HARLAN: This action was brought to recover certain rents alleged to be due under a written lease of May 2, 1883, between Charles and Edwin Bamford, of England, and the Lehigh Zinc & Iron Company, Limited, of Pennsylvania. The company acquired, by the terms of the agreement, the exclusive right for 10 years to mine, dig, raise, crush, concentrate, roast, use, and remove, sell, and dispose of all metals or minerals found or to be found upon the leased premises.

The lease contained, among other provisions, the following:

'Second. That the party of the second part, for and in consideration of the rights and privileges thus granted, hereto covenant and agree to pay to the said parties of the first part the following rents, profits, and tonnage due, to wit: Upon all concentrated ores removed from or used upon the premises, the same having been obtained by crushing, sizing, washing, jigging, or separating ores mined upon said premises, a royalty of one dollar and fifty cents per ton of two thousand pounds, (2,000 lbs.;) upon all concentrated ores which may be obtained by crushing, sizing, washing, jigging, or separating ores or minerals hauled and brought to the said premises from other estates and mines, a royalty for the use of the soil, buildings, machinery, and fixtures hereby leased shall be paid to the parties of the first part as follows, viz. during two days of each week a royalty of fifty cents per ton of two thousand pounds of such ore so concentrated when removed from or used upon the premises aforesaid, and during the remaining five days of each week a royalty of one dollar for each ton of two thousand pounds so concentrated when removed from the premises.

'Third. Upon all ores mined upon and removed from the premises, other than those above mentioned, a royalty of one dollar and fifty cents a ton shall be paid to the parties of the first part; and it is also covenanted and agreed that the said party of the second part shall put all the engines, boilers, and machinery which it shall use in good and substantial repair, and keep and leave them in the same good order, ordinary wear and tear excepted.'

'Fifth. That the party of the second part shall pay or cause to be paid to the parties of the first part or their duly-authorized agent or attorney at New York city, on the twentieth day of January, April, July, and October of each year, all sums of money found to be due by said party of the second part for ores removed during the three full calendar months next preceding, and shall accompany each remittance with a detailed statement of weights and amounts so accruing, specifying also whence such ores were originally obtained.

'Sixth. In case the royalty due and payable to the parties of the first part according to the above rates shall in any year fall below the sum of one thousand dollars, then the party of the second part shall pay to the parties of the first part such additional sum of money as shall make the royalty for such year amount to the sum of one thousand dollars, which sum shall be held and taken to be the royalty of that year: provided, always, that if sufficient ores cannot be found to yield said minimum payment, and said party of the second part shall in consequence thereof fail to pay said minimum sum of one thousand dollars yearly, then said party of the second part shall, if required by said parties of the first part, relinquish this lease, and the privileges hereby granted, and the same shall cease thereupon.'

The company acquired by the agreement the exclusive right to purchase the leased estate, mining rights, etc., at the price of $125,000, payable according to certain named terms.

The complaint alleged that the company entered upon the leased premises, and dug and carried away ores, but only in such quantities that at the agreed rates the royalties fell below $1,000 in each of the years ending May 2, 1884, and May 2, 1885. Judgment was asked for $1,000 for each of those years, less the sum of $59.49, leaving a balance of $1,940.51, with interest from May 2, 1884, on $940.51, and from May 2, 1885, on $1,000.

The company denied all indebtedness to the plaintiffs, and asserted a counterclaim for the sum of $8,000. The answer alleged that Charles Bamford, for himself and Edwin Bamford, in order to induce the company to lease the property, represented the mine to be a valuable ore-producing one; that, properly worked, it would yield, and had yielded, a large amount of zinc and other metals; that it was still a valuable mine for such purposes, and would be a source of profitable investment to the company; that when those statements and representations were made the mine was flooded to the extent of nearly

100 feet, so that it was impossible for the company's officers, agents, and servants to make actual examination of it; that, relying upon and believing such statements and representations to be true, the defendant entered into the contract; that immediately after the execution of the lease the company, in consequence of the above representations and statements, purchased from the Bamfords a large quantity of tools, wagons, material, and personal property, to be used in developing the mine, paying therefor the sum of $883.74; and that the articles so purchased were of no use or value except for the purpose for which they were so purchased. The answer further alleged that in developing the mine the company expended, in addition to moneys for materials and for cleaning the mine, nearly $4,000, the aggregate of all expenditures by it in that way being between $5,500 and $6,000; that its officers devoted their personal attention and labor to the business, the value of such services being at least $2,500; that these expenditures were made in good faith, in the character of the mine; and that these representations, so made to induce, and which did induce, the company to enter into the lease, were entirely false, whereby it had sustained a loss of at least $8,000.

By stipulation between the parties the plaintiffs had leave to amend and did amend the complaint, claiming judgment for the sum of $1,000, with interest from May 1, 1886, for an additional installment of minimum rent due May 1, 1886.

At the trial the plaintiffs read in evidence the written contract of lease, and rested their case. The company then moved to dismiss the complaint upon grounds set forth in writing. The court denied the motion, and to that ruling the defendants excepted.

The company introduced evidence tending to show that Charles Bamford, prior to the execution of the lease, made the representations stated in the answer and counterclaim. The bill of exceptions states that the defendants in the latter part of 1883 ceased to work the mine, and never resumed, and subsequently claimed that it was valueless for producing ores. The plaintiffs introduced evidence tending to show that the statements alleged to be made by Charles Bamford were in fact true; that the mine, properly worked, would be a valuable ore producing one; that plaintiffs made no statements about it; and that the company was acquainted with its character, and relied upon their own knowledge, and not upon any statements by the plaintiffs. It appeared in evidence that the company entered into possession and used for several months the mines, buildings, machinery, and fixtures described in the schedule of the lease, which buildings and fixtures cost upwards of $60,000. It did not appear that any complaint of misrepresentation, failure, mistake, or disappointment was made until the answer was filed in this action about August, 1885.

There was a verdict in favour of the plaintiffs for $3,201.58, for which sum judgment was rendered.

Sidney Ward, for plaintiff in error.

[Argument of Counsel from pages 669-671 intentionally omitted]

L. A. Fuller and M. L. Towns, for defendants in error.

Mr. Justice HARLAN, after stating the facts in the foregoing language, delivered the opinion of the court.

Appendix X

Famous owners of Minerva's

Henry Ford
Louis Bleriot
Harry Hawker

Royal patrons included

H.M. The King of the Belgians
H.H. Prince Leopold of Belgium
H.H. Prince Charles of Belgium
H.H. The Princess Stephanie of Belgium
H.M. The King of Norway
H.M. The King of Sweden
H.H. The Grand Duchess of Luxembourg
H.H. The Consort Prince of Holland
H.M. The King of Romania
H.H. The Maharajah of Pithapuram
H.M. The King of Afghanistan
H.E. Admiral Horthy
The Regent of Hungary
H.M. The King of Morocco
H.M. The King of Siam

H.M. The Shah of Persia
H.H. The Princess Nazli Helmi of Egypt
H.H. The Rajah Mida of Selancor
H.H. The Prince Chandaburi of Siam
H.H. The Sultan de Marrakech

Many world politicians, industrialists and stars of the movie industry owned a Minerva. The car had the same qualities as the Rolls Royce, but was a little less expensive.

Appendix XI

References in Wiguläus von Kreittmayr article

Johann August Ritter of Eisenhart: Kreittmayr, Aloysius Freiherr von. In: General German Biography (ADB). Vol. 17, Duncker & Humblot, Leipzig, 1883, pp. 102-115.

Hans Rall: Kreittmayr, Aloysius Freiherr von. In: New German Biography (NDB). Vol. 12, Duncker & Humblot, Berlin 1980, ISBN 3-428-00193-1, p. 741-743 (digitalisat).

Richard Bauer and Hans Schlosser (Hrsg.): Wiguläus Xaver Aloys Freiherr von Kreittmayr (1750-1790). Munich, 1991.

Anne Dreesbach: Wiguläus Xaverius Aloysius Freiherr von Kreittmayr on Offenstetten and Hatzkofen. In: Wurst, Jürgen and Langheiter, Alexander (Eds.): Monachia. Munich: Urban Gallery at the Lenbachhaus, 2005, ISBN 3-88645-156-9, p. 68.

Friedrich Ebel: Legal History. Volume II (Modern Times). C.F. Mueller Juristischer Verlag, Heidelberg, 1993.

Raimund Eberle: What used to be right in Bavaria. Rosenheim publishing house, Rosenheim 1976.

Helmut Glöckle: The guardianship right of Codex Maximilianeus Bavaricus Civilis. Dissertation, Wilhelms-Universität Münster, 1977.

Gerd Kleinheyer and Jan Schröder: German jurists from five centuries. 3. Edition. C.F. Müller Verlag, Heidelberg, 1989.

Michael Kobler: Bavarian Codifications of the Natural Lawyer. In: Adalbert Erler and Ekkehard Kaufmann (Hrsg.): Handbook on German legal history Erich Schmidt Verlag, Berlin 1971.

Peter Pöpperl: Sources and System of the Codex Maximilianeus Bavaricus Civilis. Dissertation, Julius-Maximilians-University, Würzburg, 1967.

Franz Wieacker: Private History of the Modern Age. 2nd Edition. Vandenhoeck & Ruprecht, University of Göttingen, 1967.

Genealogical Manual of the Noble, Adelslexikon Volume VII, Volume 97 of the complete series. C.A. Starke Verlag, Limburg (Lahn) 1989, ISSN 0435-2408

Hans Rall: Kreittmayr. Personality, work and continuity. In: Journal of the Bavarian State History. Vol. 42, 1979, pp. 47-74.

Welsch: Life and work of the Wigulaeus Xaverius Aloysius Freiherrn von Kreittmayr, Churbayer secret state chancellor and supreme feud. 1845.

Hans Schlosser: Principles of recent private history. 10th edition. Heidelberg 2005. (UTB 883).

Hans-Georg Hermann: Wiguläus of Kreittmayr. In: Katharina Weigand (Hrsg.): Great figures of Bavarian history. Herbert Utz Verlag, Munich, 2011, ISBN 978-3-8316-0949-9, pp. 261-280.

WEBLINKS

- Literature from and about Wiguläus von Kreittmayr in the catalog of the German National Library

- Works by and about Wiguläus von Kreittmayr in the German Digital Library

- Literature list in the online catalog of the Staatsbibliothek zu Berlin

FOOTNOTES

1. Leitschuh, Max: The matrices of the upper classes of the Wilhelmsgymnasium in Munich, 4 volumes, Munich 1970-1976; Vol. 2, p. 210.

2. a b c Eberle, p. 12.

3. Kleinheyer and Schröder, p. 153.

4. Ebel, Rn. 480

5. Member entry of Wiguläus Alois Freiherr von Kreittmayr (with picture) at the Bavarian Academy of Sciences, retrieved on 6 January 2017.

The content is available under CC BY-SA 3.0, unless otherwise stated.

Appendix XII
References in article by Jeri L. Jones

Frazer, Persifor, Jr. 1880 The Geology of Lancaster County, Pennsylvania Geol. Survey, 2d Ser., Rept. CCC, 350 p.

Freedman, Jacob. 1972 Geochemical Prospecting for Zinc, Lead, Copper and Silver, Lancaster Valley, Southeastern Pennsylvania, U. S. Geol. Survey Bull. 1314-c, 49p.

Gordon, S. G., 1922. The mineralogy of Pennsylvania, Acad. Nat. Sci. Philadelphia Spec. Pub. 1, 255p

Landis, D. B., 1904 Mineral deposits and works of the Hempfields, Lancaster Hist. Soc., v. 8, no. 8, p. 239-255

Moiser, McHenry, 1948, Bamford Zinc Mine, Lancaster County, Pennsylvania, U. S. Bur. Mines Rept. Inv. 4247, 3 p, map.

Additional Family Information

Additional Family Information

Additional Family Information

Additional Family Information

About the Author

Sarah Hartley is retired and lives in Palm Coast, FL. "The Bamfords: A Family History" is Sarah's second book. Her first title was an autobiography, "Sunset: Sunrise, A Journey of Self-Acceptance", and is available on amazon.co.uk. She currently has started work on her next book about her sailing adventures. A lover of the outdoors, she has regrettably given up her passion for sailing but continues to enjoy her garden, where she prefers to enjoy the fruits of her labour rather than the labour itself! Sarah loves to travel and has made numerous trips, mainly overseas.

To contact Sarah: *email*   mssarahhartley@aim.com
                       Twitter   @mssarahhartley
                       Facebook   mssarahhartley.13

www.ingramcontent.com/pod-product-compliance
Lightning Source LLC
Chambersburg PA
CBHW062021290426

44108CB00024B/2734